REJECT THE DANCE OF PATRIARCHY

"...I noticed how hard it was for me to keep my sexual feelings out of my dealings with women on a daily basis. I saw how I was having to deal with an immensely long-standing attitude toward women that persistently saw them as sex objects and inferior beings. I could hardly believe these attitudes were in me.

"The issue came to a boil one day when I was reading about a rape of some women by soldiers in the Vietnam war and I realized that a part of me was getting a thrill from it. I was actually enjoying it. At the same time, some other part of me knew I should have been denouncing the rapes and striving to stop them. And some other part of me was appalled and disgusted that I could be deriving any kind of fascination and pleasure from reading about it at all."

—Nicholas Mann, *His Story*

His Story boldly exposes the conflicting cultural messages that drive today's men to pervert their true masculinity. Arguing that Christianity, the American Dream, national security, and "family values" condition men to embrace diametrically opposed values, author Nicholas Mann offers men exciting alternative models of masculinity.

His Story revives powerful masculine role models based on European traditions that precede the patriarchal era. These mighty myths integrate all aspects of the human experience, encouraging a rich sex life, self-knowledge, healthy relationships, inner strength, and re-connection with the earth. Men weary of the cycle of self-defeat and find *His Story*'s alternative models inspirational and applicable in everyday life. A fundamental change in our psyches will only come when we begin to adopt new perspectives and behavior.

His Story asks men to reject a dying 3,000-year-old patriarchal system which has seduced our souls into an ongoing dance of denial, destruction, and domination. Men willing to recreate a masculine model that reflects a whole being in a meaningful universe can find the starting point in this book.

ABOUT THE AUTHOR

Nicholas Robin Mann was born September 4, 1952, in Sussex, England. Having always had a fascination with the past, he studied ancient history and social anthropology at London University. He received his B.A. (Honors) in 1982. By 1985 he became deeply interested in asking what constituted the native European conception of God and masculinity. He has pursued this question through lifestyle choices, by living simply on the land, through working ritual, in community, in men's groups, in relationships, and in guiding visitors around the ancient sites of the British Isles. In 1987 he came to the United States and currently lives in New Mexico.

TO WRITE TO THE AUTHOR

If you wish to contact the author or would like more information about this book, please write to the author in care of Llewellyn Worldwide and we will forward your request. Both the author and publisher appreciate hearing from you and learning of your enjoyment of this book and how it has helped you. Llewellyn Worldwide cannot guarantee that every letter written to the author can be answered, but all will be forwarded. Please write to:

Nicholas R. Mann

% Llewellyn Worldwide

P.O. Box 64383-K458, St. Paul, MN 55164-0383, U.S.A.

Please enclose a self-addressed, stamped envelope for reply, or $1.00 to cover costs.
If outside U.S.A., enclose international postal reply coupon.

FREE CATALOG FROM LLEWELLYN

For more than 90 years Llewellyn has brought its readers knowledge in the fields of metaphysics and human potential. Learn about the newest books in spiritual guidance, natural healing, astrology, occult philosophy and more. Enjoy book reviews, new age articles, a calendar of events, plus current advertised products and services. To get your free copy of *Llewellyn's New Worlds of Mind and Spirit,* send your name and address to:

Llewellyn's New Worlds of Mind and Spirit
P.O. Box 64383-K458, St. Paul, MN 55164-0383, U.S.A.

LLEWELLYN'S MALE MYSTERIES SERIES

HIS
STORY

MASCULINITY IN THE
POST-PATRIARCHAL WORLD

NICHOLAS R. MANN

1995
Llewellyn Publications
St. Paul, Minnesota 55164–0383, U.S.A.

FIRST EDITION
First Printing, 1995

Cover design and ornaments by Tom Grewe
Illustrations by Nicholas R. Mann
Green man faces in frontispiece by Tom Grewe

Editing, design, and layout by David Godwin

Library of Congress Cataloging in Publication Data

Mann, Nicholas R.
    His story : masculinity in the post-patriarchal world / Nicholas R. Mann. — 1st ed.
       p.   cm. — (Llewellyn's male mysteries series)
    Includes bibliographical references (p. 287) and index.
    ISBN 1–56718–458–8 (pbk.)
    1. Masculinity (Psychology)   2. Men—Psychology.
    3. Mythology—Psychological apsects.   4. Patriarchy.
    I. Title   II. Series.
    BF692.5.M37   1995
    155.3'32—dc20   95–12264
                                                        CIP

Llewellyn Publications
A Division of Llewellyn Worldwide, Ltd.
St. Paul, Minnesota 55164–0383, U.S.A.

LLEWELLYN'S MALE MYSTERIES SERIES

In recent times, the inevitable backlash to thousands of years of repressive patriarchy and devaluation of the feminine has led to the re-emergence of women's spirituality and a new respect for the ancient Goddess. Yet now the pendulum seeks balance or equilibrium—not a denial of men and everything male, but a new equality between the sexes.

Men may well and rightly revere the Goddess and seek to restore the lost feminine within themselves. Yet, in the process, they must not lose sight of the positive aspects of their own masculinity. There must be a male partner in the *hieros gamos*, the holy marriage within the psyche.

Llewellyn's Male Mysteries Series will explore these aspects and the possibilities that exist in today's world for male quests for the sacred and for the restoration of the awe and reverence due to our primordial male gods. Men must now forsake the negative and tyrannical aspects of the sexless gods of the patriarchies and embrace instead the wisdom of Odin, the compassion of Osiris, the justice of Zeus, and the moral strength of Krishna. Neither should we overlook the law-giving leadership of the god of Moses, the mercy and self-sacrifice of Jesus, the call to honor and righteousness made by Muhammad, nor the announcement of the New Aeon by Ra-Hoor-Khuit.

Today, in an age that is witnessing the return of the Goddess in all ways and on all levels, there is also a need to find, and re-define, the God within. Men—and women—need to know and to experience the Divine Masculine as well as the Divine Feminine so that the God, too, may be renewed.

OTHER BOOKS BY NICHOLAS R. MANN

The Cauldron and the Grail (Glastonbury: Annenterprise, 1985)
Glastonbury Tor (Glastonbury: Triskele, 1986, revised 1993)
The Keltic Power Symbols (Glastonbury: Triskele, 1987)
Sedona: Sacred Earth (Prescott: Zivah Publishers, 1989, revised,
    expanded edition 1991)
The Red and White Springs: The Mysteries of Britain at Glastonbury
    (Glastonbury: Triskele, 1992)
The Giants of Gaia (co-author Marcia Sutton Ph.D. Albuquerque:
    Brotherhood of Life, 1995)

FORTHCOMING

The Isle of Avalon (Llewellyn Publications)
The Secret Geometry of Washington D.C.

TABLE OF CONTENTS

FOREWORD

This book gives men a history they can use. Instead of being defined as war makers and war fodder, as being exploiters, patriarchs, creators of economic depressions or of monopolies, this book offers an alternative and positive view of men. Compared to the formative depths of prehistory, the history of the last few thousand years is but a veneer. Through returning to roots, to the continuity of tens of thousands of years of arising on the planet, a man of European ancestry can connect to his own inner native tradition. This book outlines a path that will provide him with a profound sense of self and a deeper connection to the other forms of life on earth.

This book is written for men. It is written for men seeking a new definition of being. At a time when men are either described as being too weak and "soft" or too violent and dominating, there is confusion about who we truly are. This book addresses some of the fundamental flaws in the structure of Western thought. As a result of the predominance of the myths and religion of one world view, we have been cut off from the source of our own origin. There is a division between earth and spirit, between intellect and feeling, between mind and body. From where do we come? What is our original tradition? From where do we draw our power? How do we become whole? By drawing on the pre-Christian, the pre-classical, the pre-patriarchal era, this book offers a history men can use to deal with these questions. It offers a tradition that is alive and well within ourselves. It offers a source to connect with at the deepest level of our being so that we may re-create, in the present, a true man, attuned to life's own purpose, so that his story may go on.

Part I takes the reader through some biography of the author, then through the cycles of culture in prehistoric Europe. The art of the Ice Age caves, the mysteries of the megaliths, the traditions of the Horned God, the Green Man, the Wild Man of Celtic mythology and pantheistic symbolism are all gathered up into a new synthesis. In Part II, the theme for the re-creation of the archetypal masculine identity is exposed. In Part III, the way forward is discussed. The text examines the established assumptions around sexuality upon which masculinity is defined. It exposes their shallow historical character and reveals a far deeper and wider ranging sexuality which allows men to relax into their true selves.

ACKNOWLEDGEMENTS

Over the eight years it took to move from the initiations I received to when I could find a way to record them, there are many friends to thank. I honor the part they all played in this book. I thank Chris Craig for allowing me to photograph his carving of the Horned God; Patrick Whitefield for being the Green Man that he is; Robert Lawlor for the inspiration of his work and permission to quote from it; the groups of men I have been a part of both in Britain and the United States; Steven Humphreys, Margaret Thompson, Nancy Dye, Joseph Zummach, Iain Rose, Gray Wolf, various gods and goddesses; Dartmoor, specifically the upper Walkham valley, Glendalough, Tara, Dunkeld and the Wild Wood folk. And I especially thank Maya Sutton for computerizing my efforts, proofreading and editing Chapter 9, and for the suggestions, encouragement, and motivation without which this book would still have not been written.

INTRODUCTION

A "TRUE MAN"

Some years ago at college, I wrote a poem for a girlfriend and upon reading it to her, discovered I had unconsciously included the message that women were subservient to men. This was very embarrassing to me because I was meant to be a man who held the sexes in equality. Although I tried to excuse myself on the grounds that the sentences in question were literary allusions drawn from Chaucer, Shakespeare, and the like, she would have none of it and never dated me again.

I was disturbed by this event. It showed that the weight of social conditioning went far deeper in me than I thought I had become as a latter-half-of-the-twentieth-century "liberated male." I saw, possibly for the first time, how deeply dominance over women was inculcated into me as a fact of life. I almost felt possessed by some kind of invasive force, which I later was to define as patriarchy.[1]

I recognized similar patterns of behavior in me in the following years, especially when I began long-term relationships with women. I noticed how hard it was for me to keep my sexual feelings out of my dealings with women on a daily basis. I saw how I was having to deal with an immensely long-standing attitude toward women that persistently saw them as sex objects and inferior beings. I could hardly believe these attitudes were in me.

The issue came to a boil one day when I was reading about a rape of some women by soldiers in the Vietnam War and I realized that a part of me was getting a thrill from it. I was actually enjoying it. At the same time, some other part of me knew I should have been denouncing the rapes and striving to stop them. And some other part of me was appalled and disgusted that I could be deriving any kind of fascination and pleasure from reading about it at all.

I felt torn apart by such conflicting feelings. I felt I did not possess a true center. Which was I? The man who had honest sexual feelings but allowed them inappropriate power to the point of gaining enjoyment from the infliction of pain, rape, and death on women? The man who was appalled and self-censorious? Or the man who high-mindedly could tell what was right and wrong and through litigation and control change the world? I did not feel any of these inner men would serve me. I felt like the "hollow men" of T.S. Eliot. The "captains...bankers...men of letters...the statesman and the rulers" of his *Four Quartets*—all going "into the dark."[2]

On another occasion, I was attending a gathering where there were many women who had made considerable headway in their personal growth. I could see from their actions and hear in their words that they had a sense of who they were, and were much clearer than I about what was happening and where they were going in the world. As women they showed a degree of sharing and community that I certainly did not enjoy with men. I think they would have thought of themselves as being feminists, though they did not say this. I was very impressed by them, and at some point in the group asked how I could support them in what they were doing. One woman rounded on me and said in no uncertain terms that she did not need my support. No woman anywhere needed a man's support to be who she was and do what she did. She added that if I wished to support myself and thus be a part of the joint effort to end the present planet-destroying direction of humanity, then I should find out what it meant to be "a True Man."

Again I was embarrassed. How could I have committed the social gaffe of offering support to a feminist woman? And be shamed in public at the suggestion—by implication—that I was not a true man? I reeled from this. But a part of it went in and made a big impression on me. It was true. I did not know what it meant to be "a True Man."

Over the following years, I turned my attention to this question. I needed to find out for myself what a true man was apart from the definitions and images which had been created for me by a history of male supremacy. Without trying to evade individual responsibility, I eventually came to see that the social conditioning of men in our world is pathological to the extreme. We have been pressured into becoming something that denies our true nature. Somehow along the line, we, as men, have been let down by our patriarchal culture, by our whole civilization. We have become indoctrinated by principles that a moment's clear-sighted examination would reveal to be cruel, destructive, exploitative, harmful to ourselves, each other, and the planet.

Writers, a few men, but mostly women, have shown that behind the examples of witch hunting in Medieval Europe, genital mutilation of women in Africa and the Middle East today, the rape of women everywhere, the concentration camps of the Nazis and Pol Pot, slavery, ecological destruction, factory farming of animals, and countless wars of incalculable cruelty, there is a sickness present in every man—an ethical amnesia—resulting from a patriarchal conditioning which denies him access to who he really is.[3]

We have become possessed by this conditioning to the point where we cannot see a way out of it because we cannot see that we are in it. The institution of patriarchy fills our lives. We deny that we have created and are living in a world of power, oppression, and domination. Yet this is the bottom line. And this is what is really meant whenever there is a call to return to "traditional" values.

Whenever there is a general perception that something is amiss in society and the cry goes up for a revival of "family values," what is not stated is that this means a return to the patriarchal code where the man is at the head of the family and is the leader of church and state. Of course, in some circles this agenda is quite explicit. In this view of the world, a rise in the amount of crime and violence is not attributed to the code of male supremacy reasserting itself, but to the decline of it. The blame for any crisis is placed on anything which is counter to the patriarchal code. The blame for domestic violence is attributed to the increasing numbers of women seeking independence and career outside of the home. It is blamed on the undermining of a man's confidence by improperly assertive women, by feminists, and even by their own mothers.

In male-dominated society, the biggest insult is being likened to a woman. Some branches of the current men's movement are no exception to this when they accuse men of having become "soft" as a result of listening to women, especially feminist women. They insist on men separating themselves from women and "initiating" themselves into masculine identity. This manages to ignore the fact that this is what men in patriarchal society have always done and that male domination and violence is on the increase in all parts of the world. It also ignores that the social and economic gains made by women—mostly in the '70s—have been set back in the '80s and early '90s. Men are either being told they should be tougher—more like "a man"—or that they are being too aggressive.

What should we believe? Who is right? Whatever the case, enormous pressure is being placed on men and women as a result of patriarchy. What is this monster, patriarchy? How can it be described?

Imagine, for a moment, being born into a world where every face of authority is female. Where every president had been a woman, all religious officials are women, and all but a few senators are women. A sea of female faces predominates in Congress, in the judiciary, on executive committees, and in professorships. All their secretaries are men. Imagine if most doctors were women and they diagnosed and pronounced upon "men's problems." Statistics demonstrating the innate preference of men to choose the slow-lane jobs and be of a service-oriented nature are periodically released in journals and are used authoritatively by the courts and insurance companies.

Imagine if all this were supported by ancient religious texts which state "wives are the head of the husband" and "husbands should be submissive to their wives." Imagine if "she" is employed as the collective noun and humanity is referred to as "wom-ankind." Imagine if men make sixty-five per cent of the wage women make and twenty-five per cent of husbands are regularly and violently beaten. Imagine if women politicians and religious leaders press for a return to "traditional values" on the basis that men suffer when given roles which take them from their time-honored, and unpaid, role of service in the work force and should be returned there.

Imagine a world where men submissively adore women's wealth and power and appear adorned and half-naked on the arms of the rich and famous. Imagine a world where women fashion designers come up with the next set of clothes for their bubble-head models which show their buttocks, expose their chests, set off their legs, pull in their waists, and pressure them to have silicon implants in strategic places. Or a world where thousands of films show women sexually attacking, brutalizing, torturing, and killing men, and it is unsafe for men to walk the streets at night. The only thing which saves us from the horror of imagining such a "matriarchal" world is that it is not one that women are likely to create. But it does help us to grasp its complement, the world already in existence.

My contention is this: such massive social deception exposes the issue that men do not know who they are and that masculinity as it is presently defined is a tenuous, fragile, and at the same time dangerous construct. The moment the assumptions of the dominant patriarchal ideology are made conscious—for example, "The husband is the head of the wife" (Ephesians 5:22) or "Your yearning shall be for your husband yet he will lord it over you" (Genesis 3:16)—and the homophobia is exposed which keeps men apart and at each other's throats, a man with any conscience and common sense is placed in a morass of contradictions. He is doing everything that he was told is morally right by authority and religion and yet feelings of confusion and loneliness deny him self-knowledge and separate him from the rest of life. He does not want to be a perpetrator of misogyny—hatred of women—nor does he want to perpetrate or be at the effect of homophobia—fear of the same sex—but these values keep coming up in his life.

Men suffer in the patriarchal society. It is important to keep in mind that it is not men per se being criticized here, but the system in which we all, men and women, collude. The patriarchal system oppresses women severely—by definition it exerts power over women—but it is by its nature a system of domination, so we must expose where patriarchy oppresses men.

The "Dream" in which we all thought we shared has become subverted by an aggressive, competitive, and hierarchical system in which few succeed and most fail. The promise held out to a man by the patriarchal system—the promise of money, status, power, possessions, and sex—is actually demeaning to him. Men are driven by the goals society says they should have and by the goals which say how they should be. Men have become wage slaves subjected to enormous pressures to work—to perform, to compete, to be a certain "successful" way. Men feel a tremendous amount is expected from them. The result can be depression and chronic stress. Problems in the work place are dealt with by the recourse of working harder and longer. All the time there is the threat of dismissal or of being replaced by upcoming younger men.

At the same time as men are oppressed by the nature of the marketplace, they are denied many of the qualities of home. While some men feel guilt from spending too little time with their families, other men feel they are cut out from the close bonding women and children experience at home. Forced out to work, they feel alienated from their own children and envious of their wives. Paradoxically the patriarchal system creates weak fathers and poor husbands—characters visible in many sitcoms and comic strips. If misogyny is implicit in the system, then male-bashing is so taken for granted there isn't even a word for it—misandropy? Some women may manipulate the bond they have with their children against their male partner to portray him as weak and foolish. They assert their power in the home to create a negative view of men. The system forces them to act manipulatively in an area where they at least retain some power. Men react at work and in the locker room with hostile attitudes toward women. The net result is that we all suffer. Discrimination cuts in every direction.

Men cannot make friends or they lose them as a result of the competitive and homophobic nature of the system. Men are prevented from experiencing each other in any real, caring way. Many men have no male friends at all. Young men are constantly forced into "male" modes where they have to prove their masculinity. Men are cut off from their emotions, their intuition, and nurturing capabilities. Women are credited with enjoying a natural "superiority" in these areas—effectively disempowering men. Many men by mid-life experience a loss of meaning—a "Is this all there is?"—and suffer a sense of powerlessness from the grinding wheels of the system. Great and ever-increasing numbers of men suffer time in prison, where they are subjected to abuse, violence, and rape.

We hardly know what it means to be human, and everyday we perpetuate the chain of patriarchal conditioning that—not to put too fine a point upon it—will make our own children continue to rape, torture, and kill others and exploit and destroy the planet. The conditioning tells us that it's okay to exploit and kill. This conditioning is effected through cultural ideals such as proselytizing religious belief; racial superiority (in concepts such as "Manifest Destiny"); the pursuit of happiness, profit, and "national security,"; the ending of "primitivism"; upholding of "family values" (e.g., anti-homosexuality); and the extending of the "frontiers of knowledge." With such ideas so evident in the history of patriarchy, how can a man sort out the moral dilemmas of his own life? Where did we go wrong? Or more to the point, where can we go and what can we do to go right?

Other books, some of which are listed in the bibliography, go further than this in detailing where we went wrong.[4] Any man who is not already convinced that something is amiss in the male psyche, who does not see from the increase of rape, date rape, the violence against women, the violence against men, the number of men in prisons, the fear and distance between men, the crimes of corporate business and of war that a crisis is afoot can read these for himself. They will not be delved into deeply here. It is not that there is no instruction in knowing about these things; they help to raise our awareness. But it is not the purpose of this book to drag men through more self-incrimination, guilt, and pain; rather it is to seek a solution. However, certain fallacies do need to be exposed which reveal the backbone and ribs of the patriarchal conditioning and, as in the following example, they show the fundamental structure of the psyche in which there can be reshaping and renewal.

EXPOSING OUR MINDS: GOD AND THE ENEMY

The most predominant flaw in the whole edifice of Western thought and consciousness is the creation of the concept of a singular, omnipotent, omnipresent, and transcendent god. He is accompanied by a "divinely appointed" male hierarchy of popes, apostles, cardinals, priests, prophets, kings, bishops, judges, generals, emperors, lords, and so on. It does not take much thought to realize the divisiveness such hierarchy has brought to the world: the haves and have nots; the aristocrats and the people; the priest and the congregation; the saved and the damned; the sexism, racism, and classism; the ruthless and bloody competition for wealth, status, and power over others. This is the established order. But there is no reason to believe that it is the only one, nor that the patriarchal father god is the only version of the divine.

The author, Starhawk, has pointed out that the patriarchal system of "power over"—as opposed to "power from within"—has effectively allowed those at the top to plunder, possess, and subjugate the entire world. It has placed the natural realms and those deemed inferior—other races, children, and women—somewhere down at the bottom of a hierarchy.[5] People and things are not appreciated for what they are, but for where they stand in the order of the hierarchical system. In the words of William Greider: "A society (America) that regularly proclaims democratic pieties also devotes extraordinary energy and wealth to establishing the symbols and trappings of hierarchy, the material markings that delineate who is better than whom."[6]

Patriarchy and its system of hierarchical ranking, made explicit in and sanctified by its religions, forms the conceptual basis for domination over everything of "lesser" worth. In the patriarchal world of vertical hierarchy, power can be defined as control by virtue of scarcity. The scarcest position is the most powerful; i.e. there is only one president at the top. If there is a lot of something, like air, ocean, forest, then it isn't worth much, but if there is only a little, like gold or diamonds, then it is worth a lot. The ultimate scarcity, then, is the most powerful, and this could be defined as the patriarchal version of the divine. In Mary Daly's words, "The patriarchal God is the ultimate scarcity—rarified to the point of zero." He does not exist—like the emperor's new clothes.[7]

A major result of creating such an ultimately powerful—yet invisible and absent—concept of god, is that in terms of the inner psyche, its opposite of equal power is automatically created. The "devil," whether portrayed as the enemy, absolute evil, witches, communism, women, or the infidel, will have reality in a psyche structuring itself upon the hierarchical principles of the patriarchal cosmos. This is compounded by literal readings of "divine" texts. Forced to accept a real god in heaven, the fundamentalist has no choice but to accept real demons here on earth.

The universe is pluralistic and complex in its nature rather than singular and reducible to simple ideas. The universe also is twofold in its nature, as expressed by male and female forces. But when muddled by patriarchal thinking, a simplistic duality is created where one side inevitably becomes good—in this case the male—and the other side evil—in this case the female. This is exemplified in the duality of culture and nature. One is made by the effort of masculine will; the other naturally exists. As such, it threatens culture.

It comes really as no surprise, therefore, to find the judges of the Inquisition were projecting onto women their own inner fantasies defined as evil. Or the devil, having no more existence outside the mind and imagination than the patriarchal god, lives in the wildly beautiful, untamable, and deep places of the earth. Or, in this dualistic cosmos, it really is okay to kill tribal peoples and chop down their forests, or pour pollutants into the rivers. For there is nothing holy or sacred to be found within them. Holiness is all to be found in a transcendental heaven or in an "ascended" spirit. The world in this cosmology is an evil, daemonic place, imprisoning the soul.[8]

The hierarchical, dualistic system defines itself by projecting all that is good upon its own leaders and institutions and all that is bad upon an enemy. A warrior mentality results where men through heroic efforts of their will can save society through self-sacrifice or by killing the enemy. Death is necessary for life. In the case of no external enemy being available, then attention focuses on the enemy within. As a result of its identification with Christianity, the Western world found its external enemies in non-Christians and its internal enemies in heretics and women. With the replacement of the Christian world view by the secular world view and the exposure of the injustice of the hierarchical mode of domination over women, the question is, where will the system now turn to find transcendence in heroic combat with the foe?

The answer seems to be that nature is now the foe. And we, through the exertion of our will in the industrial economy, are creating a culture whose goal is supreme technological control of and transcendence over the natural world.

I call this the split between the sacred and the world, or the duality of spirit and matter. I believe it to be the result of the creation of the idea of a transcendental god by ascendant philosophies and religions and that it lies at the heart of the sickness of the Western psyche. There is nothing holy left in the world.

We need, therefore, to be sure that in re-creating the symbolic structure of our cosmos—a principle aim of this book—we reclaim the parts of ourselves which have been separated. We integrate the parts either driven to a sacred but unattainable transcendent other-world or to a profane and profoundly negated natural world. In the new world view, power is immanent throughout the cosmos. It is seen everywhere and in everything. There will be a source where it is possible to rest, relax, recharge, and draw power. The goal is wholeness in plurality, rather than ranked singular fragments. The goal is where the value of an individual or the worth of a thing is appreciated for what it is and for the part it plays in the whole. The goal is being-from-within, rather than from a mental idea.

Hierarchy, reductionism, the spirit-matter duality, and the placing of ultimate power outside of the psyche and outside of the cosmos has resulted in many of the sicknesses that are visible in the patriarchally defined male. Created in the attempt to control and have power over the daemonic and chthonic natural world, with which women were closely identified, patriarchy has resulted in the disempowerment of men. As blind obedience characterized the hierarchy of the church and military—a priest would be excommunicated for disobeying his superiors, a soldier shot for disobeying orders—so those unwilling to obey the dictates of the industrial economy in its war against nature will be relegated to the borders of society. They will be abandoned by the system. Only those willing to "sacrifice" themselves to the industrial economy and work harder for the "good of all" will be honored.

In a ranked system, people are either superiors, inferiors, failures, or competitors. If we choose to use our individual conscience and not compete on the ladder of hierarchy, social mores do not give us any other source of power, of self-esteem, or any other valid definitions of masculinity by which to live. We are left lonely, demeaned, disconnected from and set against the rest of the world. How can we end those things and put something else in their place? What is the "dream" that really is for all the people? Something which provides us with an alternative definition of a man?

To answer those questions, the method that this book will follow will be to draw from the past ideas and concepts which pre-date those imbued with patriarchal values. Those ideas will assist us in re-creating a definition of masculinity that is capable of locating us as whole beings in a congruent, mythologically rich and meaningful universe.

One difficulty with such an approach is that history—patriarchal history—cannot be ignored, and there is no such thing as a wonderful golden age only waiting to be retrieved. Another difficulty with such a process is that we actually know very little about the ancient past. What has survived has been reinterpreted many times, and we already view it through acculturated eyes. I therefore do not claim that the ideas and values presented in this book are "how it was" in the past. But I do claim that from what little we know of the past, combined with our current perception of what is needed today, it is perfectly valid to make the effort to re-create a deep and satisfying sense of ourselves from an alternative view of history. This re-creation will serve us as we shape the future.

In my own life, I recognize the principle that if I focus on something, I give it energy, even when my aim is to dispel it. I find the quickest way to dispel something is to focus on a positive alternative and simply allow the unwanted thing to atrophy. I recognize the power of being driven by what I want rather than by what I don't want. I don't want to be anti-patriarchy or anti-nuclear or anti-anything. This perpetuates the singularity and competitiveness of the patriarchal world view. I do want to be for the equality of all people, for sustainable energy sources and for a pluralistic system that respects and honors all the many ways of being and all life forms. I want to be for a masculinity that harmoniously integrates with and contributes to all life on the planet. A masculinity that uses its power to positively relate to women, children, animals, and other men. That loves and is loved. This is the goal that I think men can expect to get from this book. It is not by pushing through the obstacles that we obtain the goal; we focus on the goal and we find the obstacles moving away. The goal, in this case, is the creation of a new definition of what it means to be a man, and the obstacles moving away are the overlaying principles of patriarchy.

Please note that throughout this book, the word "man" is always used to refer to the male sex. It is never used in the sense of referring to humanity as a whole.

Throughout this book, B.C.E., "before the common era," is used to replace B.C., and C.E., "common era," replaces A.D. This avoids perpetuating the implicit values of a particular theism, while keeping the familiar structure of dating intact.

At the close of each chapter in Part II, a visualization is offered. The purpose of these is to support the reader in gaining an internalized understanding of the "re-created" archetype of the masculine rather than simply a mental description of it. Creating a visual image of the symbols involved is a powerful way to access their content. The reader is therefore encouraged to take the time to practice the visualizations apart from reading the text. Figure 4 on page 159 will be of great help in this.

NOTES

1. Patriarchal: "rule by fathers." Patriarchy: a society in which all religious, economic, political, and social relations are defined in terms of ownership by fathers. Patriarchy = patrimony.

2. T.S. Eliot, *Four Quartets* (East Coker, 1943).

3. For example, Mary Daly, *Gyn Ecology* (Beacon Press, 1978).

4. Ibid. Also: Mary Daly, *Pure Lust* (The Women's Press, 1984); Susan Faludi, *Backlash: the Undeclared War Against American Women* (Crown Publishers, 1991. This well researched and documented work brings the story of women's rights up to date but fails to provide an analysis of patriarchy. As a result it does more to help women pull away from domination than it provides ways in which men and women can

work together to change the system); Monica Sjoo and Barbara Mor, *The Ancient Religion of the Cosmic Great Mother of All* (Norway: Rainbow Press, 1981). For a man's perspective, see Rupert Sheldrake, *The Rebirth of Nature: The Greening of Science and God* (Bantam, 1991). Here, the blame for the assault upon the planet is pinned onto the Newtonian-Cartesian world view. See Sheldrake's Note 7 for a critique of the impact of patriarchy upon the Church.

5. Starhawk, *Dreaming the Dark*, ch. 1 (Beacon Press, 1982). This book is a must-read for its perspective on the god as well as the goddess.

6. William Greider, *Who Will Tell the People: The Betrayal of American Democracy* (Touchstone, 1993), 411.

7. Mary Daly, *Gyn Ecology*, 79.

8. "Daemonic": a chthonic (earth arising) force, often personified as the "spirit of place." It would be appropriate at this point to express my belief that no amount of tinkering with the dominant religious ideology of Christianity will change it for the better. Christianity, built upon its historically specific base, is implicitly and definitively hierarchical, dualistic, and patriarchal. For egalitarian,, earth-honoring, sex- and body-positive spiritual attitudes to grow, I am of the opinion that it is necessary to abandon institutional Christianity altogether. There have been attempts by theologians to find an alternative tradition within Christianity. See for example *Women-Church: Theology and Practice of Feminist Liturgical Communities* by Rosemary Radford Ruether (Harper & Row, 1985). But despite her excellent analysis of the patriarchal content of Christianity, the rites Ruether offers are still patriarchal. They remain predicated on original sin, martyrdom, and hierarchical dualism. "Out, demons, out!" is the response suggested for the "exorcism" of oppressive Biblical texts.

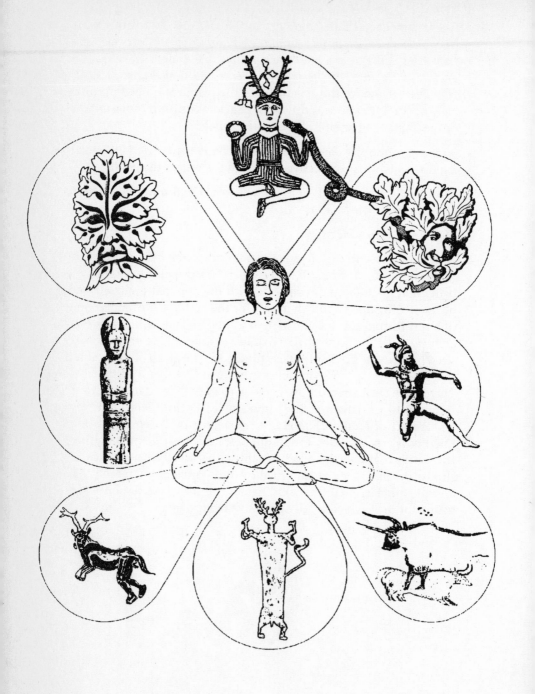

PART I

CLEARING THE PATH

WHAT IS A MAN?

MY EDUCATION

When I was at school, an English teacher pointed out to us in the class that many of the questions in the Elizabethan and Greek dramas were about what it meant to be a man. The question "What is a man?" resonates as much through the soliloquies of Hamlet and Macbeth as it does through those of Oedipus and Orestes. The second major question "What can I do?" invariably followed hard upon the heels of the first. That there was never really an answer to what constituted a man has sent a hollow laughter through all these plays, which have invariably ended in tragedy—at least for their main participants. The moral seemed to be: stop philosophizing and get on with it. Yet the question remains, and in contemporary society we are exposed from birth to definitions of manhood which bombard us from all sides without ever really letting us know that there is a question and a choice in the matter. "What is a man?" is a very good question to ask indeed.

A man is: honest, fair, decent, proud, loyal, hard-working, tough, generous, skillful, competitive, aggressive, patriotic, commanding. He doesn't show pain. He is willing to make sacrifice. He

3

is ready to obey. He is committed to his work and family. He is ready to assert justice....

This list begins to flag either through my own lack of conviction or because these answers are superficial. They do not really get to the heart of the question. They express values which are socially imposed. They are standards that a man is as likely to feel judged by and condemned for a lack of. Standards he will spend his whole life pursuing, only to find empty. They are the tragedy rather than anything about what a man really is.

These values present themselves to us from the media, our parents, teachers, friends, and institutions. I remember that in the school I attended from age five to eleven, there was a wooden board with the names upon it of local men who had died in World War II. Along the bottom of the board was engraved, "Greater love hath no man than a man who lays down his life for his friends." I knew I was supposed to feel that way. That this was good, that this was A MAN. But every time I read it, I wanted to leave the grade I was in and join the "backward" class, for I certainly wasn't good enough. I wasn't a hero. I didn't want to die. In not wanting to lay down my life for my friends, in wanting to join the "backward" class, I was refusing the highest tenets of my society. I was an outsider, an outcast, a failure. I did not belong anywhere, for I could not explain to myself why I knew—implicitly—that success or death was not what constituted the greatest love of a man.

It was only years later that I realized the other side of the message. A man being willing to "lay down his life for his friends" meant, in fact, that a man should be willing to kill for his friends. Or rather, to kill for the society of which he was a part.

To put it bluntly, the man society wants us to be is a rapist and a killer. Stepping back a little from the rawness of that statement—I can hardly believe I wrote it—the man it wants us to be is one that maintains the system of hierarchy, oppression, and domination. Rape as the degradation of women is one of the prime means by which this is done. It also wants us to be at least a soldier and at best a heroic warrior. At any rate, that's the gloss. But plain down at the bottom of it, men are all trained to kill. As Sam Keen writes in *Fire in the Belly,* "Men are systematically conditioned to endure pain, to kill, and to die in the service of the tribe, nation, or state. Nothing shapes, informs, and molds us so much as society's demand that we become specialists in the use of power and violence..."[1]

As a result of hierarchy and crude dualistic thought, the "god or the enemy" consciousness has pushed us as human beings to a place where nature and its biological progenitors, women, have become identified as the "enemy." This is the inevitable result of transcendentalism. Men and the world are at war. A culture in this situation exalts asceticism, sacrifice, martyrdom, and death. These concepts are central to the ideology of the cultures which have dominated Western and Middle Eastern history. Through facing death in religious martyrdom and in battle, men supersede the biological order and replace it with a cultural order. This order is legitimated by the claim it comes from God, but it is created by men. And now, in the twentieth century, by having the ability to hold the threat of destruction over the entire world with nuclear weapons, men can claim to be the creators of a new world. If nature is life, then only through culture as death achieved through the effort of mind and will in rape and war can men create and sustain the hierarchical, transcendental order. The philosopher Michel Foucault writes: "The principle underlying the tactics of battle—that one has to be capable of killing in order to go on living—has become the principle that defines the strategy of states."[2]

The violent nature of the system maintains itself through the creation of a constant and pervasive atmosphere of fear of intimacy with others of the same sex—homophobia. The effect of homophobia is to keep men apart and in competition with each other. Nowhere is this so clear as in the military where contempt and fear of homosexuality is encouraged and rampant. Through the constant and often violent accusation of homosexuality on the part of others or by direct attacks on homosexuals, any attempt by men to bring a gentler, more communicative and non-hierarchical character into their lives is effectively destroyed. Without touch, contact, and love, and with competition, fear of discrimination, and loss of privilege, men in the armed services are kept apart and ready to kill. At the same time, the military, and the patriarchal system as a whole, encourages prostitution overseas because this supports both imperialistic attitudes and the dogma of male supremacy.

The system is also maintained through the internalization of submissive attitudes on the part of women. Self-sacrifice is taught to young women as a defining act of life. Genital mutilation in Africa is upheld and enforced more actively by women than it is by men. Women in many places form the backbone of patriarchal religion. Marriage, an institution upholding patrilineal rights, is maintained most enthusiastically by women. Women are taught that to be raped is to be shamed. But the shame comes from the breaking of a father's or husband's rights over the woman. Throughout history women have been taught to submit to men's sexual rights over them. A terrible contradiction is thus created where the patriarchal society punishes rapists for their violation of patrimonial rights while fostering dominant values in men and submissive values in women. These attitudes make it nearly impossible for a woman to prove she was not "asking for it" from a man.[3]

It can hardly be looked at squarely and truthfully for what it is, for we all, men and women, are caught up in the need for domination, submission, and control and in the death urge of the system itself. And all the while, the second major question of the actors in the tragedies, "What can I do?" remains as equivocal as ever. Instead of living in a civilized culture supposedly created to lift us above the cruelty and injustice of nature, the barbarities and abuses of culture far exceed those created by our chthonian nature. Oedipus was not condemned by his natural aggression and sexuality but by the cultural codes placed upon him by society. Hamlet died not because he lacked anything in his character as a man but because of cultural values and stereotypes which confined his role.

And there it is, broken and acculturated before they ever get to the crossroads of free choice, men shudder and turn away from the anomie, the alienation, the ostracism that would result from the choosing of the course that uses individual conscience and asks, "What difference can I make?" So the reply, "Every difference in the world," is rarely heard and left to blow away in the winds of resignation. And the difference, I believe, is not so much in knowing what we can do—we can never fully know the outcome of our actions, and would we really want to?—but in who we are and what we want to become. What is a man?

THE ULTIMATE QUESTIONS

When I finally finished school at the age of sixteen, amid the frenzy of taking examinations, we had to attend one compulsory subject. Not mathematics, as you would expect, not English, but religious education. A local minister came to give the classes, but having long since failed to hold our attention, allowed us, the boys, to do our homework. Near the end of term, the last class on a Friday, the minister, catching something of the jubilation in the school, proposed something different. We would all write a question and put it in a hat.

I was excited. Here at last was a chance to ask the questions of ultimate importance that I had never had the opportunity to ask. Laboring over my questions, I finally wrote "Who am I?" and "Why are we here?" To me they seemed to capture the whole grand sweep of existence. The questions went into the hat and one by one the minister pulled them out and read them. As they came, I became increasingly embarrassed. The questions were overwhelmingly sports oriented, who beat whom in some final two years ago, or were related to current studies.

The questions kept on coming and I knew that when mine was read everyone would know it was mine and I would be exposed—vulnerable to their jeers. Only I seemed to possess angst. However, we were running out of time and as soon as the clock struck four, I knew I would be safe. The minister lacked the power to stop us from taking our leave. I became hot and tense as the minutes crept up to four o'clock. Surely we would run out of time. But no, one last question remained in the hat—and it was mine.

The minister pulled it out and read aloud, "Who am I?" and "Why are we here?" At that moment, the bell rang. The class roared with laughter. But to my intense relief, not at me, but at the foolish and pitiable minister, who could ask such a question and be so incapable of telling a class to hold its seat. We swept out of the room, echoing the words "Why are we here?"

It was the grandest joke, the most superlative timing. Maybe the minister had been set up by the writer of the questions. Eyes turned to me. "You wrote those questions?" My fear returned. "Go on, admit it."

I choked an affirmative. I needn't have feared. From that moment on, every boy's estimation of me as a prankster went up tenfold. I was relieved, but left with a bitterness in my throat.

I caught the minister hurrying up the corridor. "You understood my question?" I asked. I needed to know that at least this man of god understood. He turned and snapped at me. I could not see his eyes through his glasses. I did not comprehend what he said. All I saw was that he was mortified and furious with me for making him into a bigger fool than he already was.

A week later, the patriarchy caught up with me again. One by one, the boys were going for an interview about their future. A "careers interview" it was called. When my turn came, I entered the huge concrete and glass hall with a tiny desk at one end of it. Like inquisitors, the minister and the art master sat behind the desk. The art master was a sadist who had banned me from his classes because I had told him, by virtue of my size, that if he laid his hands on any of the smaller boys again, I would stop him. The minister kept silent. I could feel hostility oozing through his milky-thick spectacles. The art master waited a few moments, looked me up and down, and then announced, "It is pointless for you to attend this interview, Mann, for you will never have a career." I hesitated. He motioned me to go.

"You bastard!" I said and walked out.

I never attended a day of school after that. Nor did I spend much longer at home. Within a week, I was living in a house in town. In fact, I had run away, seeking my own solutions to what it meant to be a man—asking the questions about life that the education system never came close to answering and seemed to wish to deny me even the opportunity of asking.

POST-EDUCATION

I remember the following years—1968 through the seventies and eighties—as a difficult time. They had their moments—with a great amount of civil rights legislation being passed into law. But the hand of patriarchy came down over everything. The wars around the world seemed to crush the hope of change. Even the realization by many sent to fight in Vietnam that they were duped by the cause and made less than human by its effect was eventually neutralized and assimilated by the establishment. Politically, the 1980s saw a powerful re-entrenchment by the established hierarchies in the West, supported by all those who had an investment in keeping things the way they were.

Reagan and the Republicans in the United States, Thatcher and the Conservatives in Britain, won astonishing terms of leadership because they promised to maintain and even increase the benefits of capitalism. In fact, they managed to put such a benign face on capitalism and make it appear so attractive that, by the end of the eighties, pretty much the rest of the world wanted what the capitalists had. The fact that they could never have it and that capitalism was as exploitative and destructive as its counterpart, communism, was irrelevant. Many of the civil rights won in the seventies were rolled back in the eighties. In America, perhaps nowhere was this so clear as in women's rights, where wages compared to men dropped and the right to abortion was limited. Corporations moved to "green" their facade; to make it appear that their soil-loosing, forest-felling, animal-torturing, aquifer-poisoning, wage-slave-creating, consumer-family-maintaining policies were a benefit to all life.

In 1983, I wrote the following poem, after reading Shelley and realizing things were not so different back in 1823. It is a decidedly negative poem—the poor are not helped by the destruction of the rich—but it expressed my feelings then.

Behind the city's marbled fronts
Run the desperate men in banks
Trying to avert the squeeze
The one that will bring them to their knees
And make them cry out
"Why did we not listen then!"
Behind the corporations' "caring" facades
For workers, forests, and the law
Lie the means which chop the trees
Make the poor and take away
The workers' rights to land, justice
And feeling one with all.
It's time the people gave the shout

"They would not listen then
They will not listen now!"
Inside the State's still tottering towers
Sit the men who, desperate
For reputation and for power
Decide that we, the people, need defense
From "them."
And pay the rich to make more bombs
To win their vote, despite our cries
"The bomb is for us, not them!
To keep us in line and make us starve!"
And all around the fruits of war
Lie rotten and sour and go to prove
"They did not listen then!"
All down the ailing Main Street fronts
The tyranny of Mammon is screwed up
Another notch, just so
We the people are made to feel
The pinch is all our fault.
It was we who did not work
Who cheated and stole.
When all the while it was the men
In banks and ties and up in towers
With an economy to support
Based on property, rivalry, and retort
On extortion, pollution, and on war
That stole from us—the people.

And now in 1995 there is little cause for renewed hope. The
armed struggle of male power elites in former Yugoslavia, the
Middle East, and many parts of Africa appears to be for the worst
of reasons and we are all victims: men, women, and children.
Indeed, there is some renewal of anxiety on my part that the
Western capitalistic power elites will not take the struggle of the
Eastern European and former Soviet countries as an example and
reform their own shortcomings. Rather we will sink into the complacency of having been ideologically right all along and export
our own brand of exploitation eastward to simply perpetuate the

death wish, homophobia, and misogyny of patriarchy in free market instead of communist form. It does appear that the fear of losing the benefits the system currently provides takes precedence over the fundamental changes which are necessary for future life.

While a vast amount of expenditure is on weapons that kill and violence is everywhere in evidence—war being essential to the patriarchal society—death itself is virtually denied. This would conflict with the transcendental, aesthetic, Apollonian values we have chosen at the expense of the natural, raw, chthonian, and Dionysian. Bodies and terminally ill people are rushed away from view and no provision is made for conscious dying—they are too ugly. But such repression and denial creates a pathological fascination with death and violence. We are desensitized to violence and at the same time excited by it. It appears nightly on our television and cinematic screens as an act devoid of its very real messiness.

Violence also appears as there is an assessment—which is accurate—that the patriarchal culture is under threat and in order to compensate for its decline, male violence is being clandestinely, and in some places openly, encouraged. The beauty of Apollo is maintained by his right arm not knowing what his left arm is doing. The "assassins" of patriarchal culture are out on the streets right now in every kind of uniform asserting the death wish of patriarchy with actions which they believe to be true and right. Minorities, prostitutes, gays, and other marginalized people are the targets. As are mainstream figures who commit acts counter to patriarchy, such as abortionists.

I doubt whether the bigotry, racism, and national chauvinism that is resurging throughout the world would succeed if the staring, listless eyes of the Holocaust survivors, and the piles of the slain, were remembered.

I once wrote that we would become so compulsive about and obsessed with war that in order to consume sufficient amounts of it "seats would be sold on mountaintops." War could be wrapped in packets "ready to serve to our prison camp suburbs…. Fashionable satisfaction could be achieved from sleek, death-dealing magazines." This seems to have come true with the media's presentation of the high-tech war with Iraq over Kuwait—especially the SCUD missile attacks on Israel—and the popular response to it. The bodies were ignored—as much as possible.

Needless to say, objectors to that war—or any war—were accused of anti-patriotism. It was as though love of war and love of country were the same thing; which, of course, they are—under patriarchy. The objectors' very sense of self-definition was questioned. It was un-American—by implication un-human—to oppose the war. It was weak—by implication un-manly—to choose not to fight. The same undermining of identity and the disempowerment created by a deadly set of moral values also took place during the war Britain waged against Argentina over the Falkland Isles.[4] And it continues to happen today to anyone in any country who joins the peace movement. We have come such a long way from any life-affirming definition of self and especially of what constitutes a man that it would seem to war is human—to want peace is inhuman.

MEN AND THE WOMEN'S MOVEMENT

Before I can go on and define a masculinity whose values do not contain the injustices and contradictions of patriarchy, I must pay dues to the Women's Movement. Women have suffered the effects of the violence of patriarchy to an extent men cannot imagine. The witch burnings and African genital mutilation have already been mentioned. But add to this the rape, the everyday threat of it, and the constant disempowerment—psychological, economic, political, and physical—and we come closer to the zone in which women have been forced to live.

Patriarchy is by definition anti-women, make no mistake about it. It will seek to minimize or destroy any challenges made to its power structure by women. It will go to any length to keep women "in their place," insisting that where women are dominated and raped it is because they want it and are "asking for it." In the Old Testament one of the tribes of Israel is given license to repeatedly gang-rape women. This reveals a prime way in which a man in the patriarchal society can visibly prove to his peers that he is "a man" (Judg. 19:23–25). If it is difficult to find out what it means to be a man, for women the task of finding out and then fulfilling what it means to be a woman in a culture that systematically denies and oppresses them is unimaginably difficult.

Yet, as is often the case, it appears the "victim" has built character, sense of purpose, unity, direction, and inner power, while the "oppressor" has wilted by degrees as a result of complacency and values which keep him apart from other men. This is no excuse for oppression; it merely points out that women are now far ahead of men in terms of a new definition of self. Of course, the problem is more complicated than this. It is not that all women have been the victims and all men the oppressors. It is rather that we are living in an historically created culture of domination whose nature is patriarchal and patrimonial. In such a context, men are also victims of the system and perhaps nowhere is this clearer than when older men send younger men off to war. Sam Keen goes so far as to suggest that men suffer as much at each other's hands as do women at the hands of men, and as a "battlefield sacrifice" endure "wounds every bit as horrible as the suffering women bear from the fear and the reality of rape."[5] Although the comparison is questionable—armed soldiers in battle are in a very different situation to the woman on the street—it is true that both men and women suffer and die in the maintenance of the hierarchical system of dominance. But it still remains the case that men have a long way to go to reach the point of mutual empowerment, support, sharing, spirituality, and ethics that the women's movement has achieved.

Glance at what in our society is supposed to be the leading edge of thought, the managerial, philosophical, and theological sections in a bookstore, and you will see patriarchal thinkers rehashing the same old tired stuff. Tired and, this is the sad part, dangerous, for they perpetuate the same old oppressive values. On the other side of the store, the women's section reveals new directions in all the areas mentioned. It seems new ground is being broken every day. Women have reclaimed the feminine divine principle—the Goddess. Women have developed a personal, empowering, flexible, open, and networking style of management. Women are redefining history—realizing the power of the past in influencing and determining the meaning of the present—and if necessary retelling the past, to make it useable, good, and empowering. Monique Wittig: "Make an effort to remember. Or failing that, invent."[6]

Men need to do the same. Women are redefining themselves, society, politics, medicine, management, leadership, the Church, spirituality, sexuality, and language itself. Monique Wittig's and Mary Daly's re-evaluation of the use of words from as simple as the employment of "man" to the obscurity of "Holy Ghost" reveals the implicit codes on which patriarchy has raised itself.[7] Women are challenging the very definitions on which our lives are built, including normally accepted criteria of what constitutes femininity and masculinity.

Men need to do the same. However, women are not defining men—except in describing the exact details of the patriarchal oppressor and their many weapons and devices. When they do attempt to define men, some holes begin to appear. In fact, here lies a feature for both the men's and the women's movements. We cannot define each other. We need to define ourselves. If we focus on the failings of each other, we will not be truthful about the changes we need to make in ourselves.

At its best, feminist thought has inspired men to re-evaluate themselves and join with the effort to end patriarchal domination. At its worst, the critique of patriarchy by women has meant an attack on men and has led to a widening of the gulf between us.

Valerie Solanas writes, "The male's normal method of compensation for not being female, namely getting his Big Gun off, is grossly inadequate, as he can get it off only a very limited number of times; so he gets it off on a really massive scale, and proves to the entire world that he's a Man."[8] While such writing is understandable, it is not true that the reason men are violent is because they need "compensation for not being female." While women's anger at men is justifiable, hostility is not. The same can be said for men. But there is a point where we, as men, must look closely at ourselves and present a new self-defined masculinity which is contrary to the destructiveness and emptiness that many women currently perceive in us. It may take a while to get there, but this masculinity has a fullness, a power, a quality that will be what we, as men, are needing to take our rightful place in the world.

This book is as much pro-women as it is pro-men. As in the physical world where women give birth to men, I suggest that in the process of the transformation of the social world women have a vitally important primary role which needs to be honored. At the risk of being stereotypical, it may be that what women are men can augment and develop. In this area men can be honored. Nature and culture do not need to be in opposition. For whatever new definitions we may make of and for ourselves, the ultimate goal is to come together as equals and enact every potential of life.

NOTES

1. Sam Keen, *Fire in the Belly: On Being a Man* (New York: Bantam Books, 1991), 37.

2. Michel Foucault, *The History of Sexuality,* trans. R. Hurley (New York: Vintage Books, 1980), 137.

3. I am not arguing that the victim creates the crime. I am saying that both women and men are responsible for the perpetuation of patriarchal attitudes and must work together to overcome them. For feminism to take an anti-male stance will result in the sociological phenomenon of "deviancy amplification," where men will fulfill the definitions thrust upon them. The backlash against feminism and further "male-bashing" by women will exacerbate the issue as long as we remain in the polarizing duality of patriarchal consciousness.

4. On ship to the Falkland Isles, pornographic movies were shown that were calculated to instill the need for each soldier to prove himself as a "man" in the eyes of his fellows—that is, to exert domination and control over others.

5. Keen, 47.

6. Monique Wittig, *Les Guerilleres* (New York: Viking Press, 1969), 89.

7. Mary Daly, *Gyn Ecology* (Boston: Beacon Press, 1978), 327.

8. Valerie Solonas, quoted in Daly, 360.

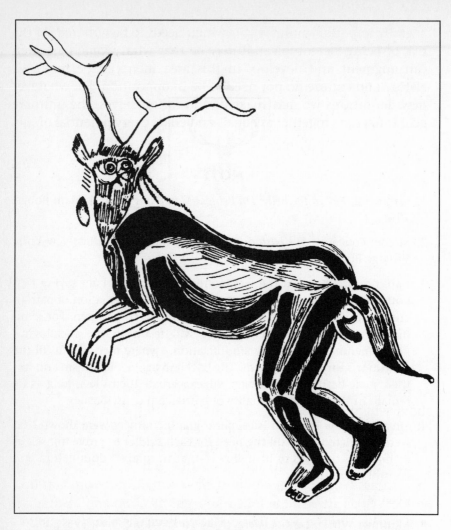

The Cave of Trois-Frères in the Pyrenees is known for this extraordinary masked and costumed figure. Set in a small side cave almost half a mile from the entrance, "The Sorcerer" was painted perhaps 20,000 years ago.

(From a drawing by the Abbot H. Breuil, who appears to have taken some liberties with his interpretation).

2

THE CAVE

THE GOD

At this point, I must be frank and endeavor to explain a little about where we are going. How do you know that you want to come on this journey, to read these pages, if you do not know the destination? We have all heard that it is not the goal but the process that is important, and this is true. But for you to consider the process worthwhile, we must have some future orientation. Besides, I was always one for instant gratification and invariably read the back of the book first. So if you have not already done so, this will save a little skipping about.

We are going to meet the GOD.

I make no bones about this. You do not have to gnaw to the marrow to find satisfaction. You do not have to flesh out a scanty structure and a few clues to find the body, or the monster in the center of this labyrinth. We are going to meet the god.

Wait, before you close the book in disgust, dismay, or disinterest, I promise you that this god-beast-man will fulfill your wildest dreams, will give you excitement, pleasure, rootedness, connectedness, renewal, and a sense of identity worthy of being called a man! This is about putting on a new skin, a new sense of self, and embodying the power that at once puts you in the center and, at the same time, allows you to touch everything.

I call this god or this power the Green Man. Others in this tradition may call it by a different name: the Horned God, Herne, Cernunnos, the Wild Man. All of these and more will come into the quest. But I call the energy of masculinity that I draw upon to nourish my true self and bring me into harmony with the world, the Green Man. For me, this image of masculinity from the past is the immanent experience of the god. The Green Man—with foliate abundance gushing from his head—is the great lover, the skillful magician, the wise warrior, the powerful healer, the poet, the true priest. He is divine. He runs with the animals. He is the man blessed with true sovereignty of self. He is the profound experience of the archetype of masculinity in a man. The reason I call this being the Green Man is because it is an inclusive term for all of the above and also because he comes from my own tradition.

WHICH TRADITION?

As people have moved from the countries of their origin to all quarters of the globe, a question has arisen—to which cultural and spiritual tradition do they belong? Is it possible to graft European branches onto American rootstock, or do we always remain a part of our own genetic, cultural, and historical lineage? Any person born upon a land can be said to be a native of that land; but when determining what constitutes a native culture, a historical and genetic depth that can only be engendered by the passing of millennia needs to be considered.

Some of the restlessness and sense of alienation present in the psyche of the white North American male is a result of a sense of rootlessness. There is no deep past, no ancient tradition, no native culture that he can call his own. Either he can remain bonded in ghettos of his ethnic origin, continue speaking, eating, and enacting the culture of his predecessors, or, because many fled the oppression of those cultures, he can abandon them altogether. The result either way is dilemma over what constitutes being an American on the one hand or a native of another culture on the other.

Neither can wholly satisfy the demands of the new land and of his own consciousness.

Take language as an example. Language is important because within it lie the values of a culture. Language tells us how and what to think because it grew up alongside the processes by which we think. The Celtic and the Germanic languages arose in unique geophysical locations in Europe and were shaped by the nature of the environment. Internalized into the people, the language, with its accompanying values, then shaped the environment. There has been a symbiosis of people and nature in every part of the world. Each has generated the shape of the other over great periods of time.

The main experience of the prehistorical European was of forests. As the ice sheets came and retreated, the climate varied, and groups of people moved over the land following the migrating herds of animals, the basic background of life was always the forest. The names of the trees, their leaves, their fruits and types of wood, the environment which they were host to, their particular shape, color, and smell probably generated the first words and grammatical sets of words. Similarities and differences between the trees, their relative hardness, combustibility, and other uses gave shape to words and categories that gave shape to the world.

In the Celtic-druidic tradition, it was always said that the first alphabets came from the trees. These possessed a sacred and divinatory use because the origins of the letters were embedded in the roots, in the trees of the world. Erma Pound, an initiate into the Tibetan tradition, has told me the same thing. The first Tibetan letters had their origin in the shape of and the patterns upon the trunks of trees.[1] In the Norse tradition, the god Odin was said to have hung upon the world tree, Yggdrasil, before being able to plunge down and draw up from its roots the magical letters, the runes. Each rune is associated with a species of tree, is shaped to express that tree's essential signature, and to make itself easy to carve upon wood.

We can guess relationships to animals also engendered language. The acts of hunting, cutting, cooking, curing, and otherwise observing the nature of creatures will have created sets of terms that then would have shaped the inner world of the psyche and then, again, shaped the outer world as similar properties, patterns, and relationships were noted. Words that were formed in communication over the processing of a slain creature would have been transferred to other processes as the millennia advanced.

It is possible to guess that early European language reached a fairly developed state by perhaps 40,000 years ago, and drew upon an even remoter experience that existed in the species Homo erectus—with pretty much the same characteristics of humanity and an even larger brain capacity—for 500,000 years. Homo sapiens appears in the archaeological record as early as 200,000 years ago, living alongside another species, the Neanderthal. The first evidence of shelter building and tool making in Europe goes back firmly to 400,000 B.C.E., evidence for ritualized burial practice as far as 80,000 years B.C.E. It is probably much older. It is this kind of development and others like them, such as inscriptions or paintings on stone, bone, or on cave walls that demonstrate the capacity for abstract thought.

The capacity for abstract thought is the marked difference between human and animal species. The creation of flint tools is perhaps the first and the best example of this development. It reveals the process whereby the mind is able to abstract itself from the object, in this case, the raw flint nodule, and project a future of an altered form which better serves the specific purpose. The thinker then carries out the act, chips the stone, and produces a cutting edge. We can be sure that such processes were accompanied by language.

As time went by, as a result of this abstracting ability, language developed to a point where it became increasingly divorced from the action, the object, and the context of the environment itself. It then became more complex and could be applied to a whole range of situations. Language became a tool of planning, of negotiating, of trading, of specialization, of metaphorical, analogical, and allegorical thought, which allowed contemplation of the universe and the place of things within it. It is through the act of naming that we understand more of what and who we are. Through naming an animal, for example, the deer, we understand that the meanings associated with the word "deer"—grace, agility, speed, shyness, and nonhostility—can exist in us.

One of the main features of all such thinking is analogy, sympathy, of like resonating with like. The word for cotton is applied to everything of a similar nature. Through analogy, language becomes a means of magical cause and effect and a provider of order through connectedness in an otherwise apparently chaotic universe. Each racial or genetic lineage in the land of its arising generates a unique language which is embedded in the matrix of the land. And this language, as it evolves over vast periods of time, shapes the culture and the order of the inner world and this, in turn, feeds back out to shape the order of the outer world.

Language embedded in its geophysical context provides an enormous sense of identity and belonging for its speaker. Words have power, for they are at once meaning and meaningful context. The shape of the word itself provides a map to the surrounding world—the contours are the same. A person who is speaking a language in its geophysical context cannot suffer from alienation. In this situation, objects have power. Everything is infused with its own essence. Each creature, stone, tree, or place is not separate from the perception that the user of the "geo-local" language has of it, even though they are capable of abstract thought. The roots of the words which shape the movement of abstract thought are the context in which the mind thinks.

By the time of the Greeks, however, writing had moved language to another level. Writing made us observers, apparently standing outside the play of life, as our thoughts no longer required an active thinker to keep them in existence. Extremely abstract world views could be created with writing, including the idea that the changing world is but a shadow of the perfectly ordered, inner one. This suited autocrats and tyrants admirably, for through insistence upon a fixed set of laws they could maintain their power indefinitely.

And so we come to the situation where an individual equipped with words and categories for describing, understanding, and acting within one context or cosmos moves to another. At first the experience can be overwhelming. The individual simply does not possess the language to order the experience of the new world and thus make it meaningful. Indeed the individual may not have the ability to perceive an object before his or her eyes. They suffer "culture shock." The words with which the experience can be described and interpreted are simply unavailable. The often

quoted (and perhaps apocryphal) example of this was the arrival
of the ships of Magellan in the straits of Tierra del Fuego. Although
the sailors could see the Indians on the shore, the Indians apparently had no awareness of them until the sailors stepped out of
their longboats onto the beach beside them. Even then, the native
people could not "see" the tall ships riding at anchor out in the
bay, much to the astonishment of the sailors.

To continue with the North American example, it does appear
that the native Americans were willing, by and large, to share with
the incoming Europeans their thoughts and words which allowed
them to perceive and order the world. Some people were very good
at getting "inside" the native peoples' frames of reference, but for
the most part the Europeans preferred to import their own categories of meaning, their own language of relationships to the land.
This was not the language that had its arising in the forests of prehistory, which could have understood the native Americans. It was
the language structured by the development of abstract, dualistic,
and hierarchical ideas which legitimated the culture of patriarchy.

The native sense of connectedness to the land, of the sacredness
of all things, perhaps most profoundly exemplified by Chief Seattle's response to Washington's request to buy land, was drowned in
the deluge of foreign words that had no meaningful context with
which to relate to the indigenous world view. This was the dilemma
for the Americans. They wanted to relate to the new land, they no
longer wanted to be Europeans, but for the most part all they had
in their possession were hierarchical, classical, and Christian concepts, which did not allow them access to their own deeply rooted
tradition that could have enabled them to understand and resonate
in sympathy with the culture of the land they were coming into.
They had, in effect, lost their tribe. They did not want what they
had but neither did they know anything else. The result was the
worst kind of gold-rush mentality and exploitation, which led to
the crushing of the native peoples, the establishment of means of
production relying upon enslaved peoples for its labor, and the
extermination of native species of animals.

Thus it is that I feel the tradition we need to work with most
deeply is the one from our own lands of origin. For us to find
meaning in our lives, wherever we are on the planet, we need to

work with the traditions that have been shaped by the thousands of years of arising in a particular place. For it is these traditions in language, in mental categories, in perceptions, that belong to our racial memory and biological code, which will allow us to resonate—albeit unconsciously—in harmony with other traditions.

I am sure that the indigenous American or any indigenous people around the world would be happier if we sat around the fire with them telling stories, myths, and legends from our own native traditions rather than if we tried to copy theirs. The problem is whether it is possible for us to find our lost stories, whether we belong to tribes which have rich and meaningful traditions.

As an example of native American emphasis upon following their own tradition, these are the words of the Hopi elder David Monongye in a message sent to the Dalai Lama in October of 1982. The italics are mine.

> We understand very well that the highest way of life can only be founded upon a spiritual basis, through loyalty to the true religion of *one's own tradition*. For thousands of years we Hopi have followed this guideline and have survived to this day as proof of the truth and strength of a way of life based on spiritual forces... If a person has eyes, ears, and an open mind, it is possible to learn from written materials, but the best learning comes from the lips of wise elders, and from the earth and nature.[2]

THE EUROPEAN TRADITION

The tradition I will be working with in this book will be one whose origin is in Europe. What I am concerned with is the people whose cultural tradition arose in the European forests. They were present there from at least 500,000 years ago. Their cultural tradition was strongly developing in all central regions from 120,000 B.C.E., when we have evidence of flint "factories" and possibly burial rites. It was formed as the people followed the migrating herds of deer, bison, horse, mammoth, and aurochs across clear areas of higher ground as glacial periods came and went. It exploded with creativity, tool-making, art, elaborate burial forms, and adornment from 35,000 B.C.E. onward—for example, in the Perigord Region of France. It changed as people settled into more sedentary modes from about 9000 B.C.E. It became a cultural tradition that was homogenous enough to flourish as a wide-reaching civilization in the Megalithic Period between 4600 and 2500 B.C.E.—a colossal length of time—during which trade, gifts, and knowledge were exchanged freely from Orkney to Brittany to Portugal. It went through a transformation of lifestyle and world view in the third millennium B.C.E.—what is often known as the "proto-Celtic." It emerged again as a widespread culture in the second and first millennia. The people were the Keltoi, Gauls, Celtae, and Galatians of the Roman and Greek historians.

At this time a loose, decentralized, matrifocal, tribal culture extended across Europe. It drew on the traditions of the past, while at the same time coalescing them, giving them form and providing consistency through the spiritual teachings of the druids. The druids, men and women, were the holy people of the Celts. However, the early Celts could not be described as an ethnic group but more as a cultural phenomenon which possessed a certain common philosophical and metaphysical outlook in all of its local diversity. Eventually the culture was influenced and then invaded by the powerful forces of Rome and of Christianity. It maintained itself a little longer in the unconquered reaches of Ireland, Wales, and Scotland. Other related but culturally distinct traditions also continued in the Baltics and Scandinavia.

All of these places were eventually thoroughly invaded by the values of patriarchy. Celts in the central European regions took to hierarchy and even monotheism as they provided unifying principles advantageous to an aggressive warrior society. And here lies the difficulty in perceiving what the prehistoric tradition of the West was in the broad sense. The literary and historical windows we have on the past are not clear. They must be reinterpreted through their classical and Christian overlay. At this point all manner of disputes break out. Who holds the key to a "correct" interpretation of the material?

The answer is you. You hold the key.

Interpretation of history is fraught with difficulties. In the case of prehistory, interpretation is practically all we have left and my interpretation is no better than yours. Perhaps, at least, I can state my bias as we proceed through the subject matter. But, at best, it is important to bear in mind that the answer to our quest lies in the realm of individual human experience. It is your experience which matters as we survey the material that remains from the lost male tradition of Europe. The history, ideas, theories, and symbols I present you with are not the answer. They are the raw materials from which you can fashion your own experience of what it means to be "a True Man." There is a dilemma here which reflects the divide between psyche and soma, between idea and experience within our own being. I felt closest to resolving this dilemma when I shared stories of my own personal experience, as in Chapter 8. For now, where do we begin on the journey toward the god?

THE CAVE ART OF EUROPE

Our search for the Source begins in the caves and with the carvings on bone and stone from the Upper Paleolithic of 35,000 to 12,000 years ago. This was a time of tremendous florescence in technology and art. Although beautiful artifacts had been created long before this time (geometrically exact ovals, leaves and triangles of flint, and the bifacet—the basic cutting tool, rounded at the base and tapering to a point), it was in this period that European culture reached a major peak.

In Europe, although the picture is far from clear, Homo sapiens (Cro-Magnon), who appear to have derived from Homo erectus, predominate over the Neanderthals, who, on a separate evolutionary path, now disappear. However, skeletons exhibiting both Neanderthal and Cro-Magnon characteristics have been found as late as the Magdalenian period of the Paleolithic, c. 12,000 B.C.E.—so it would seem the two interrelated. No evidence of warfare has ever been found, unless the paintings of men pierced by lances in the cave at Cougnac c. 15,000 B.C.E. depict intercommunal strife. The motifs at this cave, however, suggest it was a place of male initiation. The two transfixed men out of more than three hundred representations probably had a significance other than that of war.

The art in the caves of Lascaux, Altamira, Rouffignac, Laussel, Niaux, Les Eyzies, Les Combarelles, and many other locations in southern France and northern Spain reveal to us the tradition of prehistoric Europe that is our inheritance. Through its study and observation, we can begin to feel our rootedness in the land and the connection with our spiritual lineage.

The painters and engravers were men who looked like us. Being more used to physical activity, they may have looked, on the whole, tougher, but we can be sure they had the same concerns as we do as far as looks went. They adorned themselves, painted themselves, tried different hair styles, and indeed, if anything, may have looked nobler than us as a result of a confident physicality and the natural materials they used for their dress. Of course, most of this evidence has been destroyed as a result of the passage of time, so we have nothing in the archaeological record other than stone, bone, drilled shells, and teeth. But we do have the tools that were capable of working now perished materials: drills, chisels, scrapers, needles, awls, blowpipes, and sharpened drawing instruments.

If the diversity of artistic techniques is anything to go by—engraving, modeling, relief, stencilling, brush drawing, wash drawing, pointing, and blowing, as well as perspective, profile, and three-quarter views—then we can be certain that equal complexity existed in other aspects of life. Music, storytelling, basket making, dancing, body decoration and adornment, leather working, wood crafting, and clothing indubitably reached standards at least as excellent as the cave art—and may have surpassed it. For they were constantly practiced, not accomplished in what was probably a one-of-a-kind feat in the difficult and dark working conditions of a deep cave.

On the other hand, these people were not like us. A thousand other influences and changes have meant we are a long way from being able to understand what the cave art meant for its creators. It is a mystery. Yet, a mystery that still lives inside of us and which may be experienced, if not put into words.

And here we have the difference between them and us. Our language has become divorced from its context. Our words, though possessing precise meanings, are often used to say the exact opposite of what they mean. This duplicity, or rather, this psychic distance between the observer and the observed did not exist for the cave artists. In the words of Ernst Cassirer, these people possessed a "sympathetic identification" with the surrounding world which then had an immediate directness.[3] The meaning of a word lay in the word that lay in the context of daily life. We can

Three bulls from Lascaux. These larger-than-life-size aurochs were painted more than 17,000 years ago.

go one step further and say that meaning lay in the world, and words or other resonant forms could reveal that meaning. There was no duality of Spirit and Matter.

From this point, we can step for the first time into the cave. We will return again to the cave later in this book, but this is the first entry. We go in, not to talk about what lies there but to experience it directly.

In one of the passageways, bison appear. They undulate with the cave wall. Their legs are formed by fissures which arise out of an opening, a shaft, which plunges to the deep, impenetrable levels below. They rise out of the earth. Their vast bodies are packed with power, immanent, meaning-full. They are filled with an energy that their horns, legs, tails, eyes, and muzzle express but can hardly contain. We look up at an aurochs arching over the ceiling. The huge red body is the power the artist was creating. The tiny head and legs seem almost an afterthought—the signatures that make explicit the characteristics of the power being held in contemplation.

The artist did not think of drawing to draw this delicate horse, did not plan his design. He may have been alone in the dark. He became infused with the horse. The meaning that was horse came to him, filled him and expressed itself through the interaction of his hands, his tools, and pigments. Perfect in detail, but not every detail needed to be there: arching neck and flowing mane but no face, hind legs but no forelegs, belly but no back, merely a dappling of spray paint blown through a bone—was enough to express horse.

So intense is the focus on the thing itself that there is no context: no ground, no trees, sometimes not even an above or below. The figure exists of itself in limitless space or only in relationship to other creatures. The figure exists in its most powerful form, often of overwhelming size—one of the bulls at Lascaux is more than eighteen feet long—and invariably in dynamic movement or in an alert, tense stance.

And what is this? On the ground, a stone, engraved with a triangle and a slit for a vulva. Separate from the body, the parts of the self constellate themselves without reference to each other. We notice this in any other depiction that may be of a human form. Unlike the creatures, human figures are not correct in anatomical detail, they show only parts, the merest suggestion of humanity.

Talk about yourself. Communicate from within, not your view of yourself from without. Express what it is like to be inside a body and you may draw like a child does—all large head, mouth, and eyes, tiny body but great fingers. Express as a woman, fertile, possibly pregnant or breast feeding, and you may engrave a figure like that of the Venus of Laussel: spreading hips, center of gravity in the belly, pendulous breasts, small arms and legs, holding a bison horn up to her lips. Raw, natural, fecund, and given over to the body she is in her chthonian, watery power. Beside her are three other similar figures and one other, a wiry man, the "Huntsman" throwing a spear. All from 20,000 years before the present.

They may represent an experience you have had or something you would like to be, but in any case they connect you with power. Power from within yourself, from your own physical nature. Or, returning to the paintings, they connect you with power from within an animal. It is significant that the artists were not so much concerned with scenes or depictions of vegetation— which they had the skill and the techniques to execute if they had so wished—they were concerned with the creatures themselves: the mammoth, the woolly rhinoceros, the giant deer, the bison, aurochs, horse, ibex, and every now and then a big cat or a bear.

Bison in the cave of Font de Gaume at Les Eyzies. They are part of a remarkable frieze where the natural contours of the rock surface are used to great effect. The creatures emerge out of natural fissures in the cave wall, adding three-dimensional depth. Painted some time before 13,000 B.C.E.

And they were concerned with the movement and the energy of these creatures.

At Lascaux the first painting in the cave is of an extraordinary creature. A composite, fanciful beast made of parts drawn from many. Evidently possessing a phallus, it is also pregnant. Its heavy skin suggests the leopard, the hump, the bison. Its long, straight horn has meant it has been given the name of "the Unicorn," but the horn might be double. What gives it away are the human legs. Prehistoric painters understood the articulations of animal legs perfectly. They drew sinews, hooves, and joints, in correct anatomical arrangement and detail. The legs on this creature are not a mistake. They are human. The head looks like a mask. Here we have the half man, half beast with the colossal, mighty horns that weaves its way through the meandering labyrinth of the European prehistorical tradition and provides us with the clues for the way in.

We are not separate from the world. We are a part of it. Our identification with life flows out through our limbs, our bodies. Our arms throw spears, our wombs give birth, we become injured, we become sick, we die. Our minds, our language, are given shape by the world and, giving shape to it, we cannot help but express it in all its complexity, its ugliness, and its beauty. We create ourselves, but in the caves only humans remain somewhat ill defined. The horse is horse. The ibex is ibex. Aurochs is clearly aurochs. But we? What are we becoming?

MYTH AND MYTH MAKING

After the tremendous emergence of culture in the Upper Paleolithic—and how can we be sure that earlier cultural outpourings did not achieve equal peaks, long since destroyed?—the technologies and skills that had been developed appear to have become dissipated and dispersed over a broad area of Europe. In this period, the Magdalenian, between about 15,000 and the last glaciation of 9,000 B.C.E., the old technologies and industries were maintained, but attention seems to have turned away from the "high art" of the caves to the development of social and perishable cultural forms. This, after all, is a very long period of time. And it is precisely in such spans of years, through interaction with the environment, that language and the perceptual and the conceptual patterns of the brain went through their formative stages.

Although the deep past appears static or slow moving in comparison to the apparent "speeding up" of development in history, where inventions appear to proliferate as we come closer to the present, to an extent this is an illusion of our perspective. The developments we need to think about are not technical or even cultural, but cognitive, linguistic, emotional, and psychosomatic. The vast spans of time in what we tend to dismiss as "prehistory" created our patterns of thought, our perceptual categories, our social patterns of relating and bonding, our codes of behavior and communication. All were embedded in the physical context of the environment. The sense of self, of "I," of the body, was intimately bound up with the life of the immediate kin, the tribe, and the ecological context of life.

The natural world for the people of this time was perceived and conceived of in terms of the human experience, and human life was experienced and conceived of in terms of the natural world. The experience of "self" or "mind" enfolded not only the tribe but all of life. There was no cognitive dualism arising as a

Appearing to possess a leopard's skin, a bison's hump, a pregnant belly, male genitalia, human legs, and unusual horns, the "Unicorn" from Lascaux may be one of the ways the cave artists represented themselves. The horse beside it has lost its head. Possibly 17,000 years old.

result of a philosophical or religious world view which saw people and nature in separation. As a result of this experience of life, every event and phenomenon was not spoken of as an "it" but in terms of an emotionally laden relationship which H. Frankfort has characterized as one of "I-thou." He writes, "Thou experienced as life confronting life, involving every faculty of man in a reciprocal relationship." Frankfort goes on to suggest that even thought did not operate autonomously in this cognitive mode, but that the whole being "confronts a living thou in nature...and gives expression to the experience."[4] This is equivalent to the "sympathetic identification" of Cassirer.

In such a reality there must be a "will" present in the world for things to happen. There was a purpose in a storm coming at a particular time. The river communicated its wishes in flooding. The animal came to the hunter as a result of the reciprocal relationship between them. (This may be the significance of the men pierced by lances at Cougnac.) Death wills itself to be. The sun rising and the greeting of the sun were not acts of cause and effect but were of a congruent and immanent experience of life which knew time not as a uniform succession but as an emerging periodicity—as a unifying rhythm of the inner and the outer worlds.[5]

In such a reflexive universe, the live presence of the "thou" can reveal or conceal itself as it pleases, or, as a result of such unpredictability, as much as human actors participate within it. Through what we would call mythical or ritual enactment, the ancient people symbolically presented the cosmos to themselves as a compelling presence in which every aspect of their existence was involved.

This could only happen through action where events fundamental to the origin and nature of existence were dramatically related in order to perpetuate the experience of life as constant revelation. The masks, dance steps, songs, words, and other imagery recreated the experience in which the "thou" became known and thus the "I" became conscious. Through such dramatic enactments of their mythology, the people participated within the whole cosmos and could locate themselves within it. It would not be correct to think that without saying the prayers the sun would not rise or that the world was stuffed full of anthropomorphically animated "ghosts" or spirits. No. The world mirrored the people and the people mirrored the world and the two participated in an existence where there was no sharp separation between them. There was also no distinction between past and present, here or over there, individual mind or tribal mind, or living and dead—what connected them all was the physical and emotional experience of values. "Reality" was the total of all the inner and outer world. There was no division of sacred and profane. All of life was sacred.

As the experience of people increasingly became determined by anonymous urban environments, this direct perception of life was replaced by one in which the sense of individual self prevailed. Attention went inside, onto the individual. The sense of belonging to the tribe was lost. The complex and dynamic flux of inner and outer reality was replaced by dualistic concepts of mind and body, spirit and matter, and other simplistic cosmological beliefs. New myths changed the cosmology from one of being in a world of immanence to one of becoming in a world of linear time.

Personal salvation achieved in some future time replaced the awareness of living in a cosmos of immanent, perpetual, creative, changing revelation.

In recent years "myth" or "mythical" has come to mean something untrue or imaginary. And when mythology does arise as a subject among interested people, it is too often the patriarchally colored myths that attract all the attention. The supremely hierarchical and patriarchal organization of the Catholic Church has been hugely successful as a myth-maker. It has been successful in retaining its influence and power by not jettisoning many pagan mythical and ritual trappings as did Protestantism, and by understanding the deep need of people for a congruent, self-defining, and cosmically locating spiritual experience. It has done this through what I call Myths of Transition and Myths of Incorporation.[6] These tap into the ancient memories of the psyche with its sympathetic and elementally integrated experience of the world and places on top of them an interpretation, a dogma which incorporates them into the body of religious belief. When confronted, for example, by the enormous groundswell of feeling around the experience of the feminine archetype as goddess—an experience that was pre-eminent in the classical and the pagan worlds—the Catholic Church adapted its dogmas to incorporate and direct this energy into Mother Mary and so preserve itself.

What of the mythological mis-makings of the god?

When we think of god, it is usually the jealous god of the Judaeo-Christian tradition. "Thou shalt have no other gods but me." We hear the same petulant cry in all the high offices of the world, whether they are seeking a monopoly of goods, status, services, or power. Accompanying the self-righteousness is utter contempt for the other, the opposition, the enemy. Thus, we know nothing of Belial or the other gods to whom Yahweh was opposed except that which casts them in a thoroughly evil darkness. The same situation occurs in the records of the conquests of northern Europe by the Romans. Although Julius Caesar, for example, needs his enemy the Gauls to be powerful, clever, and noble, or else there will be few kudos for him back in Rome for defeating them, his invasion is justified at every step by contempt which is poured upon the inhuman, cruel, and ignorant nature of the "barbarians." This is the record we have received and we have no accounts from the other side of the story. We must be careful, because many of our own prejudices are inherited from the Christian and classical traditions.

In defense of the Gauls there is very little evidence for barbaric cruelty. War was ritualized and symbolic. It did not require killing all the enemy. The occasional corpse found in a bog or below a foundation is more likely to be evidence of a deviant local superstition than to suggest widespread sacrificial or violent practice. The Romans themselves, supposedly civilized, engaged in torture, mass killing, and cruelty, often in spectator form, on a scale far in excess of any equivalent in the Celtic world. The problem here is not war per se, but the reporting of it, the social attitudes toward it, and the scale on which it is carried out.

TWO MYTHS OF WAR

Allow me to illustrate these points with an alternative view of the conquest of the Celtic peoples. For the Celts, war was a ritual. Men trained themselves, their horses, and their dogs for the time when a dispute flared up to a point where a solution could only be found through confrontation. The opposing sides would call on their network of allegiances created through gift exchange and marriage and at the appropriate time of season plans would be laid. There would have been chariots to repair, drums and trumpets to be made, bodies to paint, horses to decorate, auguries to consult, and offerings to be made to the appropriate powers.

When all was ready the two sides would have met at an agreed-upon time and place. The chariots would have raced up and down, the young men performing spectacular gymnastic feats. Weapons and symbols would have been paraded, pyres lit, and a lot of noise made. It would have been a ritual display. The quality of painting, the tone of the skin and of muscle would have been admired. The vigor of the horses, the skill of the charioteers and metalworkers, and the quality of the adornment and weaponry would have been observed. Perhaps at this point, ceremonially and, if you like, psychically defeated, one side would have withdrawn and made gift offerings to satisfy the other. We know the druids negotiated in such situations. Their songs boast of their peacemaking powers. If all were satisfied, the dispute would be over.

Bronze Roman Figurine from the third century B.C.E. The man wears a belt, a torc, and a horned helmet that identify him as a Celtic warrior. About five inches high.

If the grievances ran deep and neither side was able to gain an advantage from the ritual display, abuse and taunts may have developed alongside challenges. Those deeply embroiled in the dispute may have already decided to put themselves forward for combat or selected a champion to represent them. Spears may have been exchanged. If a wound was sustained, then the magical power of one side was seen to be greater than the other. The spirit powers favored one side and the other would be unwise to go on. Perhaps several pairs of opponents engaged and only after severe wounding or even a death would it have been seen that right prevailed on one side, and negotiation for settlement could begin. If there was a death, then blood-guilt would have been a severe burden for the slayer, requiring assuagement through ritual and economic reparation.

By contrast, the Romans (and the later patriarchal Celts) fought war for possession. They fought to win, not ritually, not for honor, but for material gain and for power over others. They prepared for war with plans that sought to defeat an opponent through strategy. They denied the face-to-face human content of war whenever possible. (A goal perfected by the long-distance weaponry of today.) They would come at a time when every Celt honored the peace and they burned the crops in the fields. They would come with sheer weight of numbers and would keep on coming, reinforced with legions and auxiliaries drawn from the vast resources of the empire. They took hill-forts, the granaries, and the river crossings and laid down roads and forts for supply and communication.

The Roman army did not care for the life of an individual. The life of Rome lay in its whole body with the emperor at its head. It could afford to lose a lesser appendage; it would grow back. And thus war was taken to another footing. It was played for stakes other than those of the Celts, and it played to kill them. In their thousands, the Roman war machine took the lives of individuals. Took the lives of men and women, with mothers, fathers, and children and honored and ancient lineages. It took the lives of people with songs, stories, skills, peculiarities, and powers. It took away the true experience of the warrior. It took away the experience of life as emerging present in which, at any moment, spiritual revelation could take place. And it substituted plans, strategies, and defenses, based upon the experience of the past and projections into the future, in order to satisfy the goal of possession. The songs of bards could now be replaced by quartermasters' lists of provisions. The re-establishment of peace and honor in the land could now be replaced by "triumphs"—processions which displayed the authority, booty, slaves, and captives of the patriarchs.

Although I do not wish to paint a picture of the Celts as being perfect, I do not think this version of history is any more biased than that of the classical historians. It serves to ask the question—from which side were the barbarities perpetrated?[7]

Just in case you might be saying this interpretation of Celtic warfare as a ritual display does not fit the facts, that men are and always have been the most aggressive and murderous species on the planet and that this is the "natural" way of things, bear with me a bit more while we further digress into an area we have, as yet, not examined: the animals, and particularly those closest to us, the primates.

Our closest evolutionary relatives, the gorillas and chimpanzees, are fairly amicable creatures who love attention and applause. Elaine Morgan has pointed out that these characteristics have merited them least attention from the populists of evolutionary theories. Those writers have chosen to focus upon our more distant relatives, the baboons, who are described as predatory, aggressive, and vicious. Whereas social relationships are established among gorillas through attention-grabbing display—such as the chest thumping routine—among baboons they are said to be established through a reign of competition and terror.

It is clear that the baboon can be used to justify as "natural" the aggressive drives of patriarchal men. This is why they are studied. But what is of interest among baboons is a feature the populists have chosen not to focus on, which is that in successful maneuvering for dominance, the baboon does not actually fight. Elaine Morgan: "The more often he fights, the greater are his chances of being defeated. The males who get to the top are...those who keep the tightest control over their aggressive reactions and use every trick in the book of diplomacy and delay and diversion to ensure that with the minimum loss of face they never actually tangle with a member of the Establishment clique."[8] The baboons who are aggressive turn out to be insecure newcomers to a social group. The reality is that relationships within the group are maintained through highly developed forms of friendship, cooperation, and diplomacy. These center upon the females, who, unlike the males, never leave a group they were born into.

Another blow to the model of Man the Mighty Hunter aggressively making his way through the forests and savannahs of prehistory, providing for and protecting his little mate and offspring, is that "male weapons and male aggressiveness are for dominance, not protection." In other words, when creatures are endowed with means of defense, like talons or teeth, these are given to both sexes. But when male creatures are given colossal tusks or massive antlers "...the less likely it is that the male's physical superiority has any relevance to protection or to predation."9 In short, they are given for ritual display.

This is an important point. Somehow we've always known that our guns and ballistic missiles were never meant for protection and defense, but for a sort of global rutting display where the largest weapons and most threatening demeanor meant alpha male. The difficulty seems to come when men bond into groups. Here a group of men cooperating together can defeat an individual who alone could overpower them. At this point peer pressure to conform seems to dip into the creation of ideologies, which could be described as a low kind of mass consciousness. This particularly human characteristic hinges around creating an externalized enemy that will unite as many men as possible into a closely knit group. The bigger and fiercer the enemy is made out to be, the greater the incentive to bond. The displays and diplomacy that previously provided a check on aggression fail when a male-bonded group start talking about the "enemy" and generating contempt for them.

In Sam Keen's *Faces of the Enemy*, he shows how we have all become responsible for war by subscribing to the polarizing view of us and the enemy. The "enemy consciousness" is fostered by the denial of humanity to the other side. The greatest sanction a soldier can receive is when he becomes an exterminator of "criminals and vermin." We have blinded ourselves, Keen argues, to the true enemy, who is within the depths of our personal and corporate selves. We will never face that until we cease projecting the dehumanizing, stereotypical "faces of the enemy" onto others and seeking solutions by killing them.10 We need a return to the pre-patriarchal or at least a pre-Apollonian state of mind, where the chthonian forces of the earth have as much a place as the idealized and transcendental.

CLASSICAL MYTHS

Returning to the main theme, we now arrive at the deceptive sleight of hand which was dealt to the mythology of the gods by the classical world. This has wholly sullied and determined our perspective of the pre-Christian, pagan, and pantheistic archetypes of masculinity. I believe the Greeks were responsible for this. The Roman pantheon was based upon that of the Greeks, who were busily spreading themselves all over the Mediterranean long before the Romans had begun to conquer their neighbors. During the time of Roman hegemony, it was into the hands of the Greeks that education, philosophy, and mythology were placed, a situation that existed in the Hellenistic world and on into the divided Roman Empire and then into Byzantium.

I am not fully certain why the Greeks made their gods so violent and capricious. A projection of their fantasies about themselves? A result of the warrior mentality reality of Mediterranean life? The assertion of urban culture over nature culture? The rise of transcendental belief and the dualism of body and soul, spirit and nature? One of the actions of the gods is to drive the giants from the world. The giants are the personification of the natural forces of life; one of whom, Prometheus, was a supreme benefactor, giving fire to humankind.

The gods rape whichever woman they desire and become supreme creators, assimilating, giving birth to, and controlling the goddesses. Whoever the goddesses were originally, and there are glimpses in Hesiod and Herodotus of powerful, parthenogenetic deities such as Eurynome, Rhea, and Gaia, by the time we come to popular mythology and belief they have become subject to the gods. Hera has become the jealous, simpering wife of Zeus; Athena was born from the head of Zeus; Demeter was taken by Poseidon, Kore or Persephone by Hades; Semele—the mother of earthy Dionysius—was killed by thunder and lightning from Zeus, who then assumed the role of mother by completing the gestation of the child in his thigh. The stories go on and on. Only Artemis, as the wild huntswoman, refusing men, seems to have maintained her autonomy. Her sanctuaries such as Ephesus became powerful centers of the goddess cults in the ancient world.

A possible answer to the question asked about the Greeks and their gods came one rainy day when I and a friend, Diana, visited the Holy Well of Saint Canice just outside of Kilkenny in Ireland.

We huddled into the tiny whitewashed cell to avoid the rain beating down outside, and despite the rubbish, contemplated the waters of the spring gurgling by. Diana began the conversation.

"Maybe the Lady of the Lake, Canice, and the Irish Mother Goddess, Brigit, are the same. They are water goddesses. But then many of the ancient goddesses have their origin in the sea. The war goddesses of the Tuatha de Danaan were led by the terrible Morrighan. Originally she was a sea goddess who sang from the rocks, luring sailors to their deaths. Isn't it strange that the feminine in these tales should be so terrible and at the same time so enchanting? The sylphs and mermaids combing their hair and looking into their mirrors were beautiful to men and also such a trap. Do you suppose it's because men are afraid of letting go into their feelings, of jumping into the primal waters?"

"I think so," I replied. "Like everyone else I was taught to appear to be in control of my feelings. 'Be a man.' Rise above the wildness of my natural emotions, the churning feminine sea. Then there was all that stuff about women's hysteria. The biggest insult you could give another man was to call him a 'sissy' or a 'woman.' But surely water represents more than feelings?"

Diana let the waters of Saint Canice's well flow over her fingers before she replied. "The waters are ancient and primeval. They are about life and death. Which is why men are afraid of the sea and honor her when sailing on her. But they are also about rebirth. Which is why baptism by water is the most widespread initiatory rite in the world. By plunging into the waters, into the feminine ooze of the womb, we can release the old and rise renewed.

"King Arthur got his sword, Excalibur, for the first time from a stone, which represents the feminine. He got it the second time directly from the feminine. He got it from the waters, from the Lady of the Lake, which shows he had access to the realm of the deep unconsciousness. He was an initiate who had died to himself, who was willing to plunge into the waters. He had been to the other side and been reborn of the goddess. His throne and the Grail are also feminine symbols, but it is in the sword that the deeper face of the feminine is revealed."

"How is that?" I frowned as I fished some of the debris out of the basin that formed the wellhead.

"All of us must be strong in the masculine energy. It is great strength. But we must learn how to contain and direct its power, not throw it away. As all men are born of women, of the waters of the Great Goddess, their power comes through the feminine. But when they grasp the sword, it is feminine power transformed into masculine power and must be used wisely. This is why the teaching of the scabbard is as important as the sword. Power in abeyance is power held. But power projected and used is power gone. When Arthur used his power to try and force the issue of his son, Mordred, it caused his death. The sword had to be returned by Bedivere to where it came from—the Lady of the Lake."

"That may be," I said. "But Venus-Aphrodite was a sea-born goddess, and she has never struck me as being very powerful."

"Maybe she hasn't struck you yet!" Diana laughed, throwing back her head. "But you are partly right there. The Greeks replaced the ancient goddesses with male-born ones who had less power. The myths show that patriarchal values of competition and hierarchy crept into the older pantheon and the gods all began fighting each other for the succession. Kronos overthrew his father Uranus. Zeus overthrew Kronos and the Titans to establish Olympus. The goddesses did not have to fight each other. They simply transformed, giving birth to each other through parthenogenesis.

"This power was frightening to the Greek mind that was trying to put logic and rationality in the primary place. Love made men lose their reason. It was chaotic. So they took the power away from the goddesses. Zeus took the earth, his brothers Poseidon took the sea and Hades took the Underworld. Venus-Aphrodite was born of the overthrow by Zeus of his father Kronos. He cut off his father's testicles and threw them into the sea. This was an attempt to re-create Aphrodite, goddess of love, in the order of the masculine rather than in terms of the chaotic, feminine genetic principle."

"Didn't a similar sort of thing happen to Athena, goddess of wisdom?"

"Yes, she was made to spring fully formed out of the head of Zeus. You couldn't get a clearer example of male usurpation of feminine power. Athena became the model for Greek women to emulate: chaste, faithful, perfectly reasonable and matronly. Zeus also assumed women's reproductive role by gestating Dionysius in his thigh. The chthonic wildness of Dionysius who loved to be with the women was replaced by Zeus' favorite son, Apollo, the great civilizer, the perfect Sky God.

"The result of all this in the subconsciousness of the Greeks was simply awful. By fragmenting the whole image of the archetypal feminine, the negative aspects of the feminine—emerging as the sirens, the furies, the harpies, the gorgon, Medusa, Circe, and so on—were given a power that could only manifest indirectly. They came in nightmares, intoxication, and madness. In the same way that the Christian creation of one god on high created and gave existence to its opposite, the devil down below, so the Greeks created an archetype of the feminine that made women either matrons or demons. We've been virgins or whores ever since."

I was impressed by this exposition and said so. Diana grinned wryly and said not to thank her, but her namesake. "At least she kept her power. They couldn't subsume her. Oh, by the way, did you know that Diana-Artemis is not only the Huntress, Queen of the Animals and Cat Goddess, but Mistress of the Drains?"

"Of the drains?" I was puzzled.

"Yes. Remember her when you build, or farm, or manage a grove or a wood. The renewing, recycling, or filtering aspect of water, that very important part of the water cycle, the part where all the riches are—the muck, the blood, the shit—is the area she presides over. If your drains are not in order, then nothing is in order."

The rain had stopped. We left, taking the rubbish that had choked the wellspring with us. It was time, I felt, to renew the cycle of my own inner archetypal life and not allow it to be clogged with broken images of enchantresses and demons. Surely we all needed to restore the benevolent image of Brigit, the fecund images of ancient mothers, the beautiful forms of sylphs, the power of Diana-Artemis to our rivers, streams, springs, and wells, if they were to flow healthily once more?[11]

One of the explanations for the rise of the gods in Greek culture was the desire for transcendence from the suffering of life. The natural world, which women with their powerful and mysterious fertility cycles were so clearly a part of, was chaotic, cruel, and demanding. This is worth examination. In the *Oresteia,* the trilogy of the Athenian playwright Aeschylus, the case is put.

In the old world, that dominated by irrational feminine deities, feminine avenging furies and other feminine figures of nightmare, the rule is blood for blood with no way out. Because Clytemnestra killed her husband Agamemnon for killing their daughter, Iphigynia, she must be killed by their son, Orestes, who must be killed for killing her, and so on. The city, representing the new order under the aegis of Athena and Apollo, declares a new dispensation. This new order is based upon rationality and justice. It transcends the old rule of the mindlessness of nature. From now on, women will be merely the bearers of the seed of men, who will dispense order and justice.

This example is often used to demonstrate the vengeful nature of women and the cruelty and primitiveness of any anciently existing matriarchal society. In place of "justice" there are endless blood feuds. The archaeological record of "matriarchal" sites such as Çatal Hüyük does not reveal such a situation at all, nor do anthropological studies of contemporary cultures which balance power more equally between the sexes. If Diana's exposition at Saint Canice's well is correct, then we know that the feminine "furies" our urban heroes are trying to escape from are those created in their own minds by their vertical and dualistic division of the world and the repression of the feminine.

Transcendence in this case is another abstraction created by the sophistry of the Greek mind to use as a stick to beat the world with. With this stick, goddesses and women suffered especially, but so did the gods. It is no accident that at the same time as the idea of a supreme emperor-god was being raised in the Hellenistic-Roman world, a supreme god-man was being raised in the Palestinian. Christ rose above the world and the body so completely that we are told we have only to have faith in him and we will go to heaven. The final nails were being driven into the body of the world to render it a dispirited corpse devoid of its natural cyclical, phylogenetic, and rejuvenative forces by such ideas. The world was made a place of sin and suffering against which any other blows could be made, as only the transcendent afterlife mattered. The wickedness of nature had to be further defeated and driven out of the pure spiritual body of Christ—the Church, or, in the Greek case, the city.

No one seemed willing to point out that a large portion of the cataclysms, injustices, and cruelties of the world were not inflicted by natural forces but by the wishes of people, mostly men, for control and power. The Greek city, extolling democracy, was in fact a tyranny of slaves and citizens. Women had no vote and little power. This was the real issue in question: having created a world of transcendence, with the sacred—whatever that was—at the top of the hierarchical order, where was the ontological model for men that rendered them able to live as a harmonious part of the world? Or were they at essence, an emptiness, devoid of the sacred, which in attempting to fill, drove them to further capriciousness and to obsessive, insatiable transcendentalism? A self-defeating and vicious cycle was thus created and the Greek pantheon was incapable of supplying the demands made upon it.

THE GREEK GODS

Apollo, in whose culture we all now live, was a chip off the old block of Zeus for all his solar attributes. He overthrew the goddess at Delphi to establish his own temple. One of the maxims engraved there, not the ones we usually hear about, was "Keep Women Under Rule." Dionysius, for all his apparent natural wildness, ultimately comes under the same stamp. For he is born of Zeus, denying the genetic principle, and his rites do not offer the finding of self, but stupor, intoxication, and madness. Apollo and Dionysius divide the world between them into a false duality: one apparently civilized and cultured, one apparently chthonic and wild. It is not a healthy duality, for they never meet. One takes all that is perceived as good—the city and culture—and identifies it with the mind, the sun, and sky. The other takes all that is bad—lack of control, lust, and raw sexuality—and identifies it with the watery forces of the body, nature, and the world. Hermes is interesting as the divine messenger with the implicit possibility of being able to move between these worlds. But he is the servant of an already divided world and becomes like Mercury, slippery and elusive, playing tricks which can deceive as much as enlighten.

Hephaistos is much closer in his character to the gods of the chthonic, pre-patriarchal, pre-Zeus world. He is born partheno-genetically of Hera—the original divine mother—but is rejected by her for his lameness. Dwelling under the sea in the company of women, he is taught metalworking by Thetis and the ancient, pre-Olympian goddess Eurynome, forging his connection to the primeval, watery roots of the world. He is further crippled by Zeus for criticizing his treatment of his mother, Hera, to whom he is always loyal. As the smith god, he deeply interests women, for he is strong and creative and must enter the womb of the earth to find the materials he needs for his creations. Though he makes weapons upon request, his actions are always peaceful. But despite his skill he is clumsy and impetuous. The raw muscular energy with which he works is as likely to explode as a volcano, or ejaculate prematurely, or trip him up, or put him on the edge of rape, as it is to make objects of great beauty. He fails to satisfy his beautiful marriage partner Aphrodite, but it is significant that he is married to the goddess of love at all. Hephaistos may be a god that represents an aspect of the masculine in women. He is what Jungian psychologists would call an "animus" figure—working within the earth, within the womb, fatherless, unable it seems to produce children, but able to bring forth golden objects of refinement, power, great worth, and beauty. Born of a woman, taught by women, mining the precious strata of the earth, instinctive, creative, but impotent, Hephaistos is a golden boy refining the inner world of the women's realm and perhaps telling us something about the relationship of the masculine to the feminine.[12]

Ares or Mars, the god of war, is a very difficult mythic energy to approach. The version we have of him is virtually bereft of any of the principles, codes, and even the compassions of warfare that I described in my sketch of the Celtic approach to war. Ares is, or has become, the god of violence and murder. It is difficult to face him, accept that within our lives, and go beyond him to his true nature or our own true nature as warriors. Men are violent because of what has been mythologized in the name of the hero, the warrior, Ares. "Greater love hath no man than a man who lays down his life for his friends" should really read "Greater love hath no man than a man who picks up a weapon and kills with maximum effect."

Although many of the space missions have been flown in spacecraft named "Apollo," this was merely a transference of the aspects of one god to another. "Ares" or "Mars" would have been perhaps too explicit. It amounts to the same thing. The supreme weapon, with most deadly effect created by this patriarchal archetype of the warrior, is the phallic rocket, which goes up, zeroes in on the target, comes down, and the result is an explosion and destruction, a twisted and scattered mess. Similar magnitudes of phallic excess are paraded nightly on our television and cinema screens.

We have all suffered from this mess, this archetype, not just women but men also. The war system of the god Mars has resulted in unimaginable suffering to us all and to the body of the earth. Only through its recognition by us all will we find a way to be powerful without being violent, to be protective without having to fight, to be strong without having to give up being vulnerable, gentle and tender to ourselves and each other. The dichotomy of nature and culture is not absolute. We do not need to be urban Apollo any more than we need be lost in the wilds with Dionysus. Pagan nature complements transcendent mind. The two together, Earth God and Sky God, form the whole.

Let us unburden our minds of these concepts of misogynistic and violent gods and let us go and look precisely where the patriarchs, the inquisitors, the myth-mis-makers have told us not to look. Into the face of him whom they have labeled "the enemy"—the god who wears horns, who inhabits the dark and wild places, who consorts with witches and prepares a magical brew, a taste of which is said to grant the entire world.

THE HORNED GOD

In the initiations of the Knights Templar there was one rite that helped lead to their persecution and demise. The task of the initiate was to face their greatest fear. And so there was set up on a throne a figure concealed by a black cloth. At the appropriate moment the hood was removed and the goat god, Baphomet, stared down at the initiate who had been told to kneel.

If the initiate was able to push through their fear, accept the presence of the effigy, and ask why the theater of the mask and throne, the figure stepped down, removed the mask and revealed itself as one of their number. If the effigy was rejected and the initiate remained fearful, they had failed the rite and the mask was not removed.

The use of such dramatic enactment characterizes all mystery traditions in touch with the Source. To the outsider it may appear confusing, even contrary to the tradition's stated goal. It was from initiations such as this, which allowed people to meet and pass through their fear and so connect them to their denied inner wholeness and power, that Christianity drew the fuel to create propaganda about "devil" cults which then led to the time of the burnings.

Transcendental or otherworldly oriented religion did not wish people to go to the roots of their personal power and spirituality in the world. This would contradict the need for a "savior" and an intermediating priest. The doctrine of "original sin" was central to the needs of the priests. If "original innocence," wholeness, and natural sacredness could be shown, then they would have no authority. The world, the body, sexuality, and with it women, were therefore denied by the church and seen as the source of all evil things. The old, chthonic pagan cults with their dramatic ceremonies of music, song, dance, costume, masks, horns, and other paraphernalia were—albeit incompletely—suppressed. They provided the material which the priests in their pulpits and from their printed broadsheets could characterize as the trappings of evil, the devil, and the flesh.

Denied and suppressed, these things then possess tremendous power. No matter how much the priests attempted to extol the god in heaven and reify his church, it seemed the devil became stronger in hell and his minions flourished. Two sides of the same coin. Paganism could be burned out of the people; and yes, every pyre did increase the glory of God. But God was absent except in the minds of the executioners, and paganism—in terms of their own definition—also increased in the fears of their internally created demonic world.

Fundamentalist Christians forced into a literal reading of the Bible had to fill the world with real evil beings, (for example, the giants, who are the cultural opponents of the Israelites writ large) at the same time as they had to accept a real god and angelic hierarchy in heaven. It comes therefore as little surprise to discover that many thinkers today caught in this dualistic mode of absolute good and absolute evil exhibit pathological traits.[13] The intolerance, holy wars, and sanctified murders of Christian Fundamentalism and Islam reveal the danger of entrapment in such a wholeness-denying, divided, and transcendentally oriented symbolic cosmos.

In such a historical context, the pagan mystery tradition of the Horned God could not fare well. Although they became the symbol of evil, horns, like the serpent, were always symbols of divine wisdom. Both possess the capacity for renewal. However, they do make their entry in some surprising places in ecclesiastical history. The horns on the very masculine Moses by Michelangelo, for example, commissioned by a pope, is one such place. But the older horned god, Cernunnos in the Celtic tradition, usually given splendid antlers for a crown, was pretty much driven from view. In fact, so thorough was the fear of him and so persecuted were those who practiced his rites, that apart from sculpture or other craftwork there is virtually nothing in the historical record which describes him at all. We need to examine other faces of the Horned God and other sources such as mythology to gain a picture.

THE SERPENT IN THE GARDEN

Originally, according to the Book of Genesis, we lived in a garden with all the plants and creatures. The serpent was particularly significant. There were two trees that stood out among the others. The first was the Tree of Life. It is to this that we shall make reference again, for it is the symbol of our connectedness to all things. Through it our roots go deeply into the waters of the earth and draw up nourishment. The trunk provides us with strength, uprightness, and support. The branches provide shelter and the leaves provide nourishment from the sun and sky. The fruits are many and are the knowledge that flourishes in our being. They are the potentials of our creativity and imagination.

The other tree was the Tree of the Knowledge of Good and Evil, around which was entwined the serpent and whose fruits, so it was said, were forbidden.

Think about this for a moment. The details up to this point are very explicit. In the undifferentiated world of being and consciousness—the primal, natural world—there is no knowledge of good and evil. Or because such terms are created by the mind, let us go back one step and say there is no self-awareness, no self-consciousness, no abstract thought or individuated being. In an undifferentiated world such knowing of division would indeed be "forbidden." Adam and Eve did not know they were naked until they ate the fruit. This tree represents wisdom and choice—the fruits of individuation and self-realization.

Now, the serpent is there because the serpent is wisdom and choice. I do not know of a country or a culture in the world that does not associate the serpent with wisdom. Among the Maya, the Dakota, and the Celts, the term "serpent" was synonymous with spiritual elder. And in the Gnostic Gospels, which represent the wide variety of forms available to early Christians before the Church decided upon the orthodoxy of a few, the serpent is also seen in this way. The choice aspect is also very interesting in terms of Christian myth.

Lucifer, who was associated with the serpent in the garden and with the devil—who we know is the Horned God—in Christian mythology, is the epitome of evil. But looking where we must not look, understanding the psychology of dualistic consciousness, he is also the archangel "Light" who fell from heaven as a result of his disobedience of God. His name is associated with the Celtic god Llugh or Llew, whose name means "light." Sloughing aside, in true serpent fashion, the patriarchal language, Lucifer represents the "forbidden" choice. His was the spirit that dared to break out of undifferentiated consciousness into self-consciousness. In Milton's mythological epic, *Paradise Lost,* Lucifer's preoccupation with self is his sin. Milton conveniently ignores that without Lucifer's act of "disobedience," self-consciousness could not arise, there would be no choice. Free will, or as I prefer to put it, sovereignty of self— supposedly God's greatest gift—would not have arisen.

As has been pointed out by many pondering this subject, Lucifer is in need of redemption. For while the choirs of angels continue to sing around the Godhead without a choice in the matter, Lucifer's forbidden act insured the principle of sovereign autonomy of self in the Christian cosmos. This made his choice to return to God ultimately meaningful. Without Lucifer we would all be automatons. That we are pretty much anyway is a result of our denial of what he represents. It is a denial of the daemonic serpent power able to draw upon the earth and sky.

We have all broken out of the garden where stands the Tree of Life with its deep reaching roots and high seeking branches. We have all tasted of the Tree of Knowledge, which through absolute freedom of choice or will, has allowed us to pursue diversity to a vast extent. The universe, by virtue of its infinite nature, has always cheerfully accommodated whatever we have chosen to put upon it in material or theoretical terms.

There is no judgment on life. There is no good and evil. There are only the results, ramifications, and responsibilities of our own choices. Now it is up to each one of us to learn about our choices for ourselves, before we are able to say something to the effect of the following:

Yes, I am still in the garden of original innocence, even though I know free will which denies me nothing. But now I choose to return to the Tree of Life. I choose to affirm my unity with all things; to live with them harmoniously as befits one sovereign being to another. And I choose to cultivate the fruits which grow in the branches for myself, all beings, and future generations.

Through such affirmations of our earthly chthonic power and our heavenly luminous power—embodied so perfectly by the serpent, able to live below the ground, come up and live on the surface, then as dragon able to fly and totally transform itself through the shedding of its old, worn-out skin—we are able to draw on our power from within, to celebrate our individuality and union with others. From time to time, we are able to put on the horns of the god, to honor the Source from which we all came, to honor the creatures with whom we share the earth, and to honor the wisdom of our own sovereign power; which, it seems, Lucifer, the horned serpent, was the first to really try out.

THE STATE OF POSSESSION

As part of dispelling the predominant myths in Western consciousness, it is useful to realize that patriarchy is akin to a state of possession. Patriarchy equals patrimony. Patriarchy is no more the male character than it is the female. It is rather a state of induced mass hypnosis of which we all have been and are a part. It is a mode of oppression and domination. Mary Daly points out that entry into the body of the Church begins with a rite of exorcism. Baptism insures release from "original sin." This thereby presupposes and establishes an original state of possession by evil forces. "[T]he sacrament of initiation explicitly contains a rite of exorcism, blatantly belying the fact that this is really a rite of entrance into the State of Possession."[14]

Without belief in original sin, it is very hard for us to submit to an exorcism disguised as a baptism. The only thing we need exorcising from are belief systems that possess the original innocence of our minds and create a false duality of heaven and hell. I would recommend a rite of "un-baptism" for all who would like further choice in the matter. Initiation through the element of water is a universal and deeply significant ritual. It purifies and cleanses while immersing us in the subconscious realms—the collective, archetypal, and unconscious zones which bring us closer to the sources of our personal wisdom and power.

As far as good and evil go, we will find that the specters conjured up by dualistic patriarchal possessing belief have no more substance than the masked figure of Baphomet in the initiation of the Knights Templar. We have created in the structure of our language a dualistic, hierarchical code which engenders the asymmetries of racism, sexism, and classism. Categories of high or low, good or evil, are of our own making. It is through facing our fears that we will become whole. Through facing our fears we will take responsibility for our lives. We will become more powerful than if we attempt to deny or banish them. It truly can be said, there is nothing to fear. Only fear itself disempowers us.

And now, onward! Having laid to rest the invasive Holy Ghosts of overlaying belief, let us dare to continue to discover the wells and springs of daemonic immanent experience that wait to bubble up as our inheritance, our inspiration, and our creative drive. And to do this, let us return to where we left the historical narrative in the caves at the end of the last Ice Age. For it is from here on that we can really begin to see the face of the god peeping out at us from the branches of the great forests that swept in succession across Europe. This is his story.

NOTES

1. Private communication, Sedona, Oct. 1990.

2. This address to the Dalai Lama in 1982 by David Monongye is given in full by Robert Boissiere in *The Return of Bahana*, 1989. This book also contains other valuable transcripts of the Hopi and the several versions of Chief Seattle's speech of 1854.

3. Ernst Cassirer, *An Essay on Man* (Yale University Press, 1944).

4. H. Frankfort, ed., *Before Philosophy* (1949), 14.

5. Ibid., 32.

6. Nicholas Mann, *The Cauldron & the Grail* (1985), 22–28.

7. Nicholas Mann, *The Keltic Power Symbols* (1987), 38–41.

8. Elaine Morgan, *The Descent of Woman*, 219–20.

9. Ibid., 209.

10. Sam Keen, *Faces of the Enemy* (Harper Collins, 1986).

11. First written in *The Serpent's Path* (Nicholas Mann, 1988).

12. Alan Bleakley, *Fruits of the Moon Tree* (Gateway Books), 208 ff., for a fuller exposition of this view of Hephaestos.

13. For example, among individuals, Paul Tillich's pornographic fantasies reflect the essential symbolic dualism of his own theologizing. Hannah Tillich, *From Time to Time* (New York, 1973).

14 . Mary Daly, *Gyn Ecology*, 37.

3

OUR PREHISTORIC INHERITANCE

MATRIARCHY AND SETTLEMENT: 12,000–4000 B.C.E.

The people of prehistoric Europe followed the great herds of bison, reindeer, and mammoth as they gradually shifted northward with the retreat of the glacial ice-sheets. This process took place over several thousand years. On the seasonal scale, people pursued a nomadic lifestyle as the animals moved from summer to winter grazing areas. Continuing the traditions of the preceding periods, exquisite harpoons, spear throwers, flints, and other carved domestic items were made, but almost nothing remains in the way of "art." Further south the progressive warming drove the large herds away for good and the style of life changed. Hunting remained important for deer, boar, and smaller animals, but the gathering of vegetables, berries, nuts, and grains as well as seafood and snails increased significantly and led to a more sedentary lifestyle. The flint industry now specialized in miniaturization, indicating the use of the bow and arrow, the processing of smaller creatures, and the cutting of finer materials for the manufacture of more sophisticated clothing.

In northern Britain, by 8000 B.C.E., the post-glacial woodland was well advanced, particularly with pine and birch. Elk were hunted out, and the site of Star Carr in Yorkshire revealed that the smaller species of deer came to be the most important. Many tools, iron pyrite for making fire, barbed antler points for harpoons, and a ceremonial headdress of stag frontlets were found.[1] By 6500 B.C.E., woodland covered the island, Scotland was settled, and all the marine resources were exploited.

It was from the seventh millennium B.C.E. that a veritable explosion of new activities took place. The transition from the Mesolithic to the Neolithic was accompanied by a plethora of developments which forever changed the history of humanity in Europe. Principal among these was the construction of the first permanent dwellings gathered together in villages. Land around the settlements was cleared and fenced for the sowing of barley, wheat, and other grains and for the keeping of animals.

Dwellings were arranged not so much for defense but for convenience. They typically show separation of living quarters from workshop space. The finds and detritus from the stone workshops include many tools for working in wood: chisels, adzes, drills, scrapers, cutters, and, for the first time, polished stones, usually in the form of finely worked axes. Agricultural implements have also been found, including flint sickles, varieties of picks and, by 5,000 B.C.E., fine grinding stones. The manufacture of knives, spear points, and arrowheads also continued.

Other developments included the making of pottery. This craft, introduced from the Middle East, spread across Europe in a mosaic of different styles, decorations, and designs. Most of it is utilitarian, for daily use and storage, but some of it was plainly for children, and other ceramics were certainly for ritual use in shrines or at burials. Thousands of shards have been found around the megalithic sites. Weaving and the improvement of basket- and rope-making skills, the domestication of the wild ox, the horse, sheep, goats, dogs, and eventually the pig, and the development of coracles and boats in the form of dugout canoes are all revealed in the archaeological record.

These kinds of changes would have had enormous implications for the way men and women perceived themselves. The earlier cave art suggests men saw themselves in terms of the animals they hunted. They did not make a distinction between their skin and those upon which the life of the tribe depended. The earlier view of women is also clear. They are shown as squat figures with pendulous breasts, broad hips, and other exaggerated sexual features. Women defined themselves in terms of their reproductive capacity, the male contribution to which was probably unclear—at least to him. There were no concepts of "virginity" or "monogamy," and illegitimacy was a non-issue because all children automatically belonged to the tribe. Women probably had sex with whomever they liked. In these circumstances, likely to be of extremely ancient origin, there was neither "patriarchy" nor "matriarchy," but a basic equality between the sexes who each had their own domain.

Now all this was to change. The great herds had gone and the gathering and eventually the planting done by the women came to assume more significance than the hunting done by the men. Women's work now provided constant food and storable surpluses, whereas the results of the hunt were sporadic and only of short term use.

If "matriarchy" ever existed, it is likely to have been in this time of transition. Women as providers were identified with the baskets and storage jars which they made, with the bins, the granaries, the ovens, the permanent dwelling site, the houses which they probably built, the fields which they worked, and, in their continuing reproductive capacity, with the maintenance of the life of the tribe. Women were likely to have remained in the settlements where they were born, formed its social networks, defined its boundaries, rights, agreements, and institutions. The artwork from the early settlement sites in the Balkans and the classic example of Çatal Hüyük in Anatolia supports this view of the all-encompassing role of women. Figurines of the Great Goddess as fertile, all-including womb far outnumber representations of individuals or other deities.

Where were the men? They were not bound to place like the women. They were certainly trading. Perhaps they were off at this time elevating the mysteries of the hunt; initiating young men into its ritual importance now it no longer had much economic significance. Perhaps this state of affairs still carries on today. Men are still yearning to be the Mighty Hunters—who originally it might be added were of necessity cooperative, not competitive—compensating for the insecurity they felt when their primary economic role was taken from them. There was also another insecurity looming in men's relationships with women which was going to make the lack of big game paltry in comparison.

Although we do not know the exact details of what took place nine to six thousand years ago, it is probable that men became the protectors of the fields, the storehouses, and the settled villages which were rapidly becoming the first cities. But protectors from what? Wild animals maybe, but more likely from each other. As men struggled to find their definition and status in the new urban world, politics took on a more sinister edge.

From being "protectors" of the women-defined towns, it was a short step for men to join together in bands which then preyed upon other towns. In this way the newly emerging pattern of settlement with its matrifocal values engendered its own contradiction—the warrior. As towns became walled cities, a warrior ethic arose that was supported by the women for the apparent security it gave, but in fact the sons they reared to protect them became the enemy which also destroyed them. This state of affairs can be read from the work of Homer.

In a crude sense, "matriarchy" created "patriarchy" as men lost their ancient role and struggled to find their new identity and elevate their own usefulness in a woman-dominated world. About this time it is likely that the domestication of animals allowed the male role in reproduction to be clearly understood. If the ram could not get to the folded sheep then no lambs were born that year. And, with the realization that progeny depended upon male semen, women rapidly scaled down in representation from being the great mothers of the ancient world to the slender and sexual objects of the patriarchal. Here are the roots of a huge issue which is going to dominate patriarchal consciousness up to the present day.

In its essentials, the issue focused upon the question of paternity. Unlike the women who through their natural reproductive abilities had no difficulty in establishing maternity and bonding with their children, men found their role in procreation to be exceedingly small. They could never be certain about their reproductive role. Accustomed to action, they could only set out to achieve for themselves what came naturally to women. Over the next few millennia, men constructed a cultural procreational role for themselves in order to compensate for the insecurity they felt in an area where women enjoyed a natural advantage. Codes and laws were created to establish patrilineal inheritance and to control women, their reproductive capabilities, and their offspring. To be absolutely certain of paternity and thus legitimacy, these social codes enshrined two principles at the center of the emerging institution of marriage: virginity and monogamy. Only by controlling and restricting women could men be certain of paternity. In a society that was increasingly becoming war-oriented, men wanted to know that they could live on through their sons.

Settlement and increasing population also put pressure on economic resources. Men found that greater upper body strength and greater organization gave them a big advantage when competing against other men, and soon the control of resources—which now included women—came into their hands. Fear of losing this control quickly led to the establishment of legally and spiritually sanctified forms of legitimation. The cult of the heroic warrior colluded with the religious establishment to give us the patriarchal ethos and culture which has been handed down to us to this day. It has at its center the control of women. It relegated women to her natural childbearing functions. It excluded her from cultural authority in government, in law, religion, education, medicine, war, arts, and sciences. In these men predominated.

The above description can be applied especially well to the evidence we have from sites in southern and eastern Europe, Asia Minor, and the Middle East. The Old Testament is the main sourcebook. Archaeologically, towns can be seen to follow the pattern of open settlement, then defensible settlement accompanied by often frequent destruction. The status of women can be seen to be reduced until reaching the level of slaves.

But in northern and western Europe something else is added to the pattern. Here, perhaps surpassing all other European developments, the first monumental megalithic structures make their appearance. In the fifth millennium B.C.E., capped dolmens and barrows with entrance corridors and forecourts, emulating the caves which had formed the first shelters and sacred places of the people, reveal great advances in coordination, technical skill, artistry, communal ritual and creative imagination.

THE FIRST MEGALITHIC SITES

The dolmens, appearing in the Iberian peninsular and France from as early as 4700 B.C.E., typically took the form of large straight stones (orthostats) supporting one or several capstones to form a passageway and a central chamber. The whole construction was then usually covered to form a cairn or mound. Many have a fore-court or an outside area which was used for ritual.

It would be hard to estimate the numbers of dolmens in Europe. Taking in Scandinavia, Germany, Holland, the British Isles, Ireland, France, Iberia, Corsica, Sardinia, and Malta, the numbers would run into many tens of thousands for just the known sites.[2] Most sites involve stones so large that hundreds of people would have been required to move and lift them. The capstone of the dol-men at Brownes Hill, County Carlow, in Ireland, weighs over a hundred tons and would have required seven to eight hundred people to put it in place. Many more would have been needed to dress, haul, and erect the 350-ton "Le Grand Menhir Brise" at Er Grah in Brittany. This menhir has been estimated to have stood more than fifty-five feet high and to have provided a foresight from several viewing places for all the significant lunar events.[3]

Given the small population of Europe at this time, one won-ders what inspired the people to devote such time and energy to the construction of the megalithic sites. Many ideas have been advanced, ranging from the fanciful to the functional—they were for guiding astral travellers, they were for solving complex astro-nomical problems, they were for territory marking funeral pur-poses. Somewhere in between may lie the answers.

One of the mind sets that have hampered prehistoric study, apart from the cultural prejudices and predispositions, is that old is primitive. And bedeviling the examination of European prehis-tory is the idea of slow and progressive "evolutionary" develop-ment. Things start small and simple and then become big and complicated. Even apart from examples of cultures that have started with a bang and then fizzled, let us say the empires of Alexander and Genghis Khan across Asia, we have no reason to believe that this is invariably the case, nor that, if it was earlier, it was in some way lesser. Ridding our minds of this for a moment, it may be possible to see that in the remnants of the culture that gave us the cave art of Altamira, Niaux, and Lascaux, almost 20,000 years ago; in the possibility that during the periods prior to this when humanity walked the earth with a body and brain capacity equal to and often exceeding ours; and in the florescence of the megalithic building of the Neolithic, there has been a continuity of a wealth of knowledge only awaiting certain material and social conditions to burst into tangible form.

This brings us to another bias inherited from classical culture (and classics is still the dominant department in history taught at our universities today), which views writing, social hierarchy, roads, palaces, uniformity in planning and religion, organized war, bureaucracy, centralized government—all components of patriarchal society today—as being advanced and an indication of civilization. This fosters a general attitude which refuses to recognize the value and the wealth of a culture that may deliberately eschew fixed, externalized forms. Indeed, an alternative view of civilization may be one where riches are measured in the vital, ephemeral flaring of the human spirit. Where cultures develop transitory forms such as dance, costume, dream interpretation, music, poetry, and storytelling. Where they emphasize the continuity of an ancestral tradition, nomadic existence, and an ecologically integrative and transformational world view rather than fixed, materially manipulative, and permanent forms.

The Aboriginal people of Australia possess a metaphysical, social and linguistic wealth of diversity that has allowed them to live in harmony with the delicate Australian environment for 50,000 years. Modern society will be hard put to emulate that and already laments ecological destruction and spiritual impoverishment. It is hard for us to see that more may mean less, that simpler may mean richer and more diversified, that less culturally ornate without may mean more ornate within.

Returning to our theme, I suggest that the richness of the culture that ran through the biological inheritance and the minds of the people of Europe in the New Stone Age, preferred the transitory arts for its expression. Cultural life was complex and sophisticated and, like the Aborigines, mainly existed in oral forms. But when certain conditions coalesced, when people and food were abundant and spirituality sought a means of emerging in a way that satisfied a burning imperative, then the people united to create, from the best combination of their talents and genius, a form which exemplified and represented their cosmos to and for themselves. A form which we might describe as a temple.

THE MEGALITHIC TEMPLES: 4700–2500 B.C.E.

It has been pointed out by several researchers that the first megalithic structures took the form of an opening and an enclosed area modeling a cave. In Britain the earliest barrows—c. 3900 B.C.E.—appear without the use of stone, taking the form of large earthen mounds using timber for the construction of the inner chambers. But in the Iberian peninsula and France, stone—and elaborately worked stone in some cases—appears earlier, in the fifth millennium.

In the Alto Alentejo of Portugal, the site of Poco da Gateira has been dated to 4500 B.C.E. and consists of a circular mound, curbed by some stones, containing a megalithic chamber reached by a passageway. A type destined to be developed to a great degree. In Brittany, the dolmen on the island of Gavrinis with its fifty-five-foot-long passageway, is remarkable for the carved decoration on the stones. Built at the end of the fourth millennium, the curving lines of the ornamentation cover every orthostat, even in places which would remain unseen. Gavrinis is oriented to the winter solstice rising sun. Other dolmens in France, the capstones sometimes covering a great length—the classic example of which is La Roche aux Fees in Brittany—also possess these features: carvings, sometimes recognizable as serpents or bovids, signs of ritual usage, an entrance way and central chamber with an orientation to an astronomical event, in this case to the most southerly moonrise.

Knowth in County Meath, Ireland, a site showing occupation before 3200 B.C.E., reveals the full and ideal form of the chambered barrow. The main monument consists of a large mound (average diameter 279 feet) with passageways built into it that have geometrical and astronomical relationships to the surrounding world. The entrance passageways are 111 and 131 feet long and are ori-

Curbstone 52 from Newgrange in the Boyne Valley, Ireland, circa 3,200 B.C.E. This curbstone is situated directly across the 262 foot wide mound from the entrance. It faces the summer solstice setting sun. The Celtic name for the solar goddess, Grain, may be at the root of the name of Newgrange.

ented to the equinoxes on an east-west axis. The mound is surrounded by curbstones, many of which are decorated, and the eastern inner chamber possesses side cells in which were placed large carved stone basins. The western passageway has no side cells, only an end chamber in which a stone basin once lay. Martin Brennan has shown both the lunar and the solar properties of the chambered mounds at Knowth and elsewhere in Ireland, properties which were carried over and expressed in the carvings on the stones themselves.[4]

The carvings on the stones are worth further examination. From those in Malta to those in Brittany, Ireland, and Scotland, they reveal a similarity in their nonrepresentational, abstract designs. Some, like those in Cairn T at Loughcrew in Ireland, were clearly located and designed to be picked out by and express the pattern of sun or moonlight as it moved down the passageway at a certain time of year. Similar designs can be found at Knowth and her close neighbor, Newgrange. The overwhelming impact of the patterns on the stone is one of energy, of the flow of cosmic forces, whether perceived externally in the movement of the elements or in the rhythms and cycles of time, or perceived internally in the flux of the heartbeat, the breath, and the patterns of coalescence

Entrance stone of Newgrange, County Meath, Ireland, circa 3200
B.C.E. The spirals provide a visual metaphor for joining together the
experience of different dimensions of life. The union of air and clouds
with earth and water is suggested by the movement up from the
ground and by the movement downward through the center line.

and dispersal which characterize the movement of the biological
tissues and the mind. A predominant image is that of the double
spiral. The movement is simultaneously in and out.

At Stoney Littleton Longbarrow in Southwest England, the
upright stone beside the entrance has the fossil impression of an
ammonite upon it. The natural spiral pattern, bigger than a football,
was intentionally located and clearly had significance to the barrow's builders. Stoney Littleton is oriented to winter solstice sunrise.
Bones found in the side chambers of the barrow and in other sites
during the nineteenth century have led to the popular description
of the barrows as being "burial mounds" or "passage graves." Other
early sites, such as West Kennet Longbarrow in Wiltshire, with a
clear orientation to the point on the horizon where the equinox sun
rises, have led to much speculation over the use of such sites as calendrical markers, or even as instruments capable of measuring subtle astronomical shifts and predicting eclipses of sun and moon.

The early phase of Stonehenge c. 3100 B.C.E. is a good example
of this. The eclipse prediction capability of Stonehenge is dubious.
But the four "station stones" of the outer circumference form a rectangle two sides of which have a solar alignment—the solstices—
and whose other sides have a lunar alignment—the northernmost
setting and southernmost rising points of the moon. The northeast-

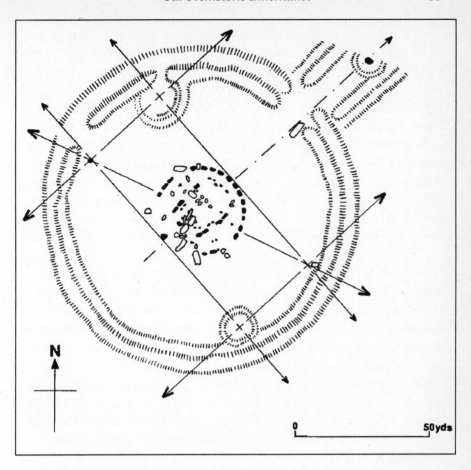

The ditch, bank and the four "station stones" are all part of the earliest phase of construction at Stonehenge. The sides of the rectangle formed by the stones indicate solar and lunar extremes while a diagonal indicates cross-quarter sun rises and sets. Similar orientation appears at other megalithic sites but such symmetry and economy is rare. Later construction at Stonehenge appears to neglect this complexity in favor of emphasis upon summer solstice sunrise.

southwest diagonal indicates the rising sun at Imbolc and Samhain and the setting sun at Beltane and Lughnasad. These are the calendrical points midway between solstice and equinox marking the four cross-quarter festivals of the Celtic year. In total, this is a remarkable synthesis of purposeful, astronomical observations using an absolute economy of markers for their measurement.[5]

The creators of these sites however, were not solely concerned with scientific observation of sun and moon, with being able to read a calendar, with burial of the dead, with ancestor cults, or with anything else which we wish to impute to them that is separated from the total context of the site. Although indubitably all those things are present within them, the megalithic sites are, in a sense, about meaning itself. They are about locating the life of humanity within a totality, which then imparts meaningfulness, aiding recognition of where we have come from, who we are, and where we are going. For these ancient people, life itself was its own meaning and purpose. And not possessing a dualism which divided spirit from matter, they did not need to create theologies or complex metaphysical theories in order to try to fill the gap between the two. The construction of the megalithic monuments with all their sophistication mirrored the people back to themselves and enabled them to directly know who they were. The meaning of the stones was the stones' own meaning. They did not require any explanation.

Any part of Knowth taken individually, examined and categorized, any theory applied and tested (which is exactly what is going on there in the archaeological excavation and has been going on for over twenty-five years), will only prove the contents of our own minds and the ability of Knowth to microcosmically exhibit the reflexive nature of the universe. Knowth, Stonehenge, or any other site stands meaningfully only in the total context in which it is embedded. If the wish is to really know that meaning, then the only way in is within, through the inheritance of our memories and our cognitive and genetic coding. The meaning is arrived at through dramatic, ritual re-enactment. It is not achieved through picking over and dissecting the dead bones of an expression of cosmic order externalized in space and time.

Knowing this intuitively, the function most persistently attributed to the barrows and dolmens by the archaeologists is that of being a place of burial. This ignores the fact that many do not supply any evidence of this at all. When they do contain bones, this only indicates the ability of bones to survive among all the other things that may have gone on or been present in the structures. Furthermore, such burials that have been found could only have been a tiny fraction of all who died during the period the sites were in use and who would had to have participated in the dolmen's construction. The case for their being used only for burial of an elite is not borne out by the evidence; if anything, it shows the opposite. Yes, bones are a part of the cosmos, they represent the ancestors and continuity. Burial may well have been appropriate for some in these cave chambers. But burial and death are no more the total cosmos than is the womb; they are only a part. For us to understand the significance and meaning that constellated itself around the megalithic sites for their builders, we need to look at the psychic maps and temples within our own minds.

This is the meaning of the cave. To go within. To connect with and explore the roots of our own needs and desires. To explore our inner being and power, to journey the Great Round. As writers such as Neumann and Eliade have shown, the cave leads us to the central symbolism of the feminine—the vessel. Around this are grouped further sets of symbols, around which it is possible to travel due to their transformational character. In the same way as the purpose of life is identical to life's own purpose, so the vessel as cave, as womb, is identical to its own contents. The symbolism includes the cauldron, the tomb, the oven, the moon—because of its constant process of transformation— the seed, the mountain, the chalice and basin, the mound, water, ocean, milk, fruits, eggs, stones, spirals, horns, snakes, the body, the throne, and the world.[6]

These symbols constellate themselves according to the psychic projections of the cultural group. Their place in the Heavenly, the Earthly, or the Underworld order as revealed in myth, religion, or art, will reflect the characteristics of that society. Patriarchy tends to extol the light and the sun and devalue the moon and the dark. Patriarchy tries to deny the genetic principle and claim the transcendental and spiritual one—placing the male in position as Source. In patriarchy the body will be denied and women will be born of men. Eve comes out of Adam. Where the feminine is valued, the transformational symbols will appear: womb as Source, the throne as sovereignty, the stone as power, the body as sacred, the chalice or cauldron as life-giving, and horns, serpents, fruits, and spirals will figure strongly in myth, art, and ritual.

We are now in a better position to understand the nature of a society that will create barrows, chambered mounds, and dolmens modeled on the cave. A society that will carve spirals upon their stones, but basically leave them uncut and roughly hewn; orient them to lunar and solar events; place within them vessels—such as the stone basins at Knowth and Newgrange—some bodies, but basically leave them empty as unknown, dark inside. A society which saw its monuments as constellating the whole, the Great Round, and therefore numinous; and therefore worthy to play with light in the form of radiant shafts that, at important times in the transformational cycle of the year, illuminated the passage-ways, central chambers, and symbols carved on the stones within.

Such a society is oriented to participation within nature, to express its great cycles in ways that are of its own kind. Meaning was not an abstraction from the thing itself but was conterminous with it. Stone circles, dolmens, or chambered mounds did not function only as calendar markers, initiation or burial sites, nei-ther did they function as microcosms of the sacred order which allowed their builders to experience social bonding and meaning within an apparently arbitrary universe. They were the sacred order. The alignment of two stones to a solstice sunrise was not separate from the event. The significance of the dance taking place in the dolmen's forecourt was the dance's own significance. The woman giving birth outside of the chambered mound was giving birth to the world. The spirals and the dark inner places of the mound was the world giving birth to the people.

The cosmos or world view conceived as the ever-changing womb of the Great Goddess was all-inclusive. Within her dynamic—the Greeks would call it "chaos"—lay all of life, includ-ing masculine and feminine. The archaeological record of the megalithic cultures reveals a fundamentally egalitarian society, which honored its members and the world around it.

Later, when we touch on the Grail myth, we will see that the establishment of the central symbol of the feminine, the vessel, in the temple of our bodies and our lives, allows us, as men, to recon-cile conflicting elements of our own inner psyche. It is through con-stellating the cosmos that is built upon the Great Round and thus the principles of transformation, holism, integration, and regeneration, that we can come to meet the dualistic, the shadow, and the feminine parts of ourselves. We can find that out of the dark inside of the cave there shines a potential for renewal, unification, and sovereignty of being. The empty cave always did imply rebirth.

THE POST-MEGALITHIC AND THE COMING OF METAL

From the beginning of the third millennium B.C.E. and later in the extreme north and west, the human population retreated from the vast communal undertakings which created the ceremonial monuments and early enclosures and concentrated on agricultural development dispersed over wide areas of land. Deep plowing is evident by oxen and ard. Dairy herds came into existence. Impressions on pottery and carbonized seed show the development of a good size of wheat. The forests were substantially reduced and kept back by grazing. Much wood went into building rectangular, planked dwellings. The estimated population of the British Isles was 200,000 people. In central Britain from about 2900 B.C.E., scrub began to invade monuments such as Avebury, indicating abandonment, and the longbarrows were blocked off. In some areas, cleared woodland regenerated itself. Toward the end of the millennium, powerful social centers asserted themselves as political forces, and we enter the age of what appears to be the grand burial of individuals. Round barrows emerge as the principal monuments. These feature single inhumations with considerable wealth in artifacts. They do not serve as places, except for the one event of burial, where all members of society can participate as communicants in ceremony.

These developments were certainly not uniform throughout Europe. If anything, regional diversity and uniqueness seems to be the rule. No two monuments are exactly alike, but communal burial in chambered mounds and construction of small stone circles continued, especially in the more isolated and maritime regions. Large dolmens continue to be built in France through c. 2500 B.C.E. This brings us to the final period of the Neolithic, marked by the introduction of metal.

The earliest metal industries appear in the Iberian Peninsula and the Balkans at an extremely early date, possibly before the fifth millennium B.C.E. But it is not until 1,500 years later that copper objects begin to find their way into Europe along the rivers through the networks of allegiance and gift exchange. These networks were already trading polished stone axes. Axes of jadeite from southern France appear in fourth-millennium contexts in Britain, where their use was primarily ceremonial.

Throughout the second millennium B.C.E., copper, gold, and tin for bronze are found in raw or finished forms in the archaeological record of Europe. In central Britain—the Wessex area—round barrows containing single burials have produced bronze helmets, daggers, spearheads, decorated rectangular or lozenge-shaped gold breastplates, and other gold ornaments. By the middle of the millennium metal almost entirely replaced flint. Axes, arrowheads, ornate daggers, and body adornments of finely worked metal proliferate.

Just as swords began to make their appearance, along with many other domestic, agricultural, and military bronze objects, experimentation with alloys resulted in the discovery of iron. This new metal rapidly flowed through the now fully developed trade routes of Europe c. 750 B.C.E. At first, the new swords, sometimes forged to the hardness of steel, took on symbolic and ceremonial significance. It was in this time that legends grew about the right use of the power they contained—legends that eventually came to us in stories of Excalibur and the Sword in the Stone. Later, especially with the conquests, swords took on a more mundane and macabre significance.

In the first and second millennia B.C.E. the rise of powerful hierarchical societies in Egypt, Greece, and Mesopotamia, and the increasing dominance of patriarchal methods of control, slowly made their presence felt in Europe. They reached northward with objects, invariably metal or of a luxurious nature such as silk or wine, stimulating the beginning of competition for status, power, and wealth among what we can now call the Celtic communities.

THE CELTS

The word "Celt" or "Celtic" is sorely in need of definition. It is used so loosely and broadly that its value as a category is minimal. It has political implications, because contemporary Celts are still subjected peoples; e.g., the Basques, the Bretons, the Welsh, the

Scots, and the Irish. The word has usually been used by linguists studying the development of the root Indo-European language. This appears to have originated in the arc of land to the north of the Black Sea many thousands, perhaps tens of thousands of years ago. Pursued linguistically, common words unite the two main branches of the Celtic language with the Germanic, Sanskrit, Slavonic, and other Near Eastern tongues. (To this day the Irish, great linguists with even greater imaginations, are claiming their Gaelic is the original and purest form of the mother language.)

Historians, wishing to narrow the definition of Celtic, would have it confined in its origins to Hallstatt in Austria. Here in the seventh century B.C.E., a social hierarchy grew as a result of being able to benefit from the control of trade through the riverine networks. It was indubitably patriarchal. Hallstatt itself sat upon salt mines. Iron and luxury items from the Mediterranean formed the basis of its controlling and elite-creating wealth. We are in a situation that the classically trained historians can be happy with: a hierarchical society with a rich material culture that can be easily excavated and thus provide prestige for its investigators. As I have said, the fact that a rich material culture existed during certain periods of European history does not mean that cultural life declined in other times.

The Hallstatt people and those in their hinterland to the north went for the creation of the tumulus or round barrow in a big way. Hochdorf near Stuttgart provides the model. A "prince" was interned on an elaborate bronze couch. He was accompanied by a bronze cauldron—once full of mead—weapons, drinking horns, silks, gold utensils, and an iron-plated, four-wheeled wagon. This was covered by a mound more than twenty-five feet high. Changes in the fifth century B.C.E. by the "La Tene" Celts replaced the wagon with a chariot, indicating increased social stratification and the rise of a governing warrior class over that of the farmers. However, it is to the farmers that we will be returning. Through them the line of the prehistoric tradition was maintained and found expression, rather than through the brief firework displays of an expropriating elite.

If it should be said that I am being unfair to elites and without them we would not have the peaks of culture in which the craftsperson can excel, let me reply that it is the definition of "peaks of culture" that we need to examine. Returning to the Hopi, they do not have an elite, yet their creativity is prodigious and their energy, instead of going into the prestige of a few, is directed into a tradition of dance, costume, ritual, and music in which all can participate. Their cultural forms exceed in spiritual wealth any equivalent in the surrounding culture, which, as any encounter with business or politics will inform you, contains many elites. But it would not be visible in the archaeological record.

Troublesome to excavate, difficult to write about, the continuity of the life of the people and the land of which they are a part forms the true wealth of our inheritance and ultimately determines the fate of empires. The historians who concentrate on economic depressions, political struggles—which often turn out to be a few thousand in one army versus a few thousand in another—the historians who focus on castles, cathedrals, the role of "great men" and of intellectual life; those who focus on the tangibly remaining visual and literary evidence, they do us a disservice in misrepresenting our heritage to ourselves. They form a part of the maintaining of a system of elitism by keeping things the way they are. That is, if elites and hierarchies and institutions and male leaders have always been there, then that proves their right to be there—it must be the destined order. Such a view conveniently ignores, worse, deliberately conceals, that the true life of the world lies not with the elites but with the relationship of humanity to itself, to its body, to the soil, to the physical substance, creatures, and plants which form its world.

As the historical record of the Celts currently exists, I do not have much more to say about it. It is a mass of documents revealing and exalting the lives of "chieftains," brawling, competitive warriors and heroes as seen through the eyes of authors, ancient and modern, who had particular interests to serve.[7] What I am interested in is the lives of men and women who lived close to the land over the European continent, who by and large resisted being controlled, who resented taxation, interference, and urban life and who maintained a rich spiritual and artistic tradition. Even after four hundred years of conquest by the Romans in Britain, within a decade of Roman withdrawal, the traditional from-the-bottom-up lifestyle of the Celtic people reasserted itself over the land. In the fifth century C.E., the towns decayed and died and the old mythological themes went through so powerful a renaissance that they have inspired us ever since. I am referring to the Grail and the Arthurian legends.

THE NATIVE EUROPEAN TRADITION

We need to back up to begin our re-examination of the Celtic material. I hope the reader is aware of why it has been important to exhume the ghosts in the barrows of our tradition. Through the control of history, men have maintained their control of the structures of political, economic, and religious power. If we are to redefine ourselves as men, we need a past that we can use.

The masculine revolution begins with the removal of the patriarchal blinders that we, as men, have been forced to wear to narrow our historical field of vision and, as a result, have kept us relentlessly moving on in the old, dominating, exploiting, competitive, aggressive, and violent style. By expanding our view of history, we can see that there has always existed a source of creativity for men to live by, that, in fact, is none of those things. We no longer need to be at the effect of a historical interpretation that says men cannot be anything other than war makers and war fodder, and that the ancient past was primitive and repressive. We need no longer be at the effect of a cosmology that exalts particular religious doctrines, has no place for women, and denies that in the deep and continuous process of our arising on the planet there exists a direct connection to a Source of immanent power.

If we allow ourselves to release the old interpretation, we can relax into a definition of a man that has always prevailed in his story but never made it into the history books. We can relax into a spirituality that is deeply rooted in elemental life, in the daily relationship with wood, water, earth, air, and fire; that seeks continuity of life and well-being into the future just as it has been given by our ancestors to us. It is perhaps best exemplified by the archetype of the Green Man that now begins to shine through the branches of the prehistoric, Native European Tradition.

TIME CHART

Date B.C.E.	Period	Key Features
750	Iron Age (Celtic)	Iron, swords, horse bit, druids
2500	Bronze Age	Metals, extensive agriculture
4600	Megalithic	Passage mounds, stone circles, dolmens, animal husbandry
7000	Neolithic	Settlement, first agriculture, domestic animals
9000	Mesolithic	Pottery
10–12,000	Upper Paleolithic (Magdalenian)	Cave art, bone carvings, Homo sapiens
50,000	Middle Paleolithic	Flint industry, burial rites
100,000	Lower Paleolithic	Huts and shelters, Neanderthals
500,000	Homo erectus	Flints and fire
2,500,000	Ancient Paleolithic	First tools

NOTES

1. For a reasonable view, see *Prehistoric Britain* by Timothy Darvill (B. T. Batsford, 1987).

2. Although the author subscribes to the narrow funerary function, for a thorough examination of European dolmens see *Dolmens for the Dead* by Roger Joussaume and B. T. Batsford (1987).

3. A. Thom and A. S. Thom, *Megalithic Remains in Britain and Brittany* (Oxford University Press, 1978), 98–102.

4. Martin Brennan, *The Stars & Stones* (Thames & Hudson, 1983). For the archaeologists view of the Irish passage mounds, try George Eogan, *Knowth* (Thames and Hudson, 1986).

5. For a comprehensive survey and discussion of the issues surrounding the "decoding" of Stonehenge, see *Megaliths, Myths & Men: An Introduc-*

tion to Astro-Archaeology by Peter Lancaster Brown (Blandford Press, 1976). See Thom (1977), for his contribution to the debate.

6. Mircea Eliade, *Patterns in Comparative Religion* (1958), and Erich Neumann, *The Great Mother* (1955). These two books map the dynamics of the archetypal feminine.

7. For example, Lloyd Laing's *Celtic Britain* (Paladin, 1981). Apart from spicing his text with words such as "barbarian" and "Celtic terrorism," his conclusion on the druids is that they were "little more than 'witch doctors' to a primitive and undoubtedly very ancient religion" (p. 112). "Primitive" is used to mean "crude," and "witch doctor" is employed without noticing that it is a nineteenth-century colonial word revealing cultural assumptions of a racist nature. The "witch doctors" of the world are probably the pharmacists and agriculturalists of the future.

PART II

RE-CREATING THE ARCHETYPAL MASCULINE

4

DYNAMICS

THE THEME

In this section, the narrative will no longer take the form of a linear progression through prehistorical time but will jump around a bit as I attempt to put the pieces of the theme into place. We had arrived at the Celtic period of history and it is here that the many parts of the theme emerge and can be woven into a coherent whole.

Originally, the subtitle of this book was to have been *A New Model for the Masculine.* But, as was pointed out to me over tea one day, the concept of a model is a static and reductionist thing, however refined. It is of the old, mechanical, simplistic, singular, mental, and paradigmatic view of the world. It is not of the direct, complex, pluralistic, immanent, and somatic experience of the new masculine that I was seeking. To simply exchange one model for another, to attempt—with a new set of beliefs—to fill the aching hole created in us by the mind-body split or spirit-matter dualism, is not going to resolve the problem of being cut off from the Source. It will simply give us another paradigm to live by and worry about whether we have it right.

Allow the theme to be stated:

By proposing the continuity of a living tradition from before the patriarchal, the classical, the Christian, and transcendentally oriented recent past, a tradition that has its arising in tens of thousands of years of European history, a tradition that is with us cognitively, linguistically, archetypically, genetically, biologically—is encoded in the very movements of our bodies themselves, we—in this case men—can connect directly to the Source of our being, which is in harmony and life-affirming relatedness to the world around us.

This tradition is self-initiatory—there are no leaders, none with the "true" teaching—and it lies within. The sources are: direct transmission through our lineage; the collective and unconscious mind; the somatic codes of our own bodies; the RNA and the DNA; the intelligent codes around us in the form of elements, plants, and animals which shared in our specific geographical arising; the cycles of nature and of time; and the life energy itself.

This life energy is always available, yet enters into us in deepened and heightened ways through such practices as ritual, sexuality, and initiation. The Source is immanent, inherent, pluralistic, integrating, and regenerating. It is intimately associated with the deep patterns of the unconsciousness, the realm of myth and archetype, the calendar, and the ecology of the living earth. It is us discovering our true selves.

Once relaxed into, the wholeness and integrity of the continuum of life that stems from the Source—and is, as it were, our past and our present—allows creative activity to take place. This activity does not derive from a cosmological dualism with a simplistic mental view of our origins. It derives from a consciousness which experiences wholeness in diversity, unity in plurality, harmony in complexity. It recognizes every strand of the vital life-force. This has the possibility of re-creating ourselves and our culture.

THE MASCULINE ARCHETYPE

At this point I wish to move forward into the idea of the masculine archetype as something which can be represented as being in constant linear but recurrent motion. This is schematically represented by figure 1. I will describe it in contradistinction to the sphere as a representation of the feminine archetype.

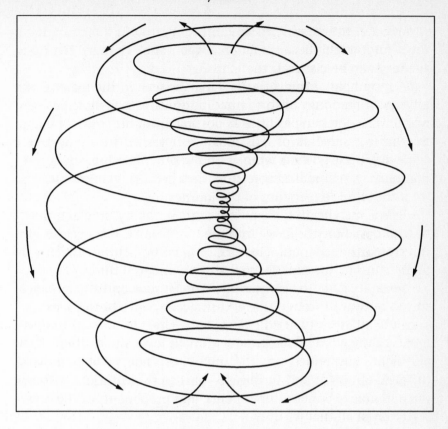

Figure 1.   Schematic of the Masculine Archetype

Unlike the feminine, the masculine mode of operation is not to move freely—and apparently chaotically—around the totality of the contents which constellate its cosmos. The masculine movement is through them in a linear process which might be described as passing from the "within" to the "without" and back again. The masculine mode is based upon an act of will. The movement is always toward achievement and transcendence in a single-minded and linear fashion. An assessment of men many women would agree with. "One track minded," I can hear them say. This is a shame, for it does not go as far as recognizing the masculine ability for total renewal through death and rebirth. Such a radical shift is often what it means for a man to change his mind. This is in direct contrast to the feminine mode. Most women can move easily in any direction around the contents of their inner world like a spider on a web. "She's changed her mind again," I can hear men say.

An example of this difference may be seen in the making of a journey. A man may wish to travel as quickly as possible between two points, deviating as little as possible from his course, making no "unnecessary" stops. His pleasure is gained from effectively achieving these goals. A woman on the other hand may linger on the journey, will make more stops and detours, gaining pleasure from the whole experience of the journey.

Before men begin to be pitied for their rigidity, single-minded-ness, and inability to move into the transformational cycle as glo-riously parthenogenetic creators, it must be realized that to be totally "inside" an experience is also a wonderful thing.

Sexuality gives the game away. Women surround and embrace, spread outward through space, contract and give birth to, experi-ence the all as unity amid change—the Great Round—the move-ments of the womb. Men enter within, as lover and as child. They are held, suspended in the mystery. Then, when moving through—in birth and in release—pass to the without. They are the dynamic exponents, opponents, and proponents of the diver-sification of all that is.

A man's genitals illustrate this process exactly. They are visible, objectified, worn outside the body. They are not unfathomable, mysterious, and ultimately unknowable like a woman's. When a man is sexually excited the penis rises into an upward reaching, one-directional, hard-edged, and precisely defined tumescent organ. His orgasm is unmistakable. A woman's sexual excitement by con-trast is not so specific. It embraces the whole of her body. It is secret, interior, watery, soft-edged, giving, and omni-directional. Where excitement does stiffen and rise, it is on two soft and undulous breasts. Orgasm is diffuse and, to the man, uncertain. During inter-course most women wish for stimulation in every erotic place. For most men the penis concentrates it all. After intercourse the woman may be still aroused, ready to continue. For the man there is no going on. The penis has collapsed, emptied of blood and semen within the apparently limitless temple of the vagina. This may be a problem for men. A man's uni-linearity has become so identified with performance and achievement that he cannot accept the rising and falling of nature's cyclicity as the order of things.

A woman's archetypal identity is based upon the visible periodicity of the natural reproductive functions of her body. In her life, her womb, her menstrual cycle, and in procreation she is the cosmos. A man's archetypal identity has to be carved out of the cosmos. He has to impose meaning and culture upon the natural world in acts of will and achievement. This has usually resulted in a preoccupation with external forms and in the making of laws, most of which are concerned with material possessions. All early law in Judaic, Mesopotamian, or Celtic history reflects this. The perfect—and perfectly rigid—geometrical patterns of Euclid, Pythagoras, and Plato reflect this.

The trouble begins when men refuse to die, refuse to go back "within," and attempt to fix their particular piece of the all as "it"—as the "real thing" forever. We have all seen the trouble that degenerate lines of descent, blind inheritance laws, hereditary dictatorship, empires on which "the sun will never set," tyrannical laws, dogmatic institutionalized religions, and fixed tenure of office, have gotten us into. They are all attempts to fix, establish and institutionalize, in effect, the permanently erect and upward-reaching phallus. Well, we can relax. As the poets like to point out—how heavily the mighty fall!

Returning to the archetype, it is the god/man moving from the within to the without in an essentially linear movement, in a dual rhythm of contraction and expansion—paralleled in love-making—which allows him to experience the transformational cycle of the world. Microcosmically, a man must give birth to and die to each action as he does in every lovemaking. Macrocosmically, he must continually experience the round of birth, love, and death. Taking him out of this cycle with the crude duality of hierarchical transcendentalism is the fundamental departure from the pagan mystery religions by Christianity and, I think, its primary error. The Christian god died and then was resurrected "forever," his efficacy operating through a vicarious redemption rather than through the direct experience of a recurring cycle.

The result of this belief is to maintain an exclusive, masculine, and transcendental focus and to deny the power and the importance of the continual dying and rising cycle of the god in the nature of the masculine archetype. This cycle repeats itself in archetypal expressions of the god the world over. Only Christianity (and perhaps Mithraism), through its concept of redemption by a savior, departs from the pattern.

The goddess/woman moving around her womb, the cosmic egg, the web of all, is able to travel freely to the diversities of every edge. She is not tempted to reify what she finds there. She is the unity of all things and the cornucopia, the outpouring and blessing of all things. At the same time, she is able to move to the center—this is why the web is such an exact analogy—to experience the innerness of her womb as cosmos. Through the experience of her fluid womb, its contraction and expansion, its eternal process of change, she understands the very nature of the universe itself—transformation. The god/man, by contrast, journeys around the transformational cycle—which is made possible and manifest by the goddess—as her son, her lover, and her ritual-maker, and ultimately as the lifeless body in her arms. This is why the fundamental symbols of the goddess are transformational ones: the cauldron, the oven, the womb, the tomb, the spiral, eggs, serpents, and horns. Her mysteries are those of transformation through cooking, weaving, baking, fermenting, potting, and, of course, lactation and gestation.

When understood in this transformational way, the archetypal mode of operation for the masculine and the feminine differs greatly from that created by patriarchy. There is no crude duality or hierarchy to maintain and a considerable amount of tolerance for ambiguity. Both god and goddess turn the Great Round of being in this cosmology and thus move the constellation of self into wholeness. Both are born and die, both are dark and light. They ultimately join masculine and feminine together within the psyche.

An ancient image arising from the cosmology of the Great Round is that of the world egg, or omphalos, being surrounded by a serpent. The egg is primal unity; the serpent is often conceived of as a dynamic opposing and activating force. When the energy of the dragon harmonizes with the egg of creation then every potentiality is realized.

I like this scheme for the masculine archetype, despite its coming ominously close to being a model. Others may prefer to view it in a different way. A schematic representation should not be mistaken for the thing itself nor how it works every time. I believe similar schemes exist in Chinese, Tibetan, and Hindu mythology for describing creation, and in science for illustrating aspects of the space-time-matter continuum. So we are on convivial ground. Every part of the cycle is significant, but I feel where the transitions are effected, the within to the without and back again, are particularly important. These are the extremes of the cycle. As points of transformation, as points of death and rebirth, they bring men closest to touching the transformational mysteries of the feminine archetype.

Before I continue with how these mysteries are expressed in the European pagan tradition, there is a topic which needs to be addressed. Men may be feeling criticized at this juncture—criticized for their one-dimensional, upward-seeking penile view of things. Feminists attack men for their thrusting sexuality and phallic excesses, which they say lead to war, rape, and exploitation.

I argue that it is not the masculine archetypal nature that is at fault here but what monotheistic, patriarchal definitions of masculinity have done with it. While it is true that in the patriarchal society cultural values do not address the imbalance of power between the sexes and encourage dominance, exploitation, and violent male sexual aggression, it is also true that masculine energy is responsible for many extremely positive aspects of culture. Men are the builders, the technicians, the farmers, the researchers, the engineers, the creators of bridges, roads, plumbing, electricity, cars, and ships. They are responsible for developments in science and medicine that have staved off disease and hunger and which go toward making life for us in the Western world very comfortable. Of course, women's masculine energy is involved in these achievements also. It is only as a result of reductionist, hierarchical, and dualistic cosmological thinking, separating the masculine from the fullness of its transformative archetypal character, that these achievements are not accompanied by people- and earth-honoring attitudes.

THE CYCLE OF THE YEAR

The next topic I ask you to consider brings the rich inheritance of our past closer. It is a cycle of the year expressed in terms of a calendar drawn from the Celtic world (see figure 2, opposite). Again, the word "Celtic" is fairly arbitrary. As we have seen at Stonehenge, the alignments contained within the monument indicate the "Celtic" cross-quarter festival dates at a time of construction over 2,000 years before the Celtic! This reinforces the case for there being a considerable continuity of tradition from the pre-Celtic ancient European world from which I would like to draw the material. Having said that, the evidence for this tradition is very slight. Much of what is ascribed to the cross-quarter festivals can be shown to have its origin among "Celtic Revivalists" in recent years. To this I am no exception and the reader must bear in mind the subjectivity of this calendar.

The cross-quarter days are defined as the points midway between the solstices and the equinoxes and are shown in the accompanying diagram. Technically speaking, the dates on which the festivals are now celebrated are incorrect. They are all a few days too soon. In 1991, for example, the midpoint between the autumnal equinox and the winter solstice fell on November 6—the dark of the moon—while Samhain (or Halloween) was celebrated on October 31. Beltane in 1993 fell on the full moon on May 5, but it is now celebrated on Mayday. However, we can be sure that these periods constituted the whole festival for the ancient peoples and lunar events would have helped determine the time of key festivities.

All the cross-quarter days were fire festivals. The Celtic day began at sunset and ended at sunset. The Celtic year begins at Samhain, the start of winter. The night and the dark half of the year are honored in this tradition. The significance of the calendar is underscored by the fact that the first actions of any invading and possessing force invariably are to ban the celebrations of the occupied country and enforce new festivals on different dates. It has always been understood that to change the calendar is to change the cosmology.

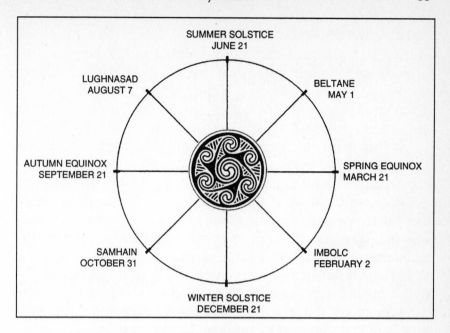

Figure 2.   The calendar cycle of the Celtic year

THE DUAL RHYTHM OF THE MASCULINE

I now ask you to consider figure 3 on page 87. In studying this diagram, two preliminary points emerge. The first is that this cycle is specific to the northern hemisphere and its agricultural and vegetative calendar. The second is that it deals with the cycle of the dying and the rising god around this calendar in which the god appears as a twofold deity. One aspect is identified with the light half of the year and the other with the dark half of the year. Such is the nature of the masculine archetype that its contents constellate themselves in this dual way. This is the secret that enables the masculine to release, transform, die, and be reborn.

According to my research, the twofold pattern is found in many places across the world. Twin gods are common in the mythologies of the North American people. They are especially common in the Southwest. For example, among the Hopi the twin sons of the goddess compete in a ball game that shapes the world and their own respective natures and destinies. Parallels are also found in the twin deities of Osiris and Set in Egyptian cosmology,

and in Queztalcoatl and his shadow self, Tezcatlipoca, "Smoking
Mirror," in the Mayan cosmos. As morning and evening star, the
latter divide the world into a dual rhythm. In Chinese mythology
and in the Tantric tradition it is the balancing of dual currents,
represented as serpents or dragons, around the "flaming pearl" or
the Tree of Life, which allows the pure creative energy to flow.

At this point the reader might be saying something to the
effect that they thought the theme of this book was about unifying dualistic or schismogenic tendencies in Western thinking and
not perpetuating them as the idea of polar twins suggests. I agree
that the theme of warring twins does occur in Western consciousness in a way that, through its either/or imperatives, the split is
maintained. Cain and Abel are an obvious mythological example.
Then there is Robert Louis Stevenson's story of Dr. Jekyll and Mr.
Hyde. Apollo and Dionysus also come to mind. But it is the
either/or mode, the way that it is carried in the mind, that is at
issue here, not the twins themselves. The antagonism and conflict
of cut and dried dualism—the god and the "enemy" consciousness—which prevents them from being held equitably is the
aspect of the twins which needs to be laid to rest. We can be
unconscious of the schismogenic tendency within ourselves and
let it rule us, or we can be aware of it and benefit from what it
offers for transformation.

Once again we need to go back to go forward. We need to go
back to a deeper tradition than Christian and Greek dualism if we
wish to empower ourselves through connection with archetypal
forces that will allow us to live in harmony with the complex
world as a result of their phylogenetic character. The Western
mind on its Greek antecedents seeks to reduce everything to the
simplest possible idea. All can be reduced to simple ideas or laws.
The most singular, the most scarce, is the most important. As a
result of hierarchical dualism it is as though we think with the
simplest part of our brains. We use the binary computer mode of
yes or no, friend or foe, good or evil, save or delete, instead of
allowing the subtleties that range within our psyches a whole existence. The Christian world is not alone in this: Zoroastrianism,
Islam, and Manichaeism share in this duality. The East with its
pluralistic tendencies and unifying concepts such as the Tao does

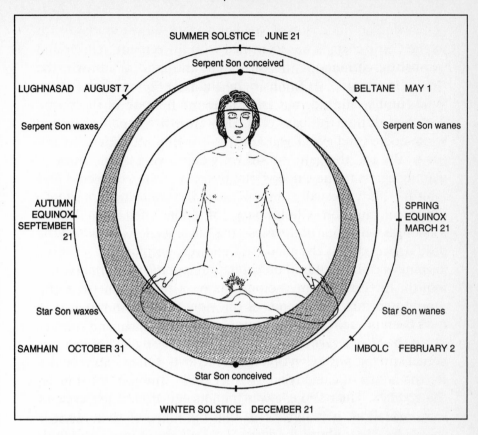

Figure 3.   The dual rhythm of the masculine around the cycle of the year.

not appear to be so category stricken. It is, however, the early European and Celtic world which mainly concerns us now.

I had been studying the Celtic deities for many years before the concept of there being a dual rhythm in the nature of the god came to me. I came upon the idea through the unwitting aid of Christian folklore. It reveals what it is designed to conceal. I was living at the time in Glastonbury in southwest England. The predominant myth of its famous landmark, the unusually shaped tor, which rises more than 500 feet above the surrounding Somerset levels, was that it was the abode of Gwynn ap Nudd, King of Faery and Lord of the Underworld. He was said to have been banished from the place by a rite of exorcism. The hill was subsequently dedicated to Saint Michael, the dragon slayer.

Gwynn ap Nudd (son of Nudd or Nodens, a river spirit—which in the Celtic cosmos was identified with the serpent, telluric and geomantic currents of the earth) was the Lord of Annwn, the Celtic Underworld. At Samhain, he and the other members of the Wild Hunt would ride out and gather up the souls of those who had died during the past year. They were accompanied by the white-bodied, red-eyed Cwm Annwn—the Hounds of Hell. Returning to the tor, the gates of Annwn would swing open. Through gaining egress to the Underworld, the soul of the Celt would find rebirth. This was usually through the process of being dipped into a magical cauldron. Glastonbury Tor is identified in myth and folklore as being one of the isles—the Isle of Avalon—to which the dead departed. It is the abode of Ceridwen, the goddess in whose keeping was the cauldron of inspiration, poetry, immortality, and rebirth. In Christian mythology, many of these elements metamorphosed into the legends of the Holy Grail. This was said to have been brought to Glastonbury and buried there.

In the *Mabinogion,* Gwynn is described as being locked in a perpetual struggle with Gwythyr ap Greidyawl—son of "Scorcher"—for the favors of Creiddylad. Neither could triumph, for she was the goddess. Their struggle was the journey around her cycle of transformation. It is significant that the scene of their struggle should be Glastonbury Tor every May Day, the cross-quarter festival of Beltane. On this occasion, Gwynn is said to have been defeated. This will prove to be highly significant. Gwynn does not appear in the mythological calendar again until Samhain, when he rides out, banishes the light half of the year, and gathers up the souls of the dead. This pattern neatly divides the year in two. Gwythyr, who was identified with Saint Michael, presides over the period from Beltane to Samhain and Gwynn from Samhain to Beltane. In the hands of the Christians, Gwynn, as the god of the dark half of the year, was to become a serpent and a monster—"in whom was set the energy of the demons of Annwn."[1]

This was fertile ground! For according to the Christian legend, not only do we have a light-identified, heavenly deity—Saint Michael—presiding over the tor, but we also have a dragon-identified, earthly, and otherworldly deity presiding in an underworld below the tor. From what we know of such dualism we can be sure that the pattern of elevating a light-identified god, or archangel in this case, to the heights, and banishing an evil-identified deity to the depths is in keeping with the transcendental urge and the denial of death and the forces of nature. But it also reveals what it attempts to conceal—a middle ground, a meeting place where the two powers coalesce in a polarizing dance, neither one side good nor the other bad, but both necessary for life. It may be that this was one of the objects of the Grail quest: to synthesize the cosmological duality of heaven and hell into a whole. A task that was made impossible with every retelling of the legend, as the Grail was pushed further and further upward into the transcendental heights and away from the immanent experience of life where the Celts held the Cauldron/Grail as symbol of the Source.

In the myth of Gwynn and Gwythyr, King Arthur mediates between them. It is almost as though he decides that Creiddylad should be with one of them for half the year and with the other for the other half. This is paralleled in Greek myth where Persephone is first with Hades and then with her mother Demeter over the two parts of the year. But myths have lives and an autonomy of their own, and it is revealing that in King Arthur's own life, he loses Guinevere—whose nature is solar like that of Creiddylad—to a dark force, his tanner, Melwas. The castle of Melwas is on top of Glastonbury Tor. Creiddylad is the daughter of Ludd, "light," and Guinevere is the daughter of Leodogranz, whose dowry, the Round Table, establishes her solar nature. These lineages reveal that we are in the realm of the Solar Goddess. Among the Celtic peoples the sun was seen as a feminine deity, frequently associated with a horse. She was known as Grain in Britain, Epona in Gaul, Macha in Ireland, and Rhiannon in Wales. It is from the Scandinavian solar goddess, Sunna, that we derive our name for the sun.[2] So we can see from these legends that it is not so much the woman passively passing from one man to another, but rather it is the men competing for and sharing in the round of the goddess.

To summarize, from these sources we find a twin male deity turning around the calendar of the solar year, intimately linked with the cycles of vegetative life as the goddess makes her way through the heavens. The image is that of two serpents around a central circle or sphere. A very interesting cosmological picture indeed.

The concept of threeness should also be mentioned here as a feature of the archetypal realm. The twin gods, being two faces of one aspect, could be seen as three, their unified state being the third aspect. The tricephalic—three headed—deity is common in Celtic art and several trinities of deities are often mentioned by classical writers as existing among the Celts. One form of this is the triad: Cernunnos, the horned god; Taranis, whose symbol is the wheel; and Esus, whose symbol is evidently the tree. The first two definitely appear on one of the finest pieces of craftsmanship from the Celtic world—the Gundestrup Cauldron.

On this cauldron, found in the depths of a Danish bog, Cernunnos is shown in the cross-legged posture that is usually ascribed to him. He grasps a ram-headed serpent in one hand, demonstrating his chthonic powers, and a torc in the other hand. The torc may represent his connection with the balanced, but nonetheless dynamic, forces of the world, indicating, among other things, his readiness for sexual intercourse. Antlers spring from his head, affirming his connectedness with the cycles of death and renewal and his role as Lord of the Animals. Creatures surround him on all sides, the wolf and the stag being the most prominent. I would identify him with Gwynn, the underworld deity, presiding over the forces of the earth during the dark part of the year. I would also identify him with Set, Tezcatlipoca, and possibly Dionysus and Attis.

On another plate inside the cauldron, Taranis is shown with his characteristic symbol, the wheel. I identify him with Gwythyr, the god of the upperworld and the light part of the year, for he has no lower body. He wheels through the sky and many of his attendants appear floating in the air. Three griffins below him have wings. Unlike Cernunnos, he is definitely not sitting on the ground. Sometimes Taranis is shown with a spiral lance representing his powers of thunder and lightning. I identify him with Osiris, Queztalcoatl, Belinus, Adonis, Tammuz of Mesopotamia, all solar gods, and thus Apollo.

These two faces of the god I refer to as the Earth God, or the "Serpent Son," and the Sky God, or the "Star Son." These two names, mentioned by Robert Graves, embody the aspects most characteristic of the dual rhythm of the god. The Serpent Son presides over the dark half of the year and the Star Son over the light.[3]

This figure on one of the inner plaques of the Gundestrup Cauldron is generally understood to be Cernunnos. He is shown in his traditional cross-legged posture, is crowned by antlers, and wears a torc around his neck. Flanked by a stag and a wolf with other creatures about him, Cernunnos is shown as the Lord of the Animals. An association with vegetation is invoked by the leaves sprouting from his horns. Found in a bog in 1891 near Gundestrup, Denmark, the cauldron is made of plates of hammered silver and dates to about the first century B.C.E.

The third face, that of Esus, who appears as the woodcutter in some Romano-Celtic art, and may also appear on the Gundestrup Cauldron, is much harder to define. But he is central to the masculine archetype and the tree most satisfactorily fulfills the role as his symbol. He may be the god of the middleworld, and sometimes I see him as the Green Man. We will see all these elements coming into focus later.

THE FIELD OF THE GODDESS

Before we embark upon the description of the dual rhythm of the god as he moves around the cycle of the year, it will be useful to say some things about the goddess and the four major festivals which fall on the cross-quarter days.

The Celtic concept of the goddess has usually been belittled or disregarded by patriarchal historians. One glance, however, at the surviving sources and, despite the later glosses, the goddess emerges as a powerful figure for the ancient Europeans and Celts.

Like the god, she was probably known by a variety of names, most of which would mean "mother." Or she would simply be known by the many names of the local deity of place. Certain goddesses shine out in their universality above others; for example the Sun and Horse Goddesses, and Brighid or Brigit of the island Celts. The name Brighid originally meant "the exalted one," and the goddess Brigantia of the British tribe the Briganti meant the same thing. From this the name of Britain is derived.

The thing about the goddess is that she originates within cosmologies utterly different from ours. It would be reductionist to say that before there were the god religions there were the goddess religions. Literary, urban cultures created gods and goddesses. Nature-based cultures may have had male and female spirits and deities, but the Great Goddess was everything. She was the cosmos, all was within her womb. She was not exclusively female; she was the all.

Brighid was the goddess of poetry, of healing, of the holy wells, of fire, of childbirth, and of smithcraft. She was the patroness of all the crafts and to her is ascribed the festival on the cross-quarter day of Imbolc—February 1, present-day Candlemas. She is the benevolent form of the goddess. Her feast day is associated with the returning light, the lactation of the ewes, and the quickening of the seeds within the earth. However, as the goddess of the land of Leinster in Ireland, she also had other functions best described by examining the more forbidding faces of the Celtic goddess.

The war goddesses are well known: Andraste in Britain, whom Boudicca invoked with devastating effect against Rome; in Ireland a triple war goddess known as Nemhain, "frenzy"; Macha; and Morrighan. All three, often appearing as crows, comprise the most terrible and devouring form of the war goddess, known as the Bad-hbh. Although the goddess has other faces—she is vigorously sexual and intimately associated with the fertility of the land and with the issues of sovereignty and wisdom—it is this terrible aspect which stands out most strongly when we come to examine Samhain, her second main festival of the year.[4]

Samhain, later known as Halloween, All Hallows Eve, derives its name from Helle, the Scandinavian death goddess. From Helle obvious associations with the Christian underworld can be drawn. Her festival is the day when the door to the otherworld stands open, the fairy realm of the Sidhe (Shee) is accessible, and spirits move freely among the living. Many kings, heroes, and deities die at Samhain, among them Gwythyr, Arthur, Diarmaid mac Cerbhaill, and Cu Chulainn. It also sets the stage for the great Battle of Magh Tuiredh.

Not surprisingly, given the belief of the Celts in reincarnation and transmigration, the places of the Sidhe and the Isles of the Dead are magical places. Sometimes known as the "Isles of Women," as the "Land of the Living," and as being the abode of the life-renewing cauldrons such as that of Ceridwen, they feature revolving or spiral castles of shining glass. One ancient name for Glastonbury is Ynis Witrin, the Isle of Glass. In the remarkable old Welsh poem *Preiddeu Annwn*, or *The Spoils of Annwn*, Arthur sets out with the intention to carry off the cauldron which lies there.

> In Caer Pedryvan four times revolving
> The first word from the cauldron, when was it spoken?
> By the breath of nine damsels gently it is heated
> Is it not the cauldron of the Lord of Annwn, in its fashion
> With a ridge around its edge of pearls?
> ...Except seven none returned from Caer Sidi.[5]

Caer Sidi is the revolving castle of a goddess, Arianrhod, and "nine damsels" is probably a reference to a triple form of the triple goddess. "Except seven" is a reference to how disastrous the attempt to carry off the cauldron was—only a few returned out of three ships. Journeys to the "Land of the Dead" or the "Blessed Isles of the West" tend to be difficult at the best of times. But, as is clear from the ambivalence of the names and the content of the realm of Annwn, although the entrance may be terrible and the guardians forbidding, the final outcome is worth the journey.

The fire festival of Beltane on May 1 has already been noted as the time when Gwythyr prevailed over Gwynn. This is the feast day of the god Belinus or Bel, "the Brilliant One," when the cattle emerge from their winter stalls and the year progresses with the return of the sun. It is a vitalizing festival, promising fertility, vigorously sexual, a time when lovers' trysts are tied. In many parts of Britain up into recent times, the festival would be celebrated with a Maypole, around which were interwoven brightly colored ribbons. A May Queen and a Summer King would be chosen—all remnants of ancient fertility rites.

On the other side of summer solstice in early August, comes the festival of Lughnasad, the god Lugh or Lleu, the "Shining" or "Skillful One." This time is connected with the reaping of the harvest. It is a festival of thanksgiving incorporated into Lammas. In Ireland, assemblies concerned with rites of fertility, with the goddesses of sovereignty and of the land, would generally meet during this time of peace and harvest dedicated to the god Lugh. In Irish mythology, Lugh becomes the most celebrated sovereign of the Tuatha de Danaan, the divine people of the goddess Danu. He is the father of Cu Chulainn, the greatest hero of Ireland. It is through Lugh's skills that the Tuatha de Danaan defeat the Fomhoire at the Second Battle of Magh Tuiredh. This is a hugely mythical event, which establishes the order of the Irish Celtic universe. So Lugh's festival is a time for celebrating the bestowing of considerable bounty.

From these brief descriptions of the cross-quarter festivals the respective natures of the gods and the goddesses begin to distinguish themselves. While the gods rise and fall, do battle, and are concerned with the order of the political world and the agricultural year, the goddesses are more pervasive, existing everywhere at all times, and have control of the other, spiritual worlds. They are the patrons of birth and death and of the weaving of the daily events which form the field of life. The gods, like men everywhere, may seem to take the limelight with their lovemaking, warring, drunken raids, and daring exploits, but without the field of the goddess they could do nothing. So as we begin the journey around the calendar, although it may appear to feature the gods, it is important to remember that the goddess is there at every stage, equal to the gods, as ardent as they, and without whom they would not be born, flourish, love, and die.[6]

THE CALENDRICAL CYCLE OF THE MASCULINE

Samhain—As this cycle of the year begins and ends at Samhain, this will be a good place to start. Through glancing at figure 3 on page 87, it will be seen this is the time of the demise of the Star Son, the aspect of the god identified with the light half of the year. It is a time of mourning of all that is identified with the light, for its heroes die. If it is not understood as a time of necessary trans-formation and renewal, then great fear could be associated with Samhain. This, indeed, is what has occurred with the festival in many Christian countries that have identified their god only with the light aspects of the Divine. However, the deeply moving undercurrent of the Serpent Son, the aspect of the god identified with the dark half of the year, is becoming more vigorous. And thus, Samhain is also a celebration of the emergence of the chthonic power of the masculine at the start of the new year. In the Celtic literature, this emerges in wild and chaotic exploits, such as those expressed in the story of *The Intoxication of the Ulster Men*. One Samhain, the men, losing their way between two feasts, rush headlong through the length of Ireland to narrowly escape death at the hands of their enemies in Munster.

Winter Solstice—The chthonic strength of the Serpent Son—the Horned God, Cernunnos—increases with the lengthening of the night until, at winter solstice, the god reaches the peak of his Underworld power. Then there is celebrated the turning point, the time of union with the Dark Goddess and the conceiving of the seed that will become the returning light. This is the moment of connection with the deep Source of being. It is the entry into the darkness of the cave. It is the time when unity is affirmed with the departed who are the ancestors. It is the time of the root of life—the time when light is born out of the darkest night.

In the older European tradition, these cosmological circum-stances are best expressed by the long barrows of the British Isles, the dolmens of the continent, and the chambered mounds of Ire-land. Frequently oriented by their passageways to the winter sol-stice rising sun, they symbolize the goddess and the god joining at the extreme of the dark cycle to conceive the return of the sun and fertilize the seeds of the cycle to come. Newgrange is the classic example, where the sun at its extreme southerly rising point on the horizon illuminates the long passageway and inner chamber with a ray of light. At every peak there follows a descent, and at the bottom the only way is up.

Winter solstice was a time of honoring the ancestors as the source of life, and one of its symbols was the tree. The bringing in of an evergreen tree and decorating it with lights affirmed the continuity of and connection with the roots of life and the illumination of its many ancestral branches.

Imbolc—The next point in the cycle is Imbolc. This is the time of the quickening of the light and of the goddess in her life-giving and maiden aspects. The bright god also emerges from out of a period of gestation within the earth and takes his place alongside the still powerful current of the dark Serpent Son. In the European tradition, the feast day of Candlemas was celebrated by the bringing in of light, usually by a young woman carrying a candle or with candles set in a crown of leaves upon her head. As the sun returned, rising earlier and setting later each day, this, the first stirrings of spring, was a very important time for agriculturalists and also for those whose cosmology had no place for a dark goddess and a god of the waning year. Brighid, whose festival was celebrated at this time, was incorporated into the Christian tradition as a saint and her pagan character expunged.

Spring Equinox—By the time of spring equinox, the Star Son has waxed enough to be equal in strength to the waning Serpent Son. All the powers are equal. This is a time of balance, of stillness and introspection. Little is known about the observances the Celts kept at this time, if any, but it was significant in the ancient European tradition because many megalithic sites are oriented along an east-west axis to the equinoctial rising and setting sun. West Kennet longbarrow and in Ireland, Knowth and Cairn T at Loughcrew, are examples. At Merrivale on Dartmoor in southwest England, there is a pair of stone rows aligned east and west along which it is possible to imagine people moving at the times of equinox. Perhaps it was possible at a time of balance, of equal day and night, neither really in one season or another, to seek oracles or guidance as to what would come about, or the best actions to take regarding planting, hunting, and social transactions.

Beltane—At Beltane, according to this cycle, the Serpent Son has declined sufficiently to insure his demise at the hands of the Star Son, now in his element of strongly increasing light. The god of the bright half of the year replaces the god of the dark half. As the deer have lost their horns, so Cernunnos must lay down his power and transform. Great fires were lit on hilltops, and in some places cheeses, hot cakes, hoops, or other symbols of the sun were rolled down the slopes to the amusement of all. Leaping over Bel's "tane" or "fire" was considered to be purifying, and if done with a partner, was an expression of relationship. Weaving ribbons (the web of the goddess) around a Maypole (a phallus) were an established part of the Beltane festivities. They joined male and female and expressed the fecund nature of the season.

The god Belinus was adopted into Christianity as St. Michael—both possess the shining, fiery nature of the deities of the light-oriented religions—and many high places sacred to Bel became St. Michael hills and had churches dedicated to the saint built upon their summits. Glastonbury Tor and Burrowbridge Mump in Somerset, Brent Knoll in Devon, and St. Michael's Mount in Cornwall are examples of this. All these points can be connected by a reasonably straight line that not only runs to Avebury—the largest stone circle in the megalithic world—but also indicates the rising sun on May Day, the festival of Beltane. This line, brought to public attention by the work of John Michell, has been called "the Dragon Line" and further underscores the nature of St. Michael as a dragon slayer and the crusher of the chthonic power of the masculine archetype.[7] Gwythyr, it must be held in mind, does not kill and banish Gwynn into hell forever, but replaces and is replaced by him in a dynamic cycle of transformation.

Summer Solstice—From Beltane the power of the Star Son and the Solar Goddess increases until the sun reaches its longest day and its zenith in the heavens. Summer solstice is marked by some extraordinary rituals in the Celtic world, rituals that the druids presided over to insure the cycle of the year could continue. This is the time of union of god and goddess. Not goddess and god as they were at winter solstice, but at the opposite polarity. The goddess is no longer darkly powerful and introspective, but has become an earth cloaked in a rich tapestry of life and a sun glorious in bright heavenly power. The god too has become full, his arms have become long with growth and heavy with leaves, the abundance of life is pressing in on every side. The symbols that most aptly express this time are the fire in the crown of the oak—which threatens at any moment to engulf the head in flame—and the burning spear. The spear is made from ash, whose time it is in the Celtic tree calendar. It is one of the weapons of Lugh, "the Shining One." It is one of the four talismans of the Tuatha de Danaan, the others being the stone, the cauldron, and the sword. More on these symbols later.

The druids were the wise people of the Celts. They were the spiritual elders, the teachers and the keepers of knowledge and the sacred lore. They quite likely had a role equivalent to shamans or the medicine teachers of contemporary tribal peoples. The picture we have of them from classical writers such as Julius Caesar and from medieval sources much influenced by the Christian and classical world is of a class highly organized into divisions—the druids, Filidh, and Bards. This is likely to be as much a feature of the precise and ordered Latin mind or of the feudal circumstances of the Medieval period, as it is a feature of actual divisions among the druids in the first millennia B.C.E. and C.E. Nevertheless, there must be some truth, especially in the never-conquered Irish tradition. There we see them varying in degree from soothsayers and diviners, doctors and teachers, to bards and praise-poets, to highly respected and influential arbitrators of political disputes and even makers of monarchs. Such roles were quite likely to be based upon the ability of each individual.

A brief examination of the role of Merlin reveals as much. He was a keeper of the knowledge of lineages or he could not have known to blend the royal bloodlines of Uther Pendragon and Queen Igraine of Cornwall to produce Arthur. He was a teacher of crafts that included metamorphosis or shape-shifting, a skill that he taught to the young Arthur. And the sources show he also possessed architectural, calendrical, astronomical, bardic, and medical powers. He was nothing if he was not a druid. His name may even be a title meaning "archdruid." He has hung in the tau-tree, dived into its depths of wisdom, allowed the sacred sprigs of the magical alphabets to grow upon his branches, and submitted to ritual death. All that, however, is another story, for later, but for now not unrelated to our theme.

At summer solstice, James Fraser tells us in *The Golden Bough*— a vast and sometimes questionable repository of custom and mythology from the ancient and folk worlds—fires were lit from fallen oak and dancers would weave among the narcotic smoke.[8] The druid would then preside over a ceremony to cut the mistletoe from the crown of the oak, making sure the cutting implement was of gold and that the severed sprigs did not touch the ground. In essence, the spirit of summer would be captured in those berries. The sovereign power was expressed by the implements of gold. Keeping the sprigs away from the ground was a simple rule of sympathetic magic to insure the retention of their potency. Oak acorns resemble the male glans—the head of the penis—and mistletoe berries when crushed produce a sticky, semen-like juice—a fact not lost on the merrier revelers, who sought to smear it over their lovers, before going on to other activities.

The action of the druid was to sever the mistletoe from the oak, and this is tantamount to a ritual decapitation and a release of spirit. As winter solstice contained within its depth the end of its own nature and the seeding of the light, so summer solstice contains within its heights its own ending and the insemination of new forces that will bring about the return of the dark. The burning spear inevitably returns to earth even when flung by the most powerful warrior. And so it is that the cycle is renewed by an ending, by a death, even in the midst of its own glory…"The king is dead! Long live the king!"

Lughnasad—The festival of Lughnasad thus has a brilliance for several reasons. It is in the light half of the year presided over by the Bright Goddess and the aspect of the god identified with the Star Son. It is also the time of the increase of the dark powers conceived at summer solstice. This manifestation and this waning of the light is expressed in the reaping of the harvest. The grain that has grown from out of the earth and has been ripened by the sun now must bow its head to the reaper. This is the tale of John Barleycorn…he lives gloriously, to die and then find new life through the mysteries of transformation.

> They let him lie for a long, long time
> Till the rain from heaven did fall
> Then Little John sprang up again
> And he did amaze them all.

It is easy to see how the festival of Lugh differs from that of Belinus. Beltane was an offering up, its practices were to bring fertility, all was stored potential. Lughnasad is a festival of thanksgiving, the potential having been made manifest. Both festivals have their high moments, but for different reasons. The dark ends, yet gives forth to the light, which secures growth. The light ends, but gives forth to the dark, the manifest fruits of the earth. The cycle of the seed expresses this mystery in that it has to be consumed. It has to die before it can grow again. Lugh was identified with Lucifer by the Christians. Both names mean "light."

Autumnal Equinox—Moving on to the autumnal equinox, the next point in the cycle, the waxing Serpent Son is now equal in strength to the waning Star Son and the Dark Goddess equal to the Bright Goddess. All stands in balance as equal day and night. However, we are late into September. The last sheaves of grain are hurriedly being taken in from the fields with many a backward glance over the shoulder as the wind begins to rustle among the decaying leaves and autumn rapidly comes on. This is the point in transition from the overworld to the underworld. It is when the disseminating and dispensing powers of the summer have scattered over the land, the cold and the rain return, and what is left in the field will go into the earth and decay.

If this cycle were to be seen in terms of directional, daily and elemental qualities, this would be the west position, the 6:00 P.M. position, and the midpoint of the quarter governed by water. winter solstice would be the north, midnight, and earth; spring equinox the east, 6:00 A.M., and air; summer solstice the south, noon, and fire. The cycles exist microcosmically as well as macrocosmically. Other correlations can be made.

The dark increases at Samhain, as the Star Son goes rushing with the leaves and the dead into the open arms of the emergent underworld goddess. She, as Ceridwen, was never incorporated into the Christian tradition. Her close cousin, the Black Goddess, frequently found ways to appear in the devotional forms of local people. She lays him out and mourns for her lover of the past year as the people of Ulster mourned for Cu Chulainn. Not for long, however, for the masculine power is rising in the form of the Serpent Son—the Horned God, Cernunnos—to perpetuate the dynamic theme of regeneration.

The theme of two men, who are actually aspects of one man, contending for the attention of one women, the goddess, recurs throughout Celtic literature. Arthur repeats the pattern with Lancelot and Guinevere, and, as we have seen, with Melwas and Guinevere. In the Welsh *Mabinogion,* Lleu competes with Goronwy for Blodeuedd, Pwyll with Gwawl for Rhiannon, Bran with Mallolwch for Branwen. What is most interesting and reinforces the seasonal theme is that, invariably, the woman passes between them and back again. When placed in its mythological context, such a process is relieved of any sordid quality—the rather pathetic behavior of two men and one passive woman—by its cosmological significance. That is, the dual movement of the Solar Goddess and the Twin God allows us insight into the dual rhythm of the masculine archetype and the transformative character of the feminine.

This completes the proposed calendrical cycle of the masculine archetype within the context of a year shaped by the ancient European and Celtic tradition. It provides a useful schema for finding a way through the jumbled mass of Celtic mythology that has been handed down to us. Other pieces will find their place within it as we begin to trace further aspects of the tradition and our relationship to them in our lives.

If one wishes to contemplate how the fundamental scheme of the archetype integrates with that of the Celtic calendar, look ahead to figure 4 on page 159. Here the basic scheme, figure 1, is overlaid on the calendar cycle, figure 2, and the dual rhythm of the masculine, figure 3. The point where the cycle turns back upon itself at the base of the archetypal scheme corresponds to the winter solstice, and the point where the cycle emerges outward at the top corresponds to the summer solstice. Imbolc and Beltane are thus "inner" festivals, concentrating the life force, quickening and encouraging it to its full height. Lughnasad and Samhain are "outer" festivals, dispersing the harvest over the land, then reaping it, storing it away, and allowing decay, before the forces coalesce again at the winter solstice. Equinoxes correspond to the midpoints on the inner and outer cycles, perhaps signifying maximum concentration and then maximum dispersion. But as places of transition between the lower and the upper worlds, they have the quality of being crossover points rather than places of energy. Equinoxes are more about the context of movement than its content.

Expressed in terms of the four elements, the period of air from Imbolc to Beltane in the first inner quarter of the cycle nurtures the seed and then feeds the fires of the second quarter from Beltane to Lughnasad. The fire reaches its crown at summer solstice, dispensing and transmuting into the benefit of water, which falls on the land in the third outer quarter after Lughnasad. This passes into the earth quarter of the cycle at Samhain, receiving and transmuting old forms and then preparing the seed through winter solstice to be quickened by air once more at Imbolc.

Although this is presented as a schema for the masculine archetype, it is evident how frequently the feminine is brought into the dynamic. It is necessary to always keep that in mind. The dynamic as such, though, is far from complete, and we need to continue our journey to encounter the elements that constitute the masculine archetype more directly if we are to animate it and thus ourselves from the roots of our own living tradition.

VISUALIZATION: THE CYCLE

It is very simple to visualize the cycle internally as a movement coming up from within, opening out over the crown of the head, dispersing, and then gathering in again through the root of the body. This basic movement is shown in figure 1.

Each time the cycle is visualized, different aspects of it can be brought in and dwelt upon. For example: the ancestors at the root of winter solstice; the birthing qualities of Brighid at Imbolc; the concentrated power of Bel at Beltane; the soaring to the heavens with the spear of Lugh at summer solstice; the blessings of harvest over the land at Lughnasad; the close of the cycle; the time of release and the beginning of the new at Samhain.

This cycle can be meditated upon slowly until its symbols and other features form a whole. Then it may be accomplished rapidly within the movement of one breath, the in-breath drawing up from the Source through the center of the body, then the out-breath opening over the crown and descending outside of the body before gathering in again at the Source or the root.

NOTES

1. *The Mabinogion,* trans. by J. Gantz (Penguin, 1976), 159.

2. Sinead Sula Grain, *The Sun Goddess* (1986), 6.

3. Robert Graves, *The White Goddess,* 387–88.

4. An amply illustrated book on the Irish Celtic gods and goddesses is Proinsias MacCana's *Celtic Mythology* (Hamlyn, 1970).

5. See Robert Graves, *The White Goddess,* 107 ff., for a commentary on this.

6. Janet McCrickard, *Eclipse of the Sun: An Investigation into Sun and Moon Myths* (Gothic Image, 1990). This book is essential reading for an understanding of the Celtic and prehistoric goddesses of Europe and their festivals.

7. John Michell, *The New View Over Atlantis,* 73–82.

8. James Frazer, *The Golden Bough* (MacMillan, 1963).

5

THE GRAIL LEGENDS

THE FOUR TALISMANS OF THE TUATHA DE DANAAN

This material has been tackled several times with considerable success by modern authors. *The Grail Legend* by Emma Jung and Marie-Louise von Franz is invaluable. More recently, *He* by Robert Johnson contains many insights for men. The purpose here is to sketch out an outline of the legends around the Grail and, in particular, to emphasize the earlier traditions which are closer to the theme of this study than the later medieval forms.[1]

In the same way as the calendar provides a map to find a way through and make an order out of the mass of material which forms the Celtic tradition, so the description of the four symbols fundamental to the Grail Legends will help us in finding our way around that tradition. The symbols are the spear, the Grail or the cauldron, the sword, and the stone.

When the Tuatha de Danaan first came to Ireland it was said that they came "through the air." So great was their coming that it was impossible to see the sun for three days. This implies their chthonic origin was elsewhere (Danaan = of the goddess Danu = Danube?). It is curious that only later were they to gain entrance

105

to the land. With their defeat at the hands of the Sons of Mil, the Gaels, it was agreed the land should be divided into an upper and a lower part. The lower world was given to the Tuatha de Danaan, the upper world to the Gaels. The Tuatha de then became known as the fairy people or the Sidhe (shee) and the fairy mounds such as Newgrange became their dwelling places.[2]

The Tuatha de Danaan originally defeated the Fir Bholg and the Fomhoire at the two battles of Magh Tuiredh (moy tura) before they were able to settle peacefully in Ireland. It was they who were said to have brought with them the high arts and skills of a wise people. They also brought with them the four magical talismans: the Spear of Lugh from Finias, which always brought victory; the Sword of Nuadha from Gorias, which none could escape; the Cauldron of the Daghda from Murias, which could satisfy any desire; and the Stone of Fal from Falias, which cried out when touched by the rightful sovereign of the land.

The Stone of Fal (fail) found its place on the Hill of Tara, the seat of Irish sovereignty. Although it is said that the original stone is still there today, other tales say it went to Scotland, where it was known as the Stone of Scone. There it was used for the crowning of the Scottish monarchs until it was taken by the British to Westminster Abbey and placed under the coronation chair.

THE GRAIL AND THE STONE

In the books of Wolfram von Eschenbach—certainly the most esoteric medieval writer on the Grail legends—his source, "Kyot," calls the Grail a stone.[3] This equates the object of the quest with something that has gone into the earth. This theme is repeated with the descent of the Tuatha de Danaan into the underworld. It contains an allegorical suggestion of riches penetrating into the greatest depths of matter. This idea is reinforced by the concept of sovereignty eliciting a response from the Stone of Fal. The "highest" and the "lowest" recognize each other.

Marie-Louise von Franz and Emma Jung suggest this migration of meaning from vessel to stone implies that the human being on the quest needs to reconcile opposites in the receptacle of the Grail. The stone essentially signifies the shadow, the matter in need of reconciliation and redemption. The vessel of the Grail sinking into its depths makes this possible. In the same way, Christ descended into the underworld to redeem its inhabitants. Although the Grail may be the vessel of reconciliation, I feel this view is excessively transcendental and perpetuates the very psychic dualism it is attempting to reconcile. In my view, the stone is the Grail and both are the Source. The contents of the Grail's symbology is identical with the Source within ourselves. With this I follow the rubric that symbols do not mean anything other than what they are. There is no matter in need of redemption. There is only the need to clear away belief systems that see matter as sinful and to reconnect with the far longer-lived tradition of spiritual immanence within ourselves. The authors, however, may have been well aware of this and were addressing the psychology of those for whom the historical dualism of good and evil, spirit and matter, was a psychic reality.

The Grail and the stone run together as symbols. They are of the feminine archetypal nature whose characteristic is that of transformation. We saw in Chapter 4 that they are a part of a group which includes the cave, the vessel, the womb, the oven, the throne, lakes, ponds, and water in general. They are thus symbols of the primordial Great Goddess and of the cosmology of the Great Round. In this cosmology, the world serpent Ouroboros devours its tail, uniting all things in the cycle of transformation.

When we read in the Celtic sources such as *The Spoils of Annwn,* attributed to Taliesin, that the cauldron belongs to the "Lord of Annwn," but it is "heated by the breath of nine maidens," we are probably looking at later changes to an original version where the cauldron was in the hands of the goddess. The many faces of the goddess are replaced by a singular god. In a similar fashion, Apollo killed the Pytheness in her cave at Delphi and the Nine Muses came under his dominion. Likewise in the Celtic literature, cauldrons are often mentioned. There is the ever-satisfying cauldron of the Father God, the Daghda. There is the cauldron of the Irish against which Bran or Bendigeidfran cannot prevail because it restores warriors killed in battle, although it does not return their speech. But it is not until we arrive at the story of Ceridwen that we see the true feminine nature and power of the cauldron emerge.

The Cauldron of Ceridwen contained a mix which would impart knowledge and poetic inspiration. The stirrer of the cauldron, Gwion, accidentally licked three drops that fell on his hand and so assumed powers not meant for him. He knew at once that the goddess Ceridwen would be after him and he fled, assuming the form of a hare. She instantly became a hound and pursued him. When he became a fish, she became an otter; when he became a small bird, she became a hawk; and so on, until he became a grain lying among countless others on her threshing floor. She became a hen, picked him out, and swallowed him. The following lines are famous:

> For nine months I lay
> In the womb of the hag, Ceridwen
> First I was Gwion
> Now I am Taliesin.

He was reborn, thus twice-born, as the poet Taliesin, which means "of radiant brow." "Hag" is not so much derogatory as denoting the terrible aspects of the goddess which have to be taken alongside her transformational, sexual, and pro-creative powers, her ability to impart wisdom, and, what for the Celts was a supreme gift, her power of poetic inspiration.

Returning to Bendigeidfran, "Bran the Blessed," it is interesting that when he eventually defeats the Irish by destroying their life-renewing cauldron, he himself is wounded in the foot by a spear. As a result, he instructs his seven remaining comrades to cut off his head and take it to the White Mount in London as a protection against invaders. For years, the head entertains company in "as a pleasant a way as when he was alive." The relevance of this will become clearer when the symbolism of the spear is examined, but for now, it is enough to comment that the legend of Bran may actually be about the misuse of power. The destruction of the cauldron amounted to a denial of the feminine power of the Source, cutting him off from his body and the true location of sovereignty in the vessel, cave, stone symbolic sphere.

Whenever the stone emerges as a symbol in the legends, we may therefore know we are touching a deep and immanent Source of power. It is intriguing that when Parsifal approaches the Grail

Castle of the wounded Fisher King for the first time and witnesses the procession of the Grail, the stone is omitted from the talismans. Only the spear, the sword, the Grail—this time covered—and a platter appear. We do not know what takes place on his second visit, for the narrative stops at the critical moment. However, Parsifal has fulfilled all the right conditions. He has asked the right questions: "What ails thee?" "What is the Grail?" and "Whom does it serve?" We can only assume the Fisher King will be healed and the Grail—as a stone?—will appear.

THE SWORD OF POWER

The same situation appears in the story of the sword Excalibur. The first time Excalibur appears, some elements are present and others are absent. The sword is embedded in the stone on the first occasion, but on the second occasion it is lifted up out of the waters of the lake by the hand of a woman. We can be sure the issue at stake is sovereignty. The sword in the stone has the clear message that whoever draws it will be the rightful monarch. But what is the issue after the sword has been broken by Arthur's impetuousness and returned whole to him by the Lady of the Lake? This is where the symbols begin to run together and find their integrity. For power, whether from the Source as stone, from the invincible spear, from the cauldron of never-ending abundance, or from the sword must be used in the right way.

In *The Mists of Avalon,* a skillful interpretation of the Arthurian legends—if a little prone to goddess theologizing—Marion Zimmer Bradley presents the teaching on the sword in a very concise manner. The scabbard is as important as the sword. Power used is power lost. The sword out of its sheaf loses its sovereign abilities. But the sword kept in its place—in the stone, in the scabbard, in the Source—retains its power. Respect for its keepers increases as justice and generosity, not force, become the order of the land. In some versions of Parsifal's first visit to the Grail Castle, the sword which appears is broken, implying misuse of power.[4]

This idea of the right use of power symbolized by the sword in its rightful place is very important. Before metals came to be worked, the equivalent object of power to the sword was the stone ax head or mace. Hours of labor went into producing beautifully shaped and polished stone ax heads during the Neolithic period. These have been found across Europe, often many miles from their place of origin. They were frequently deposited as votive offerings and as such show little sign of use. The jadeite, hematite, and other distinctive stone axes had symbolic significance. Usually interpreted as "prestige objects" traded to cement alliances and increase personal power, we need to go one step further than this and understand them as power itself—the power that came from within the cave, from the sovereign nature of the land.

Despite persistent male associations with the ax heads—Thor in Nordic mythology wields his mighty stone ax, bringing thunder and lightning—we can be sure that this power was symbolically perceived to have its origin in the feminine. The labrys, the double-headed ax of the Mediterranean, is found in cult contexts belonging to the goddess. An exquisitely carved flint mace head found in the eastern chamber of Knowth, a context from which weapons seem to have been barred, may have represented the fusion of the masculine and the feminine. The long passage in the mound has obvious vaginal significance. In Celtic mythology it was the marriage of the spirit of sovereignty, represented by the goddess of the land, to the king that ensured his rightful place on the throne. By analogy the throne is the stone, another symbol of the feminine and of sovereignty.

When swords began to appear in the historical record, they were used for purposes similar to the earlier stone axes, as symbols of power. They are frequently found, unused, in wet places such as rivers and lakes where they had been deposited as votive offerings to a deity. Since Celtic society was matrilineal, the line of descent being reckoned down the mother's side, the idea of inheritance was linked to the feminine, with power going to the men—but it could, if necessary, be held by a woman. Boudicca is the classic example of this when she became war leader of the British tribe, the Iceni, and their allies against the Romans in the first century C.E.

This idea of power being held in the hands of an individual needs to be dwelt on a little more here. The literature we have was written down and transcribed at a time when the subtleties of the way power was held in "prehistory" were lost on those whose society reckoned descent patrilineally and contained established hierarchies of leaders who could dispense their inheritance and power as they pleased. Indeed, we can almost discern a watershed in history when the view with which power was perceived turned around 180 degrees. In place of power rising up from the Source, the land and its people, who then granted the authority to a particular individual to accomplish a specific task, such as the conduct of a ceremony or the resolution of a conflict, there came a time when power was perceived as descending from the top downward. This occurred with the spread of Roman and ecclesiastical influence. One ruler, the emperor or the monarch, possessed "divine authority," if they were not themselves a god, to dispense power over the land. Thus was created a vicious, competitive, and exploitative system which eventually gave rise to feudalism in Europe, where the drawn sword was the rule and constant war was necessary to maintain power that, inexplicably, always seemed to recede.

Feudal and hierarchical societies must, by their nature, constantly expand in order for those on top to maintain their position by dispensing wealth, status, and power to those below. Hence the need for war to obtain booty and power; the need for titles, medals, and uniforms to confer status; the need for vast taxation and obligatory conscription to support the exploits of the leaders; and the need for an army to kill those who represented a threat to the system of privilege. When there is nowhere left to conquer, the disaffected minor elites turn against the center, which collapses. This is what happened to the Roman Empire.

To return to the Celtic world, historians often refer to the Celts' inability to think of themselves as a whole, as one unified people, in derogatory or even derisory terms. But it was the fact that power for the Celt came from the land, from the place, from the individual—a view that prevented them from giving away their power to another by creating hierarchical systems of control—which gave them a diversity and a devolved lifestyle which ultimately may be recognized as the only sustainable way of living on the planet. The Celts were not fools, despite every effort of the classical historian to make them so. When asked by Alexander the Great what their greatest fear was, their reply, "That the sky might fall on our heads," was deemed as stupidity in the face of Alexander's might and the Greek knowledge of the world. In fact, from the Celtic per-

spective, it meant they had no fear. And when asked by the
Romans where the center of the world was, their reply "Beneath
our feet," was deemed as utter blindness in the face of the centralized and hierarchical power of Rome. In fact, the Celts were
responding from their own world view, which saw power as located
in every individual and stemming from a deep, inner Source.

In gathering up the pieces of the symbology of the Grail, of the
sword and the stone, of power and sovereignty in the Celtic world, it
is impossible to see them constellating separate aspects of the Source.
When Excalibur was broken and returned to the waters, the Lady of
the Lake who restored the sword to Arthur was at once symbolizing
the feminine sovereignty of the land, the matrilineal bloodline, the
deep waters of the subconsciousness, the tradition passed on through
the lineages of the ancestors, and the Grail and the stone. The teaching was about the right use of sovereign power that had shifted from
the ax and was now invested in the symbol of the sword.

Where else could the sword have been returned by Bedwyr
after Arthur had died with no legitimate heir, but to the lake? The
authority who uses power for his own ends will lose that power.
But those who maintain it from the Source that nourishes everyone, those that honor the feminine principle and thus the land
and its people, will always have the people's support and be
invested with that power. This is the cry that rises up to greet every
rightful king or queen. And this is the cry that rises up to greet
every individual who succeeds in placing the crown of sovereignty
upon their heads, while keeping their feet in the roots of the land
and in the tradition and the continuity of the lineage behind it.
This is not a cry of conservation, but one of great empowerment of
the self. It is the cry of the Lia Fal, of truly earned inner power.

THE SPEAR OF LUGH

What of the spear? How does it fit into the set of symbols, the four
talismans of the Tuatha de Danaan? In the Grail legends, the spear
is described as a white lance dripping blood. It is implied that the
Fisher King received his wound from its thrust. The wound is said
to be in the thigh—a wound shared in common with other heroes
in mythology, including Tammuz and Adonis—but this is a
euphemism for the genitals.

The Fisher King, as a result of his never-healing wound, must live in a land that remains infertile. He is unable to consummate union with the goddess of the sovereignty of the land which would ensure abundance, no matter how much he fishes from his boat upon the surface of the lake which surrounds the Grail Castle. This wounding aspect of the spear's symbology is very similar to that of the broken sword. Whereas none can escape the Sword of Nuadha, the Spear of Lugh is invincible, unconquerable, it ensures victory. Its power is more absolute than the sword and less discriminating. If not directed correctly, it turns back upon its user and defeats him. There is no in between. So it is with sexual energy.

The connection between the spear and the penis is at issue here. And to understand it we need to return to the hunter moving through the depths of the inter- and post-glacial forests of Europe. As the great herds of animals moved seasonally from one area to another, so human life was inextricably tied up with the life of the animals. As the bulls, stags, and mammoths rutted and mated, so did the people, and as the creatures gave birth the women also gave birth. The hunters knew that the male animals were the ones to kill. The females maintained the life of the herd, while competing males often endangered it. It was during the mating season that the males were most vulnerable. The spear in the hands of the hunter was the evident connection between the death wished for and sought from the powerful, virile male animal on the one hand and the skill, prowess, the very continuation of the life of the people, and thus the fertility of the male hunter on the other. The spear went both ways. When it was thrown, its intention, direction, aim, and power of impact depended upon the virility of the man, who thus slew the creature and gained the qualities present in the animal.

Deep in the Cave of Lascaux there is an extremely interesting painting of a man, apparently wounded, with his penis in a state of tumescence. Before him is a huge bison through whose genitals runs a spear. The man appears fallen while his penis is rising; the bison is rigidly upright even as his bowels/penis fall to the ground. The sympathy between the penis and the spear is evident, as is the issue of life and death. This expresses the male mystery as the woman's fertility cycle expresses the female.

The Celts were not so far from the primeval forests. It is clear from descriptions of them fighting naked in war that the connection between virility and death intermediated by their weapons was strong. They fought individually, relying on nothing but their skill—so risking everything. If they were successful, the reward was victory, the positive aspect of the unconquerable Spear of Lugh. If unsuccessful, then the reward was death, or wounding and a blight to the health of the land and the tribe. Such an association between death and virility is also made clear in the stories of Greek Adonis and his Middle Eastern counterpart, Tammuz.

Tammuz was the son of Ningishzeda, "Lord of the Wood of Life," and the lover of Innana. Like Adonis, he was gored in the groin by a wild boar and was associated with the seasonal rise and fall of vegetation. Adonis was born from a tree and became a great hunter. He was the lover of Aphrodite, whose roots take her back to Innana via Astarte, Ashtaroth, and Ishtar. In this case, Adonis was mortally wounded by the wild boar. Aphrodite was said to have made a shrine for him at Byblos, which became the center of his cult. To commemorate him, the Greeks would plant "Gardens of Adonis," quickly growing plants, mainly lettuce, that sprang up and withered away like his life. What was significant, however, was that this practice had a decidedly erotic content.

THE GRAIL QUEST AND THE FISHER KING

In terms of the schema of the masculine archetype, the stone can be seen as the root in the position of winter solstice. The Grail can be seen as the inner and upturning energies which mingle in the psyche and are quickened at Imbolc. The spear is the culminating movement of the inner-directed energies as they move up through Beltane to fly as the Burning Spear to the sun at summer solstice. The spear concentrates and directs the full and virile power of the male psyche to union with the powerful and all-embracing goddess energies at summer solstice. The result of which is the fertility of the land. The conjoined energies fall back and disperse themselves over the crops in the field, the nuts and berries in the wood, and the flocks in the meadows. Then, at the autumnal equinox, the influence of the sword comes into effect in the last quarter of

Lascaux: the "Shaman." Interpreted as a shamanistic journey by the presence of the bird and the bird-like head of the man, there is also a direct correlation being made between the virility of the man and the bison. The man appears to be slain, yet has an erection; the bison appears triumphant, yet a spear pierces his body along the line of his penis. Through the skills of the "shaman," the power of the creature is secured for the tribe.

the cycle. The sword discriminates, it cuts away. Some of the harvest goes to the barn, some is left to rot on the ground. Eventually, at Samhain, the sword's final act is to cut off and kill what remains of the old, before the cycle once again enters the quarter of the stone and its life renewing power.

These mysteries, deceptively simple, are at the heart of the Grail quest. The legends in all their complexity turn around the Grail-stone, the immanent Source of power, the spear-sword, their balanced and wise use in the world, and the cycles of seasonal and vegetative life. The image, once more, is of the cosmic egg, the grail, actualized through the balance of the opposing dragons which surround it. Through ritual participation in the cycle, a man balances the cultural with the chthonian, the Apollonian with the Dionysian, earth with sky. He resolves the hierarchy and duality of Judaeo-Christian and classical cosmology and lives within a cosmos whose daemonic and transcendent qualities are accessible and immanent.

These mysteries can be directly related to men through the story of the Fisher King. The story goes that the king is wounded. His land is blighted around him. He passes the time by fishing on the lake which surrounds the Grail Castle until the knight arrives who can heal him by asking the right questions.

The wound of the Fisher King—in the genitals—is a symbol of our own psychic crippling. It is the wound of dwelling in a divided cosmos. It is the wound of our own misused and misdirected masculine energy. Bran misused his power by destroying the magical cauldron of Ireland; as a result the spear of his own virility turned around, struck him in the foot, and cut him off from his own body. He was decapitated. The dragon-killing heroes of Western mythology—St. Michael, Hercules, Theseus, Jason, St. George—abuse that power when they try to impale, dominate, fix, control the wild and chaotic chthonian energies once and for all. Unless we are willing to jump into the lake of our own connectedness to the Source, to feel the depths of our own sublimated tradition lapping around our roots, to hear the whispers of our ancestors within our own bodies, and direct the power of the Source up through our bodies, we will remain crippled. We will remain fishing on the waters of the lake, our kingdom blighted around us. No knight is going to come along and provide for our salvation.

Answers to the Grail questions: "What ails thee, brother?", "What is the Grail?", and "Who does it serve?" can now be suggested. The ailment is our own floundering in the wasteland of dualistic patriarchal cosmology. It is our denial of the underworld and our refusal to jump into the waters of feeling and the unconsciousness. We remain fishing on the surface. It is our refusal to stop using sexuality as a means of exerting power over others—against men and women—and to begin to direct it in the right way.

The Grail is the connection to our Source of being—immanent, empowering, sovereign, with no intermediary—in which all the elements of ourselves—chthonic and transcendent, masculine and feminine, intellect and emotion, idea and desire, mind and body—

can mix and find integration. It is our connection to our roots. It is the connection to the Source of our power without hierarchical ranking or spirit-matter duality.

So in answer to the final question, "Whom does it serve?", we may reply, "The Grail serves ourselves." For from the place of connection to the Source and from our reclaimed physical sexual energy—the place, the Grail legends imply, where the greatest wound lies—we can direct our passions to creativity and to wholeness. This enables us, as men, to use our sexual energy in a true way, and so bring about the bursting from the head of the flames of oracular wisdom, poetry, song, and inspiration. The flowing from the head of the leaves and fruit of the Tree of Knowledge. And so finally, if we wish, we may find the fertility which results from our claiming and co-mingling our sovereignty with another—which then can heal the land.

VISUALIZATION: THE GRAIL CYCLE

Relax into a visualization of the basic male archetype as described in the basic figures 1, 3, and 4. Allow its energy to circulate through you. Bring the energy up from the root through the center of the body. Allow it to align all parts of you; then see it opening out over the center of the head, dispersing, scattering its energy, releasing it into the earth, until it gathers again at the root.

Now see the stone of sovereignty at the root. Allow the energy of the stone to gather there. Visualize all of its parts, shape it. Feel its power. Then draw its energy up into the body and see it gathering there as a cauldron, a grail. Feel all the parts of yourself being mixed within the cauldron.

Now bring up the energy of the swirling mixture through the throat and head. See it forming a rising vortex. Form its vortex into a spear that leaps upward. Release it from the head. Watch it fly into the heavens, connecting with the qualities there. What are the qualities of the heavens? Visualize those qualities.

Now allow that energy to fall around you. Let it drop to earth, blessing the land. Visualize a sword half in the ground, half out of the ground. Hold the sword. Feel its power. Use its discriminating energy to harvest what is needed and to cutaway what has to be left behind. Then follow the sword down into the earth. Allow its final act to be a dying to the old cycle. With that release allow the energy to coalesce into a new form at the root. See the stone gathering power. Repeat the cycle.

NOTES

1. Emma Jung and Marie-Louise Von Franz, *The Grail Legend* (Hodder & Stoughton, 1971); Robert Johnson, *He* (Harper & Row, 1977).

2. Lady Gregory, *Gods and Fighting Men* (Colin Smythe, 1904).

3. Wolfram Von Eschenbach, *Parzival: a Knightly Epic,* trans. J. L. Weston (London, 1894).

4. Marion Zimmer Bradley, *The Mists of Avalon* (Ballantine, 1982).

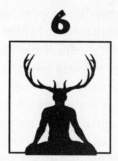

THE POWER ANIMALS

INTRODUCTION

When I first encountered the Green Man, it was through the mediumship of the animals. It was not a physical encounter, nor was it a mental one—a visualization. It was a lucid experience of creative imagination. William Blake wrote of the soul's progress from the state of innocence to that of experience to that of imagination. It is in Blake's sense I use the word imagination. Though the other two states were also present, the experience of journeying with the power animals was one of my own creative imaging power. I was innocent in that I did not know where I was going, but trusted the journey. It was experience, because it gripped my entire attention, every cell of my body, which moved and responded with actions and words, images and sensory impressions as the journey unfolded. And it was imagination, as I was at cause, willing the process, lending it my creative faculties, supplying the details. At any time, I could have stopped and returned.

At the same time, the encounter—described in Chapter 8—was with powers that appeared to possess their own autonomy and which revealed their content within me like a virtual reality program playing out its script. After the encounter, I realized what a journey into the unconsciousness to meet an archetype consisted of. It was subjective, interactive, powerful, empowering, and sometimes terrifying. I was glad it was animals that led me into the encounter and away from it. Through their mediumship I felt safe, able to trust, and able to integrate and make sense of what had taken place.

This chapter will deal with the power animals of the European native tradition and with some theory regarding the process of making inner journeys into the archetypal realm. Defining the way in which the word "archetype" is used in this book will be a preliminary step. It also needs to be mentioned that talking of making "journeys" with power animals is very close to the practices of the various shamanic traditions. In this regard there are many excellent books on shamanism. I do not pretend to have expertise on the subject. All that will be described is the experience of my own native tradition as it was shown directly to me and some of the ideas that came about as a result. Some of this material can be found in a booklet I produced shortly after the inner journeys that I refer to as my initiations.[1] For an examination of what evidence remains for a Celtic shamanistic tradition it is worth investigating the work of John Matthews.[2]

ARCHETYPES AND PROJECTIONS

The word archetype was coined by Carl Jung to describe an historically evolving "collective image" or pattern coming into a mostly unconscious existence within the individual psyche. Jung thought of archetypes as "archaic remnants" deriving from the prehistorical, biological, and unconscious development of the mind. It is a difficult concept to define, and some people reject it completely. They argue that the concept of something inherited from the collective unconscious existing in each individual psyche presents an objectionable behavioral determinism. For example, instead of giving the archetype of the little boy an existence it does not really have, why not simply leave it at boyishness? However, Jung never meant that archetypes were things, but like intelligence or natural motifs, were principles that worked through things. I think the concept provides a useful tool, a definition of which should emerge out of the following discussion.

Generally, we manifest our inner archetypes by projecting them outward onto the world: in our dress, our belief system or religion, our children, our environment, our relationships, and our lovers. An archetypal projection may be seen as having a negative or a positive character to the degree we deny or recognize it as our own. If a projection is denied, it is lived out unconsciously and usually manifests in negative results. The classic example of this is the projection of archetypal images of perfection onto a parent, a teacher, or a lover, and the pain that results when they either fail to live up to that image, or take it on and live it out. This may result on the one hand in the projector wallowing in the masochistic state of never being good enough for the other, and on the other hand in the receiver having an inflated notion of self. A similar situation can occur in religious practice, when a rigid, transcendental, and monotheistic archetypal image is projected onto the Divine. The result is inquisitions, wars, and disappointments when either others fail to conform to that image, or the self is subjected to self-accusation and self-torture when it too inevitably fails to satisfy the requirements of an unobtainable state of holiness.

There are also other factors at work within the semi-autonomous realm of archetypes which divide it into different aspects which can be termed negative or positive according to the degree we recognize and own them within ourselves. The terrible and devouring mother, for example, is only negative to the extent it is denied and shut out. But when accepted, it may be very positively experienced within the psyche. The energy of the Crone has a numinosity and richness all of its own. But if projected onto another—that is, if the cause of the experience of the inner negative and terrible mother is blamed upon someone else—then the archetype remains negative and will manifest in extreme instances as a witch hunt.

In a woman's case, if her early life experience constellated a negative image of the archetypal father, for example—distant, withholding, dominating, judging, punishing; in short, patriarchal—then it is likely that this will re-emerge in her later relationships with men. The negative aspects of the male archetype will be integrated to the degree the woman recognizes them as her own. The energies of her inner masculine—what the Jungians call her "animus"—perhaps manifesting as her "dream lover," will be accessible to her and balance her inner being to the extent she integrates the negative aspects of the archetypal male regardless of how fearful they may seem. The same could be said of the "anima" in men. Its power becomes available when we seek wholeness inside ourselves, assimilate our locked-up—because denied—negative experiences, and cease projecting them onto each other. An important task is the seeking of the inner balance, the "sacred marriage" of the masculine and feminine energies.

ARCHETYPES AND THEIR PRINCIPLES

An archetype, like a dream, has no existence anywhere except in the mind/consciousness of the individual. And yet, when encountered, it appears to have a life of its own, is historically engendered, and exists in the patterns and energies of the collective unconscious. How is this so? Around this point revolves a major component of the theme of this book—the existence within the individual psyche of an ancient, yet living and collective, European native tradition. How can an individual achieve the Stone of Sovereignty, yet apparently involuntarily share in a collective existence whose unconscious parts can come and freely engage the psyche as they will?

Firstly, I believe "The Principle of Sovereignty" is a basic universal law. By this is meant that every individual's independent and autonomous existence and free will exists as a given. No person can invade and possess another's soul or will. The power that is the self is indestructible, inviolable, and self-determining. Contrary to Plato and Christianity, there is no external hierarchy of ideal order waiting to come in and zap us at any moment.

Secondly, "The Principle of Influence" is also a universal law. Everything is connected to and influences everything else without breaking the Principle of Sovereignty.

This leads the discussion toward the concept of archetypal possession. This would seem to violate the Principle of Sovereignty. In fact, there is no contradiction, for "possession" by the archetype only sublimates the self and allows false personae or "false consciousness" to act in its stead. Archetypal possession is very common among individuals undergoing formative experience. Many teenagers, for example, exposed to archetypal projections become fascinated by them and attempt to live them out. Occasionally, an artist, a musician, a filmmaker will hit upon an archetypal theme and express it deeply and exactly. David Bowie, Madonna, and Michael Jackson come to mind. This has the possibility of enriching the lives of those who recognize the archetype by bringing to consciousness its power within themselves. If the power of the archetype remains projected onto the artist, then it can have very sad results.

And finally, although collective, sometimes on a scale that allows them to be recognized all over the world, the archetypal patterns constellate themselves uniquely for each individual. They manifest differently for every individual without losing their basic pattern. This is the factor which frees us from a collectively determined behaviorism. An open mind is able to experience archetypes from other traditions for which it has no language and no context of experience. It is able to feel their power, especially if unknown genetic and cultural traits are at work. Yet it is the case that the fundamental archetypes—father, mother, god, goddess, hero, warrior, boy, girl, crone, priestess, magician, tree, temple, and so on—constellate themselves uniquely in the unconscious of every individual as a result of their formative experiences in their present life. It is this principle which honors both sovereignty of self and the collective nature of life.

The deeper the journey into the archetype, the more collective or transpersonal the experience of the contents become. Jung talked about this in terms of extremely ancient "archaic remnants," older perhaps than homo sapiens. Toward the core of the archetype the contents can be overwhelmingly powerful. They may finally result in the breaking off of the encounter, so separate from self and universal in nature the archetype appears to be. It is this point that is important. At any moment during the journey to the archetype—and one becomes more practiced at this—the individual can close the encounter or direct his or her path away from it. It is important to remember the archetype exists nowhere but in the consciousness of the individual. It does not, under normal circumstances, threaten the integrity of the self.

There are some occasions, however, when the self is threatened. This is the reason why journeys into the archetypal realm

need to be made by the whole being and not by an aspect of the
psyche such as the astral body or the psychic body or under the
influence of drugs. When a dreamer approaches the archetype, the
state of being in a dream will determine the experience. This is not
to say the dream journeys will be unmeaningful, only that if one
wishes to have an integrative and whole experience then one
needs to go whole—in clear, waking, creative consciousness.

That there should be so much fear around the archetypes is a
result of our fragmentation of our own inner world. As a result of
"objective" and hierarchical thinking, we have created a dualistic
and divided cosmos one half of which is denied. The archetypes in
contrast, represent whole spheres of life. They are light and dark,
inviting and terrifying, giving and taking. By their nature they
contain their own opposite, which to us seems contradictory but
in fact is not. The "archaic remnants" which exist within us were
made at a time in our development when language had not developed to the point where mental categories divided the world. They
were created when language and with it thought operated in a
holistic mode. One of the chief characteristics of the Celts was that
they loved ambiguity and the juxtaposition of realities that on the
surface appear to have no relationship. Heroes can wade through
the oceans and then walk on the tops of trees; a horse may only
trot, but the fastest steed sent after it can never halve the distance.
They also loved metamorphosis, which, as we will see, is a characteristic of the inner world.

With the rise of transcendental theologizing and hierarchical
and dualistic world views, the resultant mind-body separation or
spirit-matter split created a denial of large parts of the self. Only
the mathematically perfect world had true reality. According to
Plato we all live in caves watching shadows. Only the realm of
ideas was perfect. According to Christianity the body was to be
transcended. Only the ideal realm of spirit was honored. As a
result large areas of the inner being were labeled as undesirable,
dangerous, evil, and insane. Unrecognized and unacknowledged,
this could be seen as the time when the "fairy folk" retreated from
the world. Where they did linger on, they became mischievous,
easily offended, and malevolent, a distortion of their true relationship to the unconsciousness of the self.

Without the grounding of the being in the whole vessel of the self—we may call it ego—the experience of the journey into the archetypal realm may result in a period of loss of self, even in a period of madness, rather than in transformation. Having no vehicle, no context in which to relate to the experience, the mind retreats to the place created in our social psyche for the inexplicable. There it can feel safe—labeled as insane. It is likely that truly insane people have entirely lost the sense of sovereignty of self and are tossed adrift on the currents of every archetype which manifests from the realm of the collective unconscious. In this sense they may be saints.

To enter the inner realm, therefore, requires a grounded and whole egoic vessel to facilitate the journey through the transformational nature of the archetypes. An element of ritual, concentration, and stillness is most helpful. For when the archetypal image of death finally confronts the voyager, the self must hold together and go through the fire, even when it feels like a shattering of the atomic structure of life itself.

SPATIAL ARCHETYPES

In our everyday lives, the way in which our minds experience and define space is a constant and significant activity. A task can be "straightforward," a person can be "crooked" or "bent," a film can leave us feeling "high" or "low," a concept may be "ahead" or "behind" its time. Cosmological ideas invariably turn around definitions of space, be they put forward by a scientist advocating the Big Bang theory or by a Tibetan monk describing Mount Kailash as the center of the world. Our brains are made to function using geometrical concepts. Using the information of the senses, especially the eye, they are constantly calculating the trajectory of their own body and that of surrounding bodies in four dimensional space. Compared to our geometrical abilities, which have been in operation for hundreds of thousands of years, numbers are only a recent invention. The brain is more able than a computer, no matter how large, to geometrically calculate probability, depth, speed, and movement within the apparently random forces at work in nature.

It is useful to be aware of spatial and geometrical dynamics as a characteristic of movement in the archetypal realm. Movement up or down, ahead or back, to the right or to the left, all carry specific meanings for every individual. At present, in our collective Western consciousness, we have very clear ideas that "up" and "ahead" and "to the right" are good, while "down" and "back" and to the "left" are not. Our deeper "native" consciousness may work in an entirely different manner.

Spatial patterns generated by archetypes in the collective unconscious of a specific society are indicative of the nature of that society. A culture which creates circular, spiral, or fractal forms in its art and architecture is functioning with a very different mind set to that which creates rectangular buildings and grid cities.

Mimi Lobell has created a typology of spatial archetypes which characterize different societies. Circle or "Great Round" societies generally have matrilineal social forms, egalitarian and peaceful politics, ecologically integrated economies, and a goddess-oriented religion. They don't go anywhere fast. Starburst or "Radiant Axes" societies, lines radiating from a center, tend to be hierarchical, pompous in architecture, economically centralized, and redistributive, monotheistic, and often ruled by a "divine" king. They are effective, especially in war, but they tend to be short-lived. "Grid" societies are bureaucratic, communicative, geared to production, democratic, efficient, and often atheistic. They tend to "commodify" their inhabitants, making them fit the system; e.g., children learn to sit in places where they don't want to be, respond to bells, and study grids on paper. Lobell speculates on what a "spiral" society would look like, or better still, what a combination of various patterns may produce. A return to the "Sensitive Chaos" of our primal state?[3]

ANIMALS OF TRANSFORMATION

The model of spatial archetypes was introduced here to show the importance of archetypal modes in influencing the nature of society and the shape of the world. Archetypes, once manifested, have a self-fulfilling quality—"They must be true because I can see them all around me." Once the Church and the State had succeeded in centralizing power in the capital city and building churches in every village, the social order was established, "proving" its rightness. It could thus go on proving itself to successive generations of children as it became the only known reality. This ties in with the reflexive nature of the universe, which, by virtue of its infinite nature, is able to accommodate any theory—or edifice—put upon it and so provide the evidence to prove the theory. In fact, it proves nothing but the state of our own minds and our ability for creation. Understood in this way, as patterns of our own minds, the concept of archetypes can be liberating rather than determining, because it allows us to see the manner in which we create the world.

Here we come to the quality provided by the animals—the power of immanence and transformation. For it is through the experience of the animals that we can find the ability to shed an outworn belief or a manifest norm, as an animal can shed its skin and move with its total being from one state to another. The animals are agents of the process of transformation because they are at one with the needs and the drives of their own bodies. When an animal is tired, it sleeps. When it is hungry, it eats. It is what it feels, unlike humans whose feelings are conditioned by shoulds and shouldn'ts and who will often do anything to prevent themselves from feeling. Humans will drive their bodies to exhaustion with voluntary exercise, to inertness with drugs, to starvation through denial. They will do what an animal will not do, except in a situation where there is no other choice and that is, to deny and resist their own life-force.

Because they are at one with their own life-force or Source, animals provide us with a symbolic vocabulary that is real; that is made up of actual, tangible things and somatic experiences rather than of transcendental and abstract sets of ideas. They provide us with a means of knowing that certain experiences really exist and are not just ideas. There is no separation between the animal and the world, just as there is no separation between us and the world. Only the development of abstract and then written vocabularies in which things appear to have separate existences makes it seem so. Animals speak the language of the body-mind, with all its subtle nuances of perception. They do not speak the reductionist language of a dualistic cosmology.

When a power animal is evoked by a shaman, there is no separation between the human, the animal, the spiritual, and the experiential worlds. The shaman can fly and see with the vision of a bird. They can run with the grace and agility of the deer. Move with the strength of the bear. Swim with the fluidity of the fish. Hear with the sensibility of the otter. And from these things, learn how to be, how to act, how to behave in a world where there is no division between spirit and matter. In this sense, the animal is the mediator between the worlds and can be used to facilitate rites of passage—transitions from one stage of life to the next. This is a far cry from the usual position ascribed to animals in Western society, which sees them as being somewhere lower down an evolutionary scale, without feeling and thus able to be cruelly exploited.

The power animals are essentially about transformational qualities. The power of the elk can be summoned when seeking the stamina to move through a long process. The quality of the eagle is about being able to see the way to an outcome and to achieve it through swift and efficient flight. Every animal has its power: a rabbit can get through low undergrowth, a chameleon can remain concealed, a butterfly go from one life stage to another. This transformational ability works within our psyches as symbol—as direct experience. The eagle does not mean far-sightedness, it is far-sightedness that is eagle.

As was mentioned in the section on language in Chapter 2, the experience of meaning that an animal as symbol may inspire can be lost to us as language and our lives are no longer embedded in a meaningful context. But the animals remain, and simply exposing ourselves to them restores the power to the symbol within our minds. They live in the universal realm of all being and despite our depredations, they will never give up their independence and sovereignty. They are, in a sense, as a result of their unified existence, more "evolved" than we. They can speak to us in dreams, in inner journeys and encounters with the archetypal realm. The archetypal power that is fox or coyote will unfold its message within us as we choose to journey toward it. Like Hermes, the messenger between the worlds, the trickster will turn things around in our minds and then dart away like quicksilver whenever we get too close. If we are fortunate enough to become fox, to move totally within its energy, then we will know a cunning, humorous, transformational power is working within our lives. If we, as hunters in one of the great interglacial forests, could dream of the bison, then the cycle was complete and no barrier existed between the hunter and the animal, its dream presence and real presence. To re-create the dream in waking consciousness was to manifest the creature's power. And so we return to the cave, to the dance of change, to the Source of all life-energies, and through its resonance bring into being the scenes we desire.

To be in the dream of an animal made the cycle of reciprocation complete. It allowed everything to be in its place. As animal dreams suggest a reality as tangible as their lives, it is likely that the world was as shaped and created by animal ancestors as it was by human. Thus we share with the animals the Source. Indeed, paleontology reveals they far precede us as Source. And so, in the deepest recesses of our biological arising, animal dreamings shape our cognitive and limbic modes and their power in the archetypal realm structures the collective unconscious of our lives.

Because we may attribute such processes to the "reptilian" part of the brain, it does not mean animals are in any way inferior or lacking in grace. Indeed, the instinctual modes in which animals operate generate some of the most sublime archetypal experiences, which translate in all their immediacy and power to what is considered to be some of our highest art forms. I am especially thinking in terms of movement: the dance of birds—the beating of their wings, the coordination of horses—the rhythm of their gait, the articulation of reptiles—the symmetry of their motion; the sinuousness of the water creatures—their deliberate pace, all are translated into human forms of expression. All the fluid and rhythmic patterns of art, of meanders in decoration and in dance and the forms of music and of architectural space, draw upon the archetypes that have their origin in the hindmost segment of the brain. Letters themselves are said to be derived from the observation of a flock of cranes "which make letters as they fly." We cannot escape the contribution the creatures make to the wealth of our inner lives. And, as the outer and the inner reflect each other, so it is that in the legends of all people it is the animals that first existed and gave shape to the world.

THE PICTISH SYMBOLS

The fantastic creatures and abstract designs which curl their way through the interstices of Celtic art, on stones, around doorways, in the manuscripts of the Celtic monks, are well known. What is less well known are the creatures and the symbols which appear carved on stones in the lands of the Picts, what is now Scotland, from the sixth century C.E. onward. The significance of the designs is considered a mystery.

In *The Keltic Power Symbols,* I advance the case that the carvings were done by the druids in order to preserve, or rather, to encode, ancient knowledge that was under the threat of being lost.[4] Although the European continent saw many instances where Celtic themes were expressed in artistic form, this was usually as a result of influence from the classical world. The druids themselves insisted that knowledge should not be symbolized in external form, nor should it be written down, but maintained through oral and other forms of direct transmission.

The greatest incidence of symbol stones is on the east coast of Scotland—the Pictish heartland. They commonly show two or more symbols, one of which is likely to be geometrical and one animal. The later stones of the ninth century onward become far more elaborate. In these, the earlier animal and geometrical symbols are often present but sometimes become lost among the curvilinear designs, crosses, and the depiction of mundane themes such as huntsmen, horsemen, and armed warriors. It seems the original symbols such as the boar, the fish eagle, the wolf, the horse, the bull, the salmon, the goose, the cetus creature, the centaur, the serpent, and the geometrical ones such as the crescent and V-rod and the double disk and Z-rod, began life with their original symbolic content intact. Then they were adopted as motifs on Christian monuments and as emblems of families, clans, and rulers. They became territorial markers or signs of lineage and were incorporated in much the same way as other esoteric symbols have become adopted as heraldic devices or used on bank notes in modern times—with little comprehension.

The symbols do not have literal interpretations. However one of the roadside stones at Aberlemno in Angus is worth dwelling upon and making a few comments. The stone is about six feet high and has a double disk and Z-rod symbol running through its length. There is a serpent at the top and a set of symbols known as the mirror and comb at the bottom of the stone. Evidently the geometrical symbol forms a connection between the two other symbols. The mirror and comb is usually associated with the feminine or the goddess. They appear in later literature in the hands of mermaids, the anthropomorphized dwellers of the deeps. The serpent possesses a variety of symbolic content ranging from telluric forces to sexual energy and transformation. Around the back of the stone, circular indentations are scattered over its surface. These are likely to be cup marks made in the Neolithic period. The stone has been in use as a repository of human attention and a focus of consciousness for over 4,000 years.

The cup marks; the carvings on the stones at Newgrange, Knowth, and elsewhere; the paintings on the cave walls and the early symbols of the Picts share a common intent. They are the ways in which their creators impressed their consciousness upon the world and in return received an objectification that impressed its intent back upon them, forming an interactive pathway between the inner and the outer world.

Such actions are more than simply "art." They become access ways between the different dimensions of existence which allow them to affirm

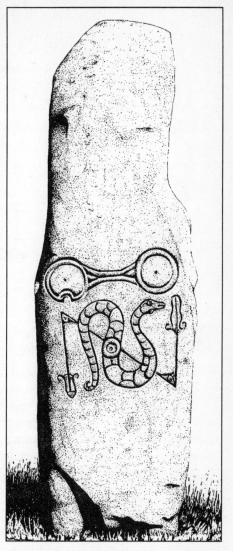

Pictish Symbol Stone from Newton House, Aberdeenshire, Scotland, c. seventh century C.E. The symbols shown are the serpent and Z-rod and a double disk.

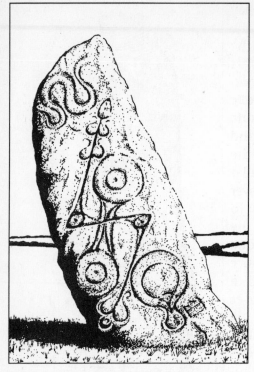

One of the three Pictish symbol stones beside the road at Aberlemno, Angus, Scotland. Showing none of the Christian influence present upon the later stones it may have been carved in the late sixth century C.E. The symbols are the double disk and Z-rod, mirror and comb and a serpent.

their ultimate unity and communicate with each other. The geometrical symbols and the animal symbols stand in a very interesting relationship to each other. They reveal that the druids, the Neolithic people and the Paleolithic cave artists, not only understood the transformational power of the animals, but sought to penetrate the other dimensions of existence. The folk traditions around the cup marks were always ones of the Otherworld. In the hollows on the stones, offerings of milk, honey, and grain would be left to the fairy people.

THE NEOLITHIC STONE SPHERES

To illustrate the point made above, I would like to introduce the example of the stone spheres carved in Scotland during the Neolithic period. Perfectly round stone spheres ranging from the size of marbles to two or three inches across have been found in the Irish passage mounds and date to the fourth millennium B.C.E. But those found in Scotland embody the various geometrical forms known as the Platonic solids: the tetrahedron, hexahedron, octahedron, icosahedron, and dodecahedron. It appears that their makers were conversant with the mathematics of three dimensions and the basic geometrical building blocks of matter itself.[5]

The carvers of the stones, which incidentally are carved in very hard stone and represent months of labor, were not proceeding from a realm of abstract ideas. They were not, post-Plato, applying rules of sacred geometry. They, along with the builders of the megalithic dolmens and circles, were making-from-within. They were allowing intuition to express the forms they encountered in life.

Given that the creators of the polyhedrons were not

A Neolithic carved stone sphere from Glas Towie, Scotland. It demonstrates tetrahedral symmetry and was made in the late fourth millennium B.C.E.

proceeding from an objective mathematical context which they then expressed in the spheres, but from a subject-object interaction, it follows they were opening up a pathway between the many dimensions of life which the emergent patterns on the stone spheres revealed like a map. The carvers of the stones were exploring the geometrical pathways by which their own brains functioned, in the same way as a computer may follow the pathways of the Lorenz Attractor or the Mandelbrot Set in discovering the order nature makes out of apparent random chaos.

The stone spheres with their complex geometry reveal the archetypal structure or resonant patterns of the universe. These manifest visibly in crystalline and other forms, but rarely precisely—as in the spheres—for every situation in nature is unique and full of cross influences. Only rarely does an apparently geometrically perfect seashell or crystal appear. By creating perfect forms, the carvers of the stone spheres were touching into and expressing the immanent causal world. One which does not exist, but is present in everything, including the way in which the brain thinks. Plato and the Pythagoreans reified this world into a transcendent reality, to be striven for at the expense of this one.

Given this cognitive process, one embedded in the context of life—the abstract processes constantly referring to the material matrix and back again—the questions I would like to ask are, what world is being referred to when an animal is carved upon the stone? And, knowing that the animals are about immanence, power, movement, and transformation, what pathways and what dimensions are being opened when they are juxtaposed with the geometrical symbols which touch upon the realm of immanent archetypal form?

The early Pictish symbol stones, carved by the druids, are symbols for the whole. Not merely geometrical or depicting animal forms, they are symbols for the whole gamut of knowledge, the interaction of all the complex dimensions of life. Facing the threat of the loss of the tradition, the druids had no other choice but to encode what they knew upon the stones. Such expression increased the risk of the knowledge becoming debased, which is what, in fact, took place. However, the knowledge revealed could only be as great as the memory or the wisdom or the right intention brought to it. Even if the symbols were deployed for other purposes, they could retain their content intact, perhaps more so than as a written form.

When we come to look into the depths of the tradition that is our inheritance, we, as a result of sharing the same modes of cognition as their creators, can touch into and release a wealth of knowledge from the Pictish stones and other native European "art." At the same time we can get an idea of what it must be like to possess a cosmology which does not divide spirit from matter. In the same way as a point may be all we perceive of three intersecting dimensions on the corner of a cube, so the symbols on the stones can tell us of an immanent archetypal reality, which the animals are an unmediated expression of. We can directly participate within that reality when we allow ourselves to open up to it. This brings our theme to the subject of archetypal re-enactment.

ARCHETYPAL RE-ENACTMENT

Journeys into the archetypal realm rarely happen in armchairs. Although, of course, they can. They come about, for me, when I go into the woods, into a cave, to the seashore, to special places with the moon at a certain phase or at a certain time or season, and I push myself to re-enact the possible, the probable, and the improbable. On the other hand, every circumstance can be auspicious and absolutely nothing takes place. But if I have the courage to go the step beyond, something always occurs. It may be my pushing through my resistance to something, but above all, it comes when I am willing to re-enact the clues the archetypal realm is giving me, to take them on and make them actual. It comes when I respond to them with my body and the power of the archetype responds to me. The somatic codes of the body, with their ancient phylogenetic memories, can connect me to the consciousness—the organizing intelligence—of the cellular organisms which constitute life on earth.

In the same way as scientists searching for a unified quantum field theory recognize that nothing can be excluded from their research—not mind, not meaning, nor any level of matter—so in searching for the nature of our being, sometimes it is the most bizarre synchronicity, the most unlikely symbol, which taps into the generative power of the Source in which all matter and mind has its origin. This is diving into complex, underlying dimensions, not simpler ones. Plato and subsequently Western science explicitly assumed the world "behind" this one would be simpler in the mechanical sense. Quantum physics now informs us this is not the case. If anything, the cellular, atomic, and subatomic realms are more complex in an intelligent sense. The universe is in a grain of sand.

I am in awe when I think through all the implications of this. What would happen if, at Beltane, I dressed in the guise of the Horned God and danced around a Maypole with the Queen of May? Would I be giving myself over to overwhelming chthonic powers? Or would I be powerfully ritualizing the currents of energy moving through the earth at this time, manifesting the archetypes my ancestors encoded in my psychosomatic memory, and so participating in the power that insures a fertile growing season and abundant harvest?

Or, what would happen if, at Samhain, I re-enacted the rites of passage between the old year and the new? Ritually, laid to rest an effigy of the God of the Waxing Year in a coffin of yew, gave away all the attachments I had formed over the year in the Samhain fires, and turned in my mask and robe of black toward the new cycle of the year? What would happen if I became Cu Chulainn dressed as the warrior and went to meet Queen Medhbh (Maeve) over the matter of the Bull of Ulster, and instead of there being war between us, enacted a solution and a peace? Would it make any difference between the forces that still find themselves on opposing sides in Ireland today? Or would it merely make peace in my own mind?

I am of the conviction that dramatically re-enacting the mythic content of archetypes in ways that heal and make whole will have profound effects, not just upon my own well-being, but upon the collective nature of human consciousness. This will be true to the extent that I—or the group I am working with—can get close to the powerful, holistic, and fundamental energies at the center or core of the archetype. It is not so much that we are determined by the archetypes but that we can determine them and the creative ordering principles they bring to life.

Sometimes the archetypes are in no need of redemption and healing. They are healthy and whole and constellate a realm in us that we vitally need. Such experiences can heal us and perhaps, above all, initiate us into the tradition of our ancestors which has as its context an intrinsic unity with the surrounding world. It is for good reason that William Anderson subtitled his book *Green Man* as *The Archetype of our Oneness with the Earth.* Through his research, the power of the archetype of the Green Man awoke in him and spurred him to take a position rarely seen in the predominant stream of Western published literature. I will refer to this book again in the following chapter.[6]

To summarize: The inner journey via the transformational qualities of the animals is into the immanent, unified, and multi-dimensional realm of being which contains the archetypal forms of life. Such archetypal forms can be said to be created out of the interaction between the elements and our consciousness, neither having an *a priori* existence. They, while being autonomous and possessing geometrical order, constellate themselves uniquely for each individual and so provide each one of us with our own unique means of access to the Source. This is accessed through ritual and other forms of intention and focus.

The Australian Aborigines refer to this creative order as the "Dreamtime," the time of the ancestors when the world was taking form. Mircea Eliade has suggested that all mythologizing and the original forms of ritual and religion are attempts to return to the time of world-creation.[7] The purpose of mythical re-enactment is to enter into the time before time. This is recurrent time, when the features of the world were being made. It locates all aspects of life in a meaningful whole. This naturally, is not a static process. Recent study has shown that the songs which accompany and reveal the paths of the Dreamtime ancestors change and adapt to incorporate new elements into the Aboriginal world view.

It is possible for us to journey into the apparently fixed and immobile edifices which structure our world and adapt them for new circumstances and new times. History is never the past as "it really was." It is always the interpretation of the historians who select certain "facts" out of the thousands at their disposal and cannot see those for which they have no context for understanding. In the same way as we use history to create, justify, and interpret our world, the Aboriginal uses the Dreamtime. I wonder which interpretation is more appropriate: the one that pretends objectivity and deals only in the "facts," or the one that deals in subjective consciousness—with the felt connection to the living world of the ancestors.

OBJECTIVITY AND SUBJECTIVITY

To illustrate the difference between these concepts, I would like to tell the following story, which was told to me by Father Charles Moore.

An old lady attended a talk on the solar system given by a professor at the local university. He explained the orbit of the planets around the sun and the forces of gravity. At the end of the talk, the old lady approached the professor, thanked him, and said he had gotten one thing wrong.

"Oh, and what might that be?" the professor asked.

"The earth is not held up in space by its orbit around the sun," the lady replied. "It is supported on the back of a giant turtle."

The professor politely hid his surprise and asked, "Well, if that is the case, what is it that supports the turtle?"

"It's standing on the back of a second giant turtle," came the reply.

The professor, thinking he now had the better of her, then asked her what she thought supported that turtle. The old lady hesitated for a moment and then rounded on him firmly: "It's no good, you know. It's turtles all the way down!"[8]

The point is that both of them are right. The scientific explanation is adequate for the material universe and chains of linear causality. It may contribute toward the creation of machines which can then explore the universe. But ultimately it will lead nowhere but to the increased exploitation of the earth's resources and to the sterility of lunar landscapes and the seeming emptiness of outer space. The old lady's explanation is adequate for the spiritual universe. It will lead to the sense of arising out of deeper and deeper inner states, out of a sense of connectedness to all things, and ultimately to meaning. This places us as ethical, responsible beings in a value-laden relationship to all life.

It is clear to me that we need both modes of operation, and this is what I mean by the interaction between the elements of the material world and our consciousness. Neither has an a priori weight; each shapes the other. So it is that we need to enter into the archetypal realms from our present understanding of life and re-dream, re-enact the ancestral acts of world creation, maintaining and learning from the ones which serve wholeness and re-shaping the ones that are harmful to life.

The animals will assist us in this process, for while they are of the elemental realm and partake in the harmony of creation, they also possess qualities that are of our world of cognition and consciousness. Indeed, in particular functions such as speed, sight, taste, smell, hearing, singing, swimming, hunting, cunning, parenting, navigation, strength, and so on, they far exceed us. It comes therefore as no surprise to find the ancestors of the Australian Dreamtime are mostly animals. When we look into the roots of our traditions, we find animals intimately associated with every deity. Did the Horned God, Cernunnos, begin life as the stag? Was Epona originally the horse? Llew or Lugh, the eagle?

Such views posit a geocentrism, the placing of the earth back in the center of the solar system, back in the center of the cosmos.

Science tells us such a view is incorrect. But in terms of our inner world—the old lady with the turtles—such a view is absolutely correct and fundamental to our well-being and that of the world.

Through what may be called a paradigmatic shift, largely as a result of advances in quantum physics where the role of the observer cannot be seen as being separate from the actions of subatomic particles, science is also beginning to incorporate the subjective world view. In the ideas of Rupert Sheldrake, David Bohm, and Fritjof Capra, intelligence or information is seen as the ordering principle between entities. The role of relationships and interconnections is emphasized rather than that of substance. Here might be grounds for discovering where the life of the archetypes actually lies—not as substance outside of ourselves, nor as unconscious contents in each individual, but a manifestation of the interactions and relationships between all forms of life on earth.

Morris Berman in his fascinating book *Coming to Our Senses* has an interesting critique of such "holistic" new thinking. He suggests it merely represents an attempt to substitute another paradigm, another world view in place of the direct experience of our own lives. Instead of treating the world in terms of Newtonian physics, we will treat it in terms of quantum theory, seeking the level where it still can be mechanically explained.

We no longer need paradigms, he writes; they are "still part of the salvation mentality, a patriarchal mind set that tells the hero to persevere, find a new form of consciousness that will give him redemption."9 What we do need is the courage to face the unknown, to accept mystery, and to know that while all world views are valuable, they are not "true"—"Only our need for truth is true."10 Berman points to the body, the somatic experience, of becoming truly embodied, as the way to go. Hence the title of his book. And once again we come back to the animals who share with us a somatic experience of great power and immediacy. The turtles can be our teachers.

The evidence shows that the world view of hierarchy, of dualism, of feudalism, of power over others, is crumbling all about us. In our case, as men—the main exponents and builders of the power-from-without and power-over world view—to simply withdraw our energy and support will be sufficient to ensure its demise.

But we must be sure to stand firmly upon the roots of our power, drawing it up deeply from within the archetypes that connect us to the elemental world. Then, like the tree, we can flourish and grow and put out branches, leaves, and fruit which will reshape the world about us in a positive, unifying way. This is where, at last, we may go into the forest and meet the Green Man.

VISUALIZATION: RUNNING WITH ANIMALS

When doing these visualizations, it is important to bear in mind that the intention is to allow the inner power of the archetypes to emerge. To aid this, personal concentration and ritual, alone or with others, establishes the right circumstances. The purpose of ritual is to reach a point of intensity beyond the current conception of self where the archetypal patterns in the unconsciousness can manifest. This often comes as energy, and ritual action such as dance provides an appropriate vehicle of response.

Run with an animal through the forest. Feel its energy and particular characteristics. Lie down and sleep with it in its nest or den. Feel every part of its life. At night, at dawn, in winter, in summer. Feel changes happening, seasons turning. Something strange is taking place within your body. Your skin is changing. A call is resonating through your animal being. Respond to it. Let it take you wherever it will. Fly with it, swim with it, run with it, burrow with it—trust its journey.

Enter the place where the essence of that animal lives. Not the particular form, but the archetypal form. The essential things that make the animal what it is. Feel the power of that place. Let it live in you. With that power return to the forest. Journey with another animal if you like. Transform, change, migrate with them and feel their particular power in its archetypal form. Then return to your human body and feel the difference made by these animal qualities.

NOTES

1. Nicholas R. Mann, *The Keltic Power Symbols* (Glastonbury: Triskele, 1986).

2. John Matthews, *Taliesin* (The Aquarian Press, 1991).

3. Mimi Lobell, "Spatial Archetypes," *ReVISION* 6:2 (1985).

4. Mann, op. cit., 19–20.

5. Keith Critchlow, *Time Stands Still* (London, 1979), 131–49.

6. William Anderson, *Green Man* (Harper Collins, 1990).

7. Mircea Eliade, *Myth and Reality* (1956). *The Myth of the Eternal Return* (1955).

8. Father Charles Moore, conversation, Sedona, 1990.

9. Morris Berman, *Coming to Our Senses* (Simon & Schuster, 1989), 312.

10. Ibid., 313.

THE GREEN MAN

THE GREEN MAN AND THE WILD MAN

The first thing to say about the Green Man is that his vitality is vast and abundant. He leaps up everywhere and anywhere, often in the most unlikely places. His vitality is not contained by his skin, for vegetation and sprigs of leaves gush from his mouth, cheeks, eyes, and brow. Considering that the world view he comes from is contrary to that of the Church, it is extraordinary that he makes his most frequent appearances in ecclesiastical architecture. This may not be surprising to those familiar with Jung's "Theory of Compensation," however, which, at its simplest, states that if something is repressed it will emerge, sometimes in a disguised form, elsewhere. In this case, the denial of a chthonic and daemonic immanent power by the Church mediating a transcendental Source of power has led to its most vital expression in the elements of wood and stone which form the places of worship of the Church. There is an irony in this, a quality much loved by the Green Man.

The next point to make about the Green Man is that he has many guises. Not least of which is the fact that his name was

applied to the foliated head so commonly found in church architecture only comparatively recently. A Green Man does exist in
folklore, as does a Green Knight, a Jack in the Green, a Leaf Man,
a Robin of the Greenwood, a Gruagach or "giant hairy man," the
Fynnoderee, Bachlach or "Wild Man," and other, local names. But
the name Green Man as applying to all, or nearly all, of these
forms was given by Lady Raglan during her research into the subject in the 1930s.[1] Since then the name has been widely taken up
and has become a favorite British pub name. Although some
authorities say the Wild Man has little or nothing in common
with the Green Man, I disagree, and would like to make myself
clear upon this point.

The basis for the separation of the Wild Man and the Green
Man lies, I believe, in a modern bias to impute intelligence only to
that which is beautiful or to that which transcends the world. It
ignores the wisdom that lies in the untamed, uncontrollable, and
often uninviting and dark aspects of the animal world and the
wilderness. The Wild Man is unacceptably shaggy, daemonic,
lusty, and Dionysian to our modern eyes, while the Green Man,
appearing in highly civilized, clean-edged contexts, is suitably
Apollonian. In the same way as Jung said his archetypes contain
their own opposites, so I feel it is necessary to understand that
these two faces of the masculine are but one aspect of a whole.

One of William Anderson's primary attributes of the Green
Man is that of intelligence. The pictures by Clive Hicks in what is
now the authoritative book on the subject, *Green Man,* are chosen
for this quality. But unfortunately he does not ascribe this intelligence to that which is born out of a deep, primary, daemonic
nature. He writes of the precursors of the Green Man as representing to the people the "transcendental impulse to experience
ecstacy and forms of awareness that took them out of their recurrent patterns of work and social life."[2] This is made doubly unfortunate by the fact that just a few pages before he writes of the word
jubilation as deriving from the Latin word *jubilus*—"the perpetual
humming song peasants and farmers used to sing while they
tended and pruned their vines and olives."[3] I see no transcendental impulse there, but I do see a joy arising out of the experience of
chthonian life.

Before we go on I would just like to say that I wholeheartedly welcome the wealth of information and interpretation that is to be found in William's book. But if we are to take seriously the "Anthropic Principle"—the theory that intelligence is innate to the universe and depends upon us as participants in its reality, a theory which William leaves us with at the close of his book—then we must allow the power of the archetype of the Green Man to inform us out of its fullness—not exclude any part of it—and willingly enter into the drama of his cycle of death and rebirth.[4]

To illustrate the necessity of incorporating the theme of wildness into the archetype of the Green Man, we only have to turn to one of the most popular legends of the day—that of Merlin. I am thinking of T. H. White's description of Merlin's teaching of the young Arthur, when he metamorphized him into the form of animals. This theme was taken up and depicted in Walt Disney's *The Sword in the Stone*. But before that there is to be found in the sources a little known episode in Merlin's life when he became wild and lived in the forest for many years. To this time Merlin attributed the gaining of his wisdom. This form of words cannot do full justice to this theme, and here I must have recourse to some crude verse.

Wild I was,
Toes hardened and black,
Eating bark and berries.
Shaggy I became,
Bent over,
Until running with the boar one day
I knew I was the same.
Wild I was,
Legs taut and thickened,
Hair matted and rank.
My bed in winter
A cave,
Lined with the forest's deep leaves,
But to this I attribute no shame.
Wild I was,
Feathered arms
Lifting from the trees.
Scales across my back

I ate
The cobs in the pool of wisdom,
Then a man once more I became.

The only anthropocentrism at work in the consideration of the Green Man is when, as a result of old forms of evolutionary and hierarchical thinking, we cannot impute wisdom to the elemental realms. Many mythological and folk traditions are expressly concerned with imparting the intelligence of the realms of nature, to the extent of peopling them with gnomes, elves, giants, undines, dryads, and other fairy forms—which contains its own hazard of making them overly human. Somewhere in between is a middle ground where the intelligence of the world can lie and tell us about itself exactly for what it is. And somewhere are the archetypes which can tell us about ourselves and who we are in relation to the whole.

An excellent example of the Wild Man is the Fynnoderee from the Isle of Man. In all accounts he is large, naked but covered in hair, ugly, and of enormous strength. He will help farmers and builders but will be offended if offered clothes as a reward. On one occasion after being offered a fine set of clothes, Fynnoderee replies:

Cap for the head, alas, poor head!
Coat for the back, alas, poor back!
Breeches for the breech, alas, poor breech!
If these be thine, thine cannot be the merry glen of Rushen.[5]

Rushen is a valley on the Isle of Man, and to arrive at an understanding of what is implied by the last line it is helpful to know that the islanders have the saying, "There has never been a merry world since the Fynnoderee lost his ground." Some of his actions are so vigorous and furious that he will round up hares and other wild creatures when folding in the sheep. When reaping he will darken the air with flying husks:

The scythe that was at him went whizzing through all things
Shaving the Round-field bare to the sod,
And whenever he spotted a blade left standing
He stamped it down with his heel unshod![6]

The name of the Fynnoderee may derive from the Irish Gaelic *Fionnadh-doiri,* meaning "Hairy Man of the Oak Woods," though it may also simply mean "hairy stockings." He has much in common with the English Wood-wose, "Wild Man of the Woods," and with the Scottish Gruagach, "Giant Hairy Man." These are often shown with clubs or branches demonstrating their affinity with the forest.

A Fachan or Gruagach. A northern European cyclops.

The Wild Man has a close relative in the Brownie and his Welsh equivalent the Bwca (buuca). These are fairy beings often attached to a specific place such as a stream, whose aid can be sought provided nothing is done to offend them. Although they like to receive offerings, especially of milk, honey, and grain, they are distrustful of anything that would bind them such as payment. In this their wild nature emerges. Among many other forms found all over Europe as giant, spirit, and fairy, the Wild Man has one other interesting relative who deserves mention. This is a giant, known in Scotland as the Fachan, who has one leg, one eye, and a shaggy and terrifying appearance. He carries an enormous club and seems to play the role of a guardian and protector of the forest.

At the center of the mystery of the Green Man is the tree. Whether we are examining the remnants of Celtic art, the stories from myth and folklore, or the foliate heads and of leaves which abound in ecclesiastical architecture, the image of the tree and its association with the Green Man and the Wild Man is constant. There is also his association with the head and horns and with the theme of death and renewal. It's time to examine these themes and the meaning of the Green Man more closely.

THE GREEN KNIGHT

The reader is probably familiar with the story of Gawain and the Green Knight, where, in exchange for meeting the challenge of beheading the huge Green Knight, after a year and a day the knight must receive a similar blow in return. All are afraid, but Gawain accepts the challenge and beheads the Green Knight. Much to the astonishment of Arthur's court the giant picks up his severed head and departs.

In his subsequent search for the Green Chapel of the Knight, Gawain arrives at the castle of Sir Bertilak. On being told the Green Chapel is nearby he agrees to stay and exchange with Bertilak whatever each had won during the day. On three occasions, Bertilak's beautiful wife enters the bedchamber of Gawain and attempts to seduce him. Gawain succeeds in containing his desires and only tells her that she is his sovereign lady. For this he receives a kiss. Gawain then gives the kisses he receives to Sir Bertilak, who gives him the game he had caught in his hunting. However, Gawain concealed a green girdle the lady had given him which protected its wearer from death.

On the day for the return of the blow, Gawain meets the Green Knight, who emerges from the Green Chapel, which is a grassy mound. The Knight makes two feints with the axe and then cuts Gawain lightly with the third blow. He then reveals himself as Sir Bertilak and tells Gawain that the wound was for concealing the green girdle.

This story, like so many others in the Celtic literature, has been elaborated and developed in the courtly context of the medieval chroniclers, which are at a remove from the power of the original archetypes. But we are fortunate in this case (as we are with the legends of the Celtic Peredur preceding Parsifal, the Grail winner) to have a precedent of the Green Knight romance in the Irish story of Briciu's Feast. In this story, the heroes Cu Chulainn, Conall, and Laegaire are disputing over who should receive the "Hero's Portion" of the feast. They are struggling for the power of sovereignty. They go on several adventures, including a visit to the land of Queen Medhbh. She is renowned for her sexuality, and the legend implies she makes love with each of the men.

Eventually they arrive at Cu Roi mac Daire's magically revolving rath or castle. Cu Chulainn is the only man to best him in a contest. However, they are still arguing as they arrive back at the court of Conchobar mac Nessa when a shaggy Bachlach strides into the hall and challenges them to a beheading game. A Bachlach is a Wild Man, sometimes shown as a club carrying "Wild Herdsman." With every blow the Bachlach's head returns to his shoulders and only Cu Chulainn is prepared to meet the reciprocal blow. The Bachlach then reveals himself as Cu Roi mac Daire and proclaims Cu Chulainn's sovereignty. Cu Roi mac Daire is a guardian of the archetypal world who challenges those who would enter and then directs the way. He is akin to the Fynnoderee. He may appear as a hairy giant, a forest man, as the one-legged and one-eyed club-carrying giant, as the Wild Herdsman, or in some other green and leafy guise.[7]

The parallels between the two stories are fairly evident. The issue at stake in each case is sovereignty of self. This is something obfuscated in the Irish story by the quarreling of the heroes, but made clear by the challenges met by Gawain. To understand the themes it is helpful to locate them in the context of the masculine archetype that we are developing in this book.

First of all, the theme of death and renewal is made clear by the character of the Bachlach or the Green Knight. He is able to die to himself and be reborn in the manner of the vegetative world. His challenge to Gawain and the heroes is that they do the same. As we see, it takes considerable courage for a man to lay down his head and expose himself to the transformational character of the seasons—which includes death.

Secondly, the theme of the tree is made evident by the nature of the Bachlach and the Green Knight. They are chthonic deities deeply rooted in the earth. Both are giants, who are none other than personifications of the forces of nature.[8] Both emerge from their magical grassy mounds—Cu Roi's revolving rath is akin to the fairy mounds of the Sidhe. They are green, the color of leaves, and the Bachlach is often shown covered in shaggy and leafy growth. But it is by applying the image of the tree to the archetype of the masculine that we can arrive at a deeper meaning for the process of attainment of sovereignty within the self. We also arrive at the third and final major theme of the Green Man—the head.

In both stories the challenge turns on beheading. We have already touched on the importance of the head to the Celtic people in the story of Bran the Blessed, and a glance through Celtic art reveals the head to be a dominant motif. This focus is continued with the appearance of the Green Man in church architecture. He is shown in most cases without a body and usually only as a head surrounded by and exuding vegetation. What does this mean?

In the scheme for the masculine archetype as presented in this book, it is clear that the Source of power is located in the earth, attendant upon which is the continuity of the line of ancestors and the symbols of the stone and the cave. This is the rath of Cu Roi mac Daire, the Fairy Mounds of the Sidhe, and the Green Chapel. The Bachlach is connected to this power, as is his other wild, forest-man forms. He is able to rise and fall like the sap in the tree due to his chthonic origin.

The test he sets for men is not only of their ability to become a part of the cycle of death and renewal, but to control and focus their inner power. That this power in its first stages is about sexuality is shown by Gawain's first real test in the story of the Green Knight. On three occasions a beautiful woman comes to his bedchamber and attempts to seduce him. Each time he insists his goal is sovereignty, and although he pledges it to her, this is a result of the relationship between the masculine and the feminine archetypes, where the feminine appears as the Source, but the quest is sovereignty of self. In Cu Chulainn's story, the goal is also sovereignty through the focus and direction of inner power. The sexual nature of this power is tested by Queen Medhbh. Although at first this is not achieved because of misplaced quarreling and strife, through the intervention of the Bachlach—the chthonically rooted tree man—it is eventually won.[9]

THE TREE

The tree provides the schema of the archetypal masculine with the symbol that helps focus and direct its inner power. At the winter solstice station—the position of the connection with power via the roots—energy is gathered and brought up through the trunk. That is, raw, chthonian, sexual energy is focused at the base of the body and directed inward up the spine. If it is directed outward, then its power is lost.

The next stage is the quickening and refining of the sexual energy as it moves upward. Conchobar knew what he was doing when he sent the squabbling heroes to Medhbh, a queen well known for her lusty sexuality. "Never without a man in the shadow of another..," Queen Medhbh is the manifestation of all that men are afraid of in the feminine—the connection to primeval, chthonian power. She tests each one and awards each of them with a beautiful cup. This reveals the balancing of the masculine and the feminine currents within the body. The cup represents the body as a vessel able to contain and mix these qualities. The beautiful lady who accosted Gawain gives him first a ring, which he refuses, then a girdle, which he accepts. The ring could not contain and focus the power in question; rather it would have bound him to her. But the green girdle, which protected its wearer from death, he could put around his lower body, his trunk, and thus focus and direct his sexual energy. Although the girdle is said to have cost Gawain a wound, it must be noted that it did indeed save his life.

The next stage is that of the trunk putting out branches. Our heroes, having accepted the inner challenge of the Green Man, literally put their heads on the line before they can reach this stage. In the Celtic tradition an ornament commanding great respect was the torc. This was several strands of metal twisted together, capped at the ends, and then worn around the neck. The word means a rotating force or even "power" and is applied to something that has achieved a stable but highly tensile state. This is the state of Gawain and Cu Chulainn as they have focused and internally directed their sexual power, have balanced conflicts and desires within themselves, and have brought their energy up to the level of the neck and head.

The head was highly venerated by the Celts, for it was the place of verbal skill. It was the seat of poetry, satire, song, storytelling, and inspiration. Those who wore the torc probably did so by right of attaining these skills. Curses and satire were as feared, if not more so, than the threat of war. The bards were given places of high honor and a kind of diplomatic protection in society. It is possible, though there is no firm evidence for it, that upon death the heads of ancestors were removed from their bodies and placed in certain locations for their protection and inspiration. Such an idea certainly underlies the story of Bran.

The Celtic tradition, perhaps more so than any other ancient tradition known to us, elevated skill in language to the highest degree. The druids of the legends are as powerful as the kings and heroes, and in most cases they worked their craft through their bardic skills. The sixth-century C.E. poet Taliesin, for example, has acquired an almost god-like reputation. His *awen* or "poetic inspiration" was reckoned to be divine. Taliesin himself attributed his inspiration to the cauldron of the goddess Ceridwen; and this, as well as other cauldrons and the Crane Bag of the sea god Manannan, was held to contain the secrets of poetry, wisdom, and the power of language itself.

Thus the branches of the tree in its application as a symbol to the masculine archetype are the many branches of knowledge, oral and otherwise, which culminate in the sprigs of wisdom, in the magical alphabets of the Beth-Luis-Nion, the Ogham, the Runic, and Koelbren. Words are objects loaded with their transmuted chthonian power. This is the meaning of the foliage gushing from the mouth, and also the eyes, cheeks, and brows of the Green Man. The abundance of the natural life force made directly available by the archetype, when focused and channeled in the appropriate manner, gushes from the head of the Green Man in inspired, oracular, and poetic outpourings. Hence the preoccupation in the legends of the Green Knight and the Bachlach with the head. The head manifests the fruit of their challenges, their tests, and their labors.

DEATH AND RENEWAL

Gawain and Cu Chulainn thus win sovereignty over self. This is not a static but a dynamic thing, as the cycle of the masculine archetype and the symbol of the tree implies. As the leaves of the tree reach upwards at the summer solstice station, we need to introduce another Celtic initiatory symbol, that of the horns. Those initiated into the highest forms of the tradition were entitled to wear the horns of wisdom. These are massive things, requiring great strength and balance to wear. The weight is something the Abbots Bromley Horn Dancers will testify to as they dance every year around their long circuit, keeping alive the vestiges of the ancient tradition.

On the first-century B.C.E. Gundestrup Cauldron, the seated figure of the deity Cernunnos provides the archetypal model. He is on the ground and draws up energy from below. No phallus is shown because the energy is turned within. In one hand he holds a torc and in the other a ram-headed serpent. This shows he has grasped the chthonic power, transmuted it sexually, balanced it in his being, and brought it up to his head—as shown by a second torc around his neck. From his head sprout great horns, and to show his affinity with the tree, some foliage sprouts from them. He is centered and poised for the circulation of the currents of masculine energy. Animals, the nearest being the wolf and the stag, approach him respectfully, lending their support for the transformational inner journey. In what may be a second depiction of Cernunnos on an outer plaque of the cauldron, he is shown holding up two deer, and his connection with the tree is confirmed by a pattern of leaves forming his hair.

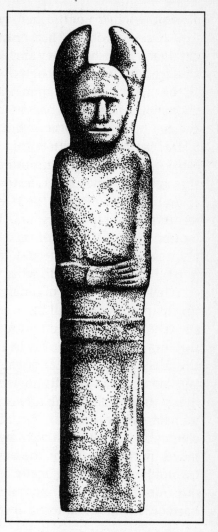

The date of origin of this carved stone figure from Holzgerlingen, Germany, is thought to be earlier than the third century B.C.E. It has a janiform head and a horn-like crown. The figure suggests the contained and inturned energies of the god Cernunnos.

In the schema of the archetype, the stage of midsummer is the time of union with the heavenly forces. It is through the horns that this is accomplished. They are like sensitive antennae requiring fine balance and tuning. Through them the subtle but powerful energies of the rapidly vibrating dimensions can be received and expressed through the mouth, perhaps as foreknowledge and prophecy. This is the quarter presided over by fire and the symbol of the spear.

Falling back to earth within the pattern provided by the archetypal cycle, fertility is disseminated over the land. This continues through the time of the festival of Lugh, to Autumn Equinox. Then the symbolism of the tree becomes exact. Having given up its fruits, the sap lowers, and the leaves fall off the tree to the ground. This is the test of the Green Knight over one full cycle of a year and a day. As the tree has to release its fruits and die, so must the man relinquish what he has accomplished through the directed inner focus of his energy and the outpourings of his head. The man must die to all his accomplishments and release them as the tree releases its fruit and foliage to the earth. He must be like the stag releasing its horns in the yearly cycle. This is the test of the Bachlach as the club or the ax that swings from his shoulder lays out the man and his powers, at Samhain, to die. Without this dying to the self in the archetypal masculine there cannot be a return to Source. There cannot be a regathering of the constituent elements of life and an acknowledgement of the continuity provided by the lineage of the ancestors. Without this death there cannot be the meeting again in the cave at winter solstice. Without this letting go the masculine power cannot be brought into harmonious interrelationship with all life on earth.

THE WORLD TREE

One tradition, that of being suspended from a tree, will serve to illustrate a further dimension of the archetype of the Green Man and also how misunderstood the tradition has become. The tree in the mythology of many people is the *axis mundi*. It is the Tree of Life at the center of and connecting all the many dimensions. In the Nordic tradition the World Tree is known as Yggdrasil, around which revolve the upper, the middle, and the lower worlds. Odin hung on this tree for nine nights and days in order to gain the runes.

I hung on the windswept tree
Swung there nights all nine
Gashed with a blade
Bloodied for Odin
Myself an offering to myself
Knotted to that tree
No man knows
Where the roots of it run.
None gave me bread
None gave me drink
Down into the depths
I peered
To snatch up the Runes
With a roaring scream
And fell into a swoon.
　　　　　　—*The Havanal*

The Germanic and Scandinavian runes form one of the branches of knowledge of the World Tree and find their equivalent in the Koelbren of the Celtic tradition. These are letters carved on pieces of wood and used for divinatory and magical purposes. They are customarily kept in a bag of crane skin. It is when we come close to the Christian version of hanging in the tree that the power of the tradition becomes lost. There, the hanging becomes a symbol of ultimate pain and death. The resurrection which follows is not of a knowledge that goes to assist in the attainment of sovereignty of self, but a once-and-for-all vicarious dispensation which robs the self of its power of transformation. This is true death, not to die in the Great Round of Transformation, but to linger on in a suspended state based upon a belief or the promise of another.

The tradition of being suspended from a tree finds expression in several legends and forms. The Tarot retains a fair image in the card of the Hanged Man, a radiant being who after his trial will achieve a truth, a gift. He is the dying and rising god. In some Tarot decks the tree is T-shaped, hence the name "Tau-Tree," which although Greek, retains symbolic veracity. Odin is the archetype of the man on the World Tree, moving with ease between the dimensions. Whether it is the realm of dreams, of visions, of our own or a transpersonal unconscious, it is Odin who joins them through his power of language and of script. He possesses all the forms of

the magical alphabets because of their ability to bring to consciousness the mysterious and unknown.

Odin's equivalent in the Celtic world is the Irish hero Lugh,
into whose keeping was placed the Crane Bag of Secrets. When the
god Ogma Sun Face first saw the Ogham script on the bark of an
oak tree, he inscribed it on a piece of birch and gave it to Lugh. But
it is Lugh's equivalent, the Welsh Llew—the pronunciation is the
same—from whom we get the full story of the ordeal to be gone
through to win the knowledge of the trees. Llew is tricked by his
wife Blodeuedd—"made of flowers"—to reveal the only means by
which he could be slain. As a result he is killed by her lover,
Goronwy, with a special spear, his own totem. Llew assumes the
form of an eagle and suffers a long ordeal in the top of a tree.
Eventually he is restored to human form. And although it is not
stated in the Welsh text, we can assume he possesses the means of
communication between the different worlds as a result of having
passed through them—the tree representing the connecting link,
or axis through them all.[10]

To return to figure 3 on page 87, which shows the dual
rhythm of the archetype of the god, we may compare the cycle of
a tree to this process and so gain further insight into the tree as
the *axis mundi* able to connect the lower, middle, and upper
worlds. To begin at winter solstice, we find the tree in the dark
and dormant part of the cycle but nevertheless drawing on the
Source. At Imbolc the sap is beginning to stir as the god in his
form as the Star Son rises and quickens vegetative life. By Beltane
his force is bursting out in blossom and new green leaf, and the
dark cycle closes. Through the pollen carried between the blos-
soms at this time the way is prepared for future fruit. At summer
solstice, the light forces reach their peak, the trees are fully
cloaked in green, and like Llew as eagle, the way is open to the
upper worlds. The fire is in the crown of the oak and the otherworldly mistletoe is cut.

This time also prepares for the coming dark and, though full of
substance, the dissolving and decaying part of the cycle. It is the
opposite to the quickening of Imbolc and the fertilizing powers of
Beltane. The god in his form of the Serpent Son after the summer
solstice begins to grow alongside the harvests of grain and fruit. The

fruit of the apple tree either rots on the ground or is eaten. Either way, only the seeds remain. and the sap of the tree has retreated.

At Samhain the god as Star Son must be laid to rest, and with him goes the last of the leaves and any remaining nuts or fruits on the branches of the trees. The time of increasing darkness to winter solstice sees the trees going into dormancy. But already on their branches, the time of the dark and the deep connection to the inner Source of life, ensures that the buds of new life are present and waiting for the next step of the cycle. This is why the mistletoe is brought in at midwinter and we kiss under it to conceive the beginning of the new cycle of the Star Son, the god of the returning sun and the waxing year. We also honor the trees by bringing in the Yule log and a tree for decoration at this time.

As Odin plunged into the depths and swept up the runes, so may we descend at this point in the cycle and touch the serpent coiled around the roots of the World Tree, Yggdrasil. This is deep, inner wisdom, not the abundant flow of summer solstice, nor the loquacity of the poets, but the daemonic Source of words themselves and their full symbolic and magical content. From the roots of the tree to its crown, through its cycle of growth and dormancy, we, as men, can find the symbol that can be placed in the center of the archetype of the masculine. It only remains to dive, with Odin and with Llew, from the tree into our depths, willing to reveal the secret of our means of death, willing to make "myself an offering to myself" to grasp the Crane Bag of Secrets. This insures the cycle can continue. Through the tree our power finds its means of connectedness and integration into the whole.

THE ARCHETYPAL MASCULINE

With that description, it is now appropriate to bring together the basic schema of the masculine archetype with the round of the calendrical cycle of the Celtic year and place the tree in its center. This is shown in figure 4 on page 159. The four elements and the four talismans of the Tuatha de Danaan, the symbols of the Grail Quest, are placed in their appropriate quarters.

Combining all the parts which contribute to this depiction of the archetype may at first be confusing, but by visualizing the cycle and journeying around its dynamic movement from the within to the without, only selected parts need to be dealt with at a time. For example, the cycle of the four elements can be visualized and gone around a few times until one feels comfortable enough to bring in the four talismans: the stone, the Grail, the spear, and the sword. Next, the visualization may include the seasonal round, then awareness of the four Celtic cross-quarter day festivals and their roles in the cycle. Alternatively, the visualization may begin with the tree, with the awareness of its deep taproot going to the Source, then of the trunk and branches, before bringing in the seasons and the other elements which make up the whole cycle.

It may at first be difficult to visualize the dual rhythm of the god in his forms of the Serpent Son and the Star Son. But by going around the cycle, the ebb and flow of their energies naturally falls into place with the peak of the Serpent Son at Winter Solstice and the Star Son at Summer Solstice. Then the relevance of the cross-quarter days can become integrated into the awareness of their rhythm. Different aspects of the cycle may be brought forward and emphasized at any one time according to what is appropriate for each individual at any particular moment in his day, or season, or time of life.

Visualization of the cycle is very powerful as a tool for meditation, as an aid for concentration, or for facilitating release of outmoded patterns or ideas. It is also wonderful as a creative process for the imagination during contemplation, ceremony, or lovemaking. It should be clear that different emphasis on the parts or the qualities and elements of the whole cycle are particularly appropriate for any of the above times or needs. For example, to aid concentration, the inner aspects of the cycle—the gathering up from the Source, the quickening at Imbolc, the fertilization of Beltane, the fire of the summer, and the singlemindedness of the spear—are all appropriate. This inner focus can then find expression through the many branches of creativity as symbolized by the spreading branches of the tree.

If the need is for relaxation and release, then the outer part of the cycle is appropriate to dwell upon. The scattering of the outer elements of air and water, the dissolving into earth, the dying to the old at Samhain, the nurturing space of the dark, are all relevant. Whatever the emphasis or the need, this archetypal pattern should be able to respond to it, being so deeply rooted in the patterns of

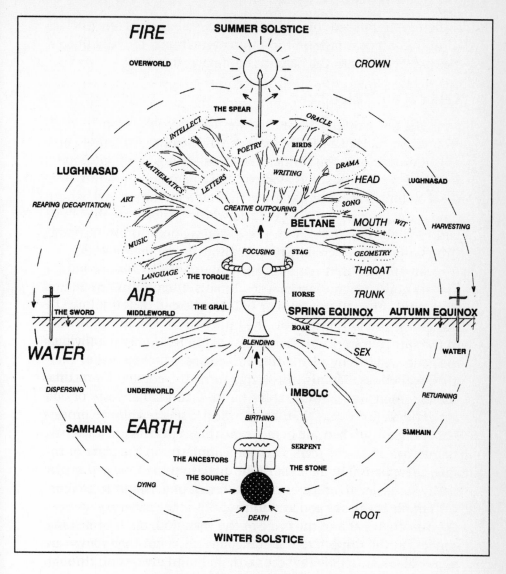

Figure 4. The Archetypal Masculine

nature, in the ground of our own tradition, and in the continuity of life which has generated our language, concepts, and modes of cognition. The most important aspect of it, however, is its dynamic—the movement around the cycle, from the Source within to the without, and back again. This alone allows the masculine energy to integrate itself into the greater whole. It allows masculine energy to find its axis of balance, and to exchange its tendency to run off in a linear fashion for a transformational movement that creates oneness with the patterns of life on earth.

THE CELTIC TRINITY

From the few written sources that we have from the Celtic period, mention is made of a triad of male deities: Cernunnos, Taranis, and Esus. Cernunnos is the Horned God, the earth god, the prototype for the devil because he is akin to the Serpent Son presiding over the dark half of the year. Taranis is the Star Son, the sky god, whose time is the light half of the year and whose symbols are the wheel and the lightning flash. Both these deities appear on the Gundestrup Cauldron, which may reveal episodes from their myths.

Jean-Jacques Hatt has suggested the myths revolve around a mother goddess who first marries Taranis, then Cernunnos-Esus. Hatt thinks the latter is known as Esus, the god of vegetation, in the spring and as Cernunnos, the underworld god, in the winter. In the spring, Cernunnos-Esus is assisted in becoming the lover of the goddess again by a hero called Smertrius, who kills one of Taranis's watchdogs. Taranis in revenge turns the goddess into three cranes. Smertrius sacrifices three bulls, enabling her to return to her goddess form, and then he sacrifices a stag enabling Cernunnos to once again become her lover.[11] These episodes are suggested as interpretations of scenes on the Gundestrup Cauldron. However, a reappraisal in the light of the dual rhythm of the god might clarify some details and advance a different understanding of Esus.

Taranis is the sky god and Cernunnos is the earth god presiding over their parts of the cycle of the year. Both are lovers of the goddess at the respective solstices. But Esus is not the springtime aspect of Cernunnos—here the earth god must give way to the sky god—he is the third face of the god to which we have yet to give any attention. In a way, Esus is like Hermes, the messenger between the worlds, who slips between them as rapidly and as elusively as quicksilver. But like Smertrius, he also facilitates the transition between the different worlds—the underworld of Cernunnos and the overworld of Taranis. He is the aspect of the deity which mediates between the two, making them accessible to the human—the middle world.

The clue to this is the several depictions that we have of Esus which show him as a woodcutter. In one relief from Trèves he is shown approaching a tree with cranes in its branches.[12] We know that knowledge of language and the divinatory alphabets are contained in a Crane Bag, so the tree he is dealing with is our Tree of Knowledge. By representing Esus as the woodcutter, the relief shows that he has the power to mediate between the sky god, Taranis—who turned the goddess into a crane, leaving her high in the tree's branches—and the earth god, Cernunnos, whose foliate associations are often shown and whose roots go deep into the earth. Smertrius's acts of restoration, whatever the details of sacrifice, are made possible through the presence of Esus, who thus gives to the human realm the properties of both the upper and the lower worlds. An examination of the scenes on the Gundestrup Cauldron reveals all the episodes that Jean-Jacques Hatt has suggested, but qualifies them with this reinterpretation of Esus. It would also be appropriate to mention that there are several depictions of feminine deities on the cauldron. These reveal episodes from the story of the goddess as she too, makes the round of the year.

Esus is really the invisible force, which by sliding through the interstices between the worlds—like the

In this relief from Trèves in France, Esus is shown hacking at a tree. The head of a bull and three cranes sit in the tree's branches. All these components, and the name of the deity, Esus, are present on a pillar found in Paris confirming the identity of the woodcutter. The relief, badly damaged, dates to the first century C.E. and reveals the cult of Esus continued on into the period of Roman occupation.

ax—while apparently dividing them, actually joins them into one. Further implications of this resonate in the beheading games of the Bachlach and the Green Knight. As often as the ax severs their heads from their shoulders, they are restored—made whole—and endeavor to transmit this wholeness to Gawain and Cu Chulainn.

It has been pointed out several times by investigators into the Culdee or Celtic Church that one of the reasons why Christianity and druidism were able to join together so easily was because of the similarity between their trinities. God the Father, God the Son, and God the Holy Ghost were interpreted as Esus being Jesus the Son. It was through their agency that the different worlds became one. Though the pattern is the same, it must be remembered that Cernunnos, Taranis, and Esus represent a trinity which includes the chthonic and underworld realms, while the Christian trinity is thoroughly transcendental. Whereas the Christian is a masculine, fixed, and the only trinity, the Celtic trio of gods is only one among a pantheon which includes many triune feminine examples. The issue we are dealing with is a dynamic, a structure of cognition, which reveals the working of the inner world and of the mind itself, not a dogmatic, reified, and absolutist belief.

THE GREEN MAN IN HISTORY

Prepared by the foregoing, I would like to give a few examples of the appearance of the Green Man throughout his story. We find him alive and well and adapting to several faces of the god in the Celtic period prior to and contemporary with the Roman conquest, perhaps the best example being on the exquisitely made Gundestrup Cauldron. Our first clearly foliate Green Man is probably to be found on the St. Goar pillar from Germany, dating to about the fifth century B.C.E. Anne Ross in her excellent book, *Pagan Celtic Britain,* gives a description, along with most of the other early material. The pillar, originally surmounted by a head, is carved on four sides with what is generally held to be a representation of Cernunnos. Leaves cluster on the brows, and foliate forms gush from the mouth, perhaps forming a beard. Forms, not obviously foliate, scroll around the head and up the column. Could two be coming out of his ears? Whatever the exact significance, the pillar conveys the fertile and abundant state of inwardly directed sexuality emerging from the intelligence of the head. Definitely a prototype for the Green Man.[13]

It is not until the fourth or fifth centuries of the common era that the Green Man really emerges as we know him as the disgorger of vegetation. In the intervening period he appears in the classical world among the rites of Dionysius, which include the stage of death where the shadowy but clearly vegetative figure known as Okeanus is introduced. Okeanus may possibly be an ancient deity whose leafy mask provides the precursor for later representations of the Green Man. His face stares out from the center of the Okeanus dish from the Mildenhall Hoard, now in the British Museum, dating to around 200 C.E. He is also found on tombs and on capitals in the classical world. He appears in a variety of vegetative and foliate forms—none of which, however, are gushing from his mouth. For this we have to return to the Celtic influence upon the classical,

Carved stone known as the St. Goar Pillar from Pfalzfeld in the Hunsrück, Germany. Possibly made as early as the fifth century B.C.E., it was originally six feet in height before the head surmounting the pillar was broken off.

and rapidly becoming Christian, world. As has been noted, it is in ecclesiastical architecture that the foliate head disgorging vegetation becomes a ubiquitous and finally triumphant motif.

He appears in the manuscripts of the Irish monks; not as a dominant theme, but continuously and steadily throughout the so called "Dark Ages." This is not surprising, given the Celtic roots of the Irish monasteries. And we even find him in his form as Cernunnos in Christian sculpture, such as on the cross shaft at Clonmacnois, probably carved in the ninth century C.E. Heads appear in the foliage used as surrounds for sculpture in many Romanesque churches, the best examples being in France; but it is not until the Gothic period really gets under way that the Green Man establishes a prominent and compelling presence.

In the early thirteenth century, one of the masterpieces of the medieval masons and sculptors was created at Chartres. The architecture and ornament of this Gothic cathedral is a sublime example of artistic endeavor incorporating mystical and esoteric principles. The site of the cathedral is said to be an ancient druidic one, and below the structure is a spring that probably once stood in a sacred grove and was the reason for the selection of the site.

William Anderson gives an inspired description of the incorporation of individualistic heads of Green Men on the water spouts of the transept portals. He points out that in each case, the sets of three heads rest upon a wavy symbol for water. The water spout on the south transept portal, for example, is composed of a trio of Green Men representing vine, acanthus, and oak. The vine suggests communion or unity, the acanthus rebirth and renewal, and the oak—central to druidic cosmology—represents the power of the Lord of the Forest. All of these themes are central to the archetype of the Green Man.[14]

To take the matter a little further, can we draw the conclusion that the heads of the Green Men resting upon water and giving it forth through the water spouts above their heads are compensating for the sublimation of their grove and spring below the mass of the cathedral? If so, the ancient, pagan archetype has succeeded in expressing itself admirably among the sculpture depicting the new transcendental cosmology.

The next example comes from England. He was carved around 1300 C.E. and is located at the west end of the interior of the church at Sutton Berger in Wiltshire. This is a head of a very individualized man from whose mouth pours leaves of hawthorn. These curl up around him, and in the foliage four birds gather berries. The leaves are outsize, but the carving of every detail is

One of the sets of three Green Men flanking the central doorways of the transept portals of Chartres Cathedral. They are vine, acanthus and oak. c. 1210 C.E.

accurate and exquisite, from the veins on the leaves to the shape of the berries, to the feathers on the birds and the facial features of the man. Every hair on the brows above the deeply set and lachrymose eyes is evident. The choice of hawthorn leaves is particularly appropriate. In the tree calendar of the Celts, its station is the time of May, Beltane, when spring festivals to promote fertility were conducted. May blossom is said to arouse desire because of its feminine musky scent. But it is significant the sculptor depicted the hawthorn in the fall with its red berries, as this suggests the inward working and fulfillment of the energy of the Green Man. The deeply introspective face confirms this. This is not the exuberance of May, but the thoughtful and self-knowledgeable face of a man who is able to provide fruit for the world around him.15 Another medieval example from Bamberg, below the famous sculpture of the Rider of Bamberg, carved about 1239 C.E., shows a furious and dynamic head formed of acanthus leaves so vigorous they as much conceal as shape the facial features of the Green Man.

Among my favorite appearances of the Green Man is Robin of the Greenwood, or Robin Hood, outside of the law, who took from the rich to give to the poor. Also from folk traditions reaching up to the present day there are characters such as the Jack in the Green, who appears at the ancient festival of Beltane, the first of May. Hidden in a costume of leaves, he dances until his time has come. Then, amid cries and groans, he is ritually decapitated, struck with staves, laid low, so that along with old John Barley-corn, the cycle of the year may end and continue in another form.

VISUALIZATION: THE WORLD TREE

See yourself as the World Tree. Visualize the details of your body. Feel your roots going deep into the underworld. Dive down into its depths. Find the Source. From that point allow its power to come upward. Upward through the genetic lineage of your ancestors. Up through the cave which contains the underworld deities. Allow their power to enter you.

Bring the power of the Source up into your body. Focus it into your trunk. Let it rise like sap, quickening and sweetening, mixing and flowing, until it reaches your head. Allow its power to open in your head. Feel branches rise, reaching skyward. Let the power course along the branches, into the twigs, and open as buds, leaves, and flowers.

Allow the full power of the Source to come up through your trunk and gush from your head. Let it take form. See words, music, movement, color, symbols, alphabets, images as the fruits of the tree. Let them pour forth. Then, when your tree is full of fruit on the branches, let them fall. See them and the leaves on your tree fall. Let them spread out over the land. Give them away to nourish others. Let them dissolve into the earth. See them fall apart and decay. Then, feel a gathering again at the Source. Allow the new cycle to draw in its power and go around it again.

NOTES

1. Lady Raglan, "The Green Man in Church Architecture," *Folklore* 50:1 (1939).

2. William Anderson, *Green Man*, 35.

3. Ibid., 56.

4. The anthropic principle unfortunately is misconceived. It assumes that "man," *anthro*, is the goal of the intelligence of the universe! Gaia theory is perhaps closer to what Anderson is really getting at. It does not assume that any one organism or environment is the goal of Gaia, other than life itself.

5. Katherine Briggs, *An Encyclopedia of Fairies* (Pantheon, 1976), 170–2.

6. Walter Gill, *A Second Manx Scrapbook*, quoted in Briggs, 171.

7. T. P. Cross and C. H. Slover, *Ancient Irish Tales* (Dublin, 1936).

8. For a study of giants, see Nicholas R. Mann and Marcia Sutton, *The Giants of Gaia* (Albuquerque: Brotherhood of Life, 1995).

9. It is well worth reading Caitlin Matthew's *Arthur and the Sovereignty of Britain* (Arkana, 1989) for further insights into the legends of the Green Knight. This book, as well as others by her and John Matthews, deal with much valuable material from the prehistoric and Celtic mysteries. Yet, although complementary, the approach taken to the material produces different results to those given in this book. Compare for example, Caitlin's wheel of the year on pages 312–3 with mine.

10. *Mabinogion*, 109–17.

11. Jean-Jacques Hatt, *Celts and Gallo-Romans*, trans. J. Hogarth (London, 1970).

12. Proinsias MacCana, *Celtic Mythology*.

13. Anne Ross, *Pagan Celtic Britain* (London, 1967),62, illus. 23.

14. Anderson, 82–8.

15. Ibid., 119–21

8

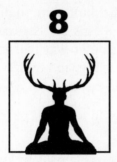

THE CAVE: RETURN

THE INITIATION OF THE HORNED GOD

In 1985 I went to Ireland for the first time. It was early May, and the yellow gorse was ablaze on the sides of the moor. The rain pelted down, the mists formed. The light seemed to come from the land itself. The already knee-high grass shone with a color that made me understand why Ireland is called the Emerald Isle.

I journeyed with two women whom I loved very much. It was a love as much engendered by the pilgrimage that we were on as it was by any attraction to them. We agreed to remain platonic in our affection. Platonic might not be quite the right word; tantric may be better. I will define tantric as the directing of sexual energy inward, making it available for creative activity in the subtle centers of the body.

At times our journey felt like a labyrinth, so many were the twists and turns from inner to outer worlds. We went from Neolithic sites to fairy ones, from Gaelic to medieval locations, from stone circles to chambered mounds, from smoky public houses to museums. But as I stood in the absolutely lifeless interior of the Archaeological Museum in Dublin and studied the engraving of the labyrinth on the stone found near Hollywood, County Wicklow, I knew I possessed a vital clue to our meanderings, and at some point I would meet the half-man, half-beast that lay at the labyrinth's center. I knew this partly because I was with women who were wise, each in her own way had access to the Crane Bag of Secrets, and partly because the land itself was directing my passage. It only remained in me to trust.

✳   ✳   ✳

"Nicholas, you're not to blame, you know."

"What!" I almost jumped out of my seat.

"You're not to blame for the wars. For what men have done."

"What are you saying, Diana?"

"I'm saying, don't take on the guilt."

We turned into the car park. Theo switched off the engine and both women swung around in their seats to face me.

"But I'm a man. I'm one of those who is responsible for what patriarchy has done. I can't escape that responsibility."

"Yes, and we are all responsible." Diana coolly replied. "Don't take away my power for determining what has happened, too. There is no blame. Your guilt will only weaken you. And for men and women to come back together again, we need you to be strong!"

Our eyes met in the silence that followed. I knew exactly what she was talking about, and so did Theo. I looked at the two of them and felt their power. Theo, no longer young, gray in hair, beautiful, as wise and nimble as a fox. Diana, steely blue eyes, steady, always ready for a fight. They looked back at me and I knew I was naked—stripped of my old self—and I knew I could no longer hold back the tide of the new self that was waiting to come in.

"Come on," I said. "Let's go to the trees."

We grabbed our boots and coats and, need pressing, crossed over the river and raced for the tree-lined slopes on the side of the glen. Soon we were climbing into a lichen-draped oak forest.

An exquisitely smelling carpet of grasses, mosses, and ferns lay beneath our feet. We had to slow down to avoid crushing tiny flowers or from going knee deep into a morass of sphagnum that

Carving of the Horned God by Chris Craig

hid tiny rivulets. Scattered over and partly submerged in the ground were boulders of shining white quartz. They had been ground down in ages long past into rounded shapes. I noticed one that was like a giant egg.

There was no path. We did not know where we were going. Only the urgency of the moment drove us on until that impetus was spent. We sank down onto the surface of an all but concealed granite rock. At that moment, a deer broke cover not ten yards away and leapt out of sight and hearing. The place felt right. A strong sense of presence filled the grove.

Images of the past few days came into my mind. I saw the stone of sovereignty on the Hill of Tara. I saw the labyrinth on the Hollywood Stone. I recalled the visits to holy wells and the teaching of the stone circles. Through the images came the spirals of Newgrange and geometrical patterns from Knowth and Loughcrew. And, peering through the boughs of the trees, like light seeking to enter a long, dark passageway, was a strange, wild face.

I lay down on the stone as the images became lucid. I was breathing hard and my sexuality was up. Theo and Diana lay on patches of moss and green shamrock on either side of me. I felt as though I was at last keeping a date that I had unknowingly spent many years journeying toward. I caught a final glimpse of the lake between three tall trees before I closed my eyes. Diana, the sea priestess, and Theo, wise woman, beside me. At once the initiatrixes and keepers of the door of my return.

"Go!" was all Diana said.

A white horse appears on the hillside ahead of me. There is no doubt of his virility, his ability to sire many foals with the splendid member that grows between his loins. He rears and strikes the air in the direction that leads deeper into the wood. I pursue him as he leaps over thickets of blackthorn covered with guelder rose. I have no trouble keeping up with him as we enter the shaggy branches of oaken groves.

We begin moving uphill. He never deviates from his course through the trees. Then, with a gasp of surprise, I see on a crag above my head a pure white hart of ten tines. Impressed by his beauty, I leap to be with his spirit. I turn as one with him as he sweeps like an arrow down the hillside.

We move fast through the forest. Groves of silver birch shimmer on either side. Green sward opens like a furrow. The powerful forms of oak gesticulate as though communicating the essence of their song in some forgotten tongue. I move with the white hart until I see, lying directly in our path, an archway made of rough, uncut stones. It is set into the rocky hillside. As we come closer I can see upon the lintel stone unfamiliar glyphs that exude power.

The darkness of the archway looms, and I feel afraid. I have a wish to halt my movement but I know I cannot. Unceremoniously, I am pitched into the threshold of the cave. I get up and continue with my movement forward. The motion is much slower, but it is still irresistibly strong. Then, in the half-light, I see the stag men. They are clad in skins, standing in two rows, one on either side of the cave. Their heads are covered by their masks. But I know who they are and they greet me.

They silently gesture for me to go deeper into the darkness of the cave. There is an incredibly musky smell. Normally I would have found it unpleasant. I now find it extremely attractive. I pass between the stag men. They gesture with the implements they carry in their arms.

As I move forward, cautiously but still compelled, I make out the form of a male figure in the darkness at the back of the cave. He is seated upon a stone throne. He is directly in my path. There is no turning back. I can see him as he generates his own pale green light. This is so subtle that for a moment I wonder if he is really there.

As I draw closer to the throne, the sense of immanence increases. I sense the wind in the trees of the forest; the odor of the woodland's earthy floor; the slow seepings of the inner earth and the rushing of the streams after rain. Invisible birds sing somewhere. A large animal stamps its foot. The man on the throne has thick and sinewy limbs, searching eyes, tangled hair and beard. From out of his brow grow a pair of horns.

All kinds of names run through my mind. Who is he? How should he be addressed? I feel slightly panicked. Is he the Green Man? Cernunnos? Herne the Hunter? The Lord of the Forest? As I'm wondering these things, he calls out...

"Welcome!"

And the word echoes around the chamber, evaporating my fears. And the sound slowly recedes to mingle with the water that trickles down one side of the cave.

Shaken out of my introspection, I take a deep breath. The stag men willing me from behind to go on, I approach the throne. Before me there appears a cup. In which, swirling of its own motion, is a green liquid. The word "elixir" forms itself in my mind. I see that the liquid shines with the same iridescence that moves over and fills the translucent limbs and body of the Green Man.

Without hesitation, I drink down the liquid. It tastes rich and strange. I find myself—as though propelled by a giant hand—turning around to face the stag men. I am moving backward toward the throne and the seated presence. The motion is irresistible.

I find myself sitting. To my astonishment I feel the limbs of the Green Man surrounding and filling my own. I feel his powerful, shaggy legs enveloping mine. I feel his deep, knotted chest enclosing my chest. I feel his thick arms filling my own. And then, the most extraordinary thing, the power of the man, the elixir, the throne, the earth itself—which, I cannot say—begins to rise upward from the base of my spine.

It is pure sexual energy. But it does not rise as I would expect, up my love member. It rises within. I have the sensation of an inverted phallus moving up my spine. It courses like liquid fire through my body. It reaches my head. It divides into two and pushes against my temples and out of my skull. I have two great horns for a crown.

I feel ecstatic. I am full of power. I am poised to act, yet at the same time I know I don't have to do anything. The horns need stillness to be worn. And when balanced they act like two antennae—organs of great sensitivity—connecting me to the heavens, to the stars, and with threads of awareness to every living thing.

I don't know how long this moment lasts. Pure consciousness of life force has replaced thought. Yet now, there is something else. I have to stand. I have to walk back between the rows of my ancestors, the stag men. I am acutely aware of keeping the balance demanded by the great and heavy horns. As I pass them by, the stag men bless me. They reach out and touch their fingers to my brow. They touch the points of their weapons to my skin. I, in turn, touch their brows.

At the exit to the cave I am faced with a grave difficulty. How do I get these horns out through the narrow opening? The problem seems ridiculous, absurd. I laugh, go down on all fours, twist my head to one side and then burst out of the cave with an exhilarating sensation of power.

I race across the meadow, zig-zagging my way through the trees. Like the lightning flash, like the deer in the fall, from the dolmen arch I fly. I run with the wind, my ears pricked back. I weave from side to side in the ecstacy of being alive. I arrive at the foot of the mountains and instantly transform. I am a wild boar, gaining in strength and momentum what I have lost in grace. In this form I climb the foothills, surging through the dense scrub. I leave the thickets behind and emerge in short pasture. I become a hare, darting over the ground, playing as I run through the boulder-strewn land. In this guise I reach the mountaintop. With one thrust of my strong hind legs, I leap into the sky.

And then I fly, peak to peak
An eagle, with the feathered host calling
A greeting to the checkered land below.
With one sharp eye I see a lake
Glistening like crystal. I dive,
Drive downward, swooping without restraint,
Crashing into the silver shine
Flinging rainbows in the spray of my descent.

In water I am a fish. Swimming with great sensuous twists of my untiring, muscled body, I leap the falls in joy. I reach a quiet pool at the head of my one mad surge, and then, surrender. The current takes me. I drift downstream. I am aware of two women. One on either side. Their hair floats in my waters. Arriving at a beach, I find myself once more a man.

And a man like I had never felt before. I feel the branches above my head as though they are my hair. I can feel the birds in the foliage of every strand of it. I can feel the plants and the mosses between my fingers as though they are issuing from them.

And I can feel the black soil between my toes as if I have grown from out of it.

"Nicholas, Nicholas," I hear a voice say. "Come back." It is Diana.

I hear myself struggling for a reply. But the words feel like leaves in my mouth, and I can only manage two...

"I am..."

Diana smiles, leans over and kisses me lightly on the cheek. I see myself standing up and walking over to the three trees at the edge of the grove. There lies the egg of white quartz I noticed on the journey up. I approach it and admire its shining color against the golden carpet of last year's leaves. Then I see that it has fractured. A piece the size of a head has broken off. It lies beside the boulder revealing the crystalline interior. I pick up a fragment and hold it in my hands until it becomes warm. Then we leave.

THE SOURCE

Some time ago, I was talking with a friend, Stanley Messenger. He asserted that it was the subtle energy fields emanating from and pervading the body that were responsible for the circulation of the blood. I replied that I thought it was the heart pumping the blood that sent it around the body. His answer was partly that the heart could not possibly reach the pressure necessary to drive the blood through all the capillaries, especially in the body's extremities, and partly to ask, what it was that I thought made the heart pump. I could see what he was getting at. For me to reply that it was a nervous or an electrical impulse would lead back to his original "subtle energy fields."

His thesis was that not only did these energies pump the heart, circulate the blood, produce and maintain the breath, but they were responsible for the continuation of the life of every part of the body. He went on to talk about our complete ignorance of the nature of electricity—something we use every day, but know absolutely nothing about. He mentioned other quandaries which beset the scientific establishment, such as the nature of light, of magnetism and gravity, of time and space and the subatomic realm.

At first, I felt there was some element of denial of the genetic principle in what Stanley was saying. But upon thinking about it, I could feel the Source of life within me went beyond the beating of my heart or my breathing, to that which made it beat and me breathe. The Source, the life force, is not separate from these things. It is these things, I thought. It is the power that enables me to see, to hear, to think, to digest. It is the power that enables all life to do what it does—for the trees to pump sap and photosynthesise, for the cells to reproduce, for the planets to maintain their orbits, and so on.

This idea of energy, not distinct from matter and its manifestations, but existing within them and through them finding its expression, in all probability comes closest to defining what I mean in this book when I talk about the "Source." To sit still and be with this energy, not to control the breath but to feel its energy breathing you, to feel every pulse of the body and every emanation of the mind, to experience the life force without evaluation or control, may be the single most important "exercise" given in this book. I hesitate to call it a visualization, as I have at the end of the other chapters in Part II, for indeed it is not. But this practice will facilitate psychosomatic visualizations or archetypal re-enactments and provide the practitioner with a central core of immanent yet infinite energy.

Once, before the notion of self became defined by an individual's own thoughts, memories, and beliefs, we lived in a world of direct perception. There was no difference between us and the creative order of nature. Meaning arose in our direct experience of the world, where perception was a function of our total being. There was no difference between mind and body. Consciousness was likely to have been not only tribal but an experience which extended into animal life and pervaded every aspect of nature. Only through letting go of our ideas of a separate self and by merging with the deeply interactive orders of reality will we find the transformative power of the unlimited creative Source.

PART III

THE WAY AHEAD

TOWARD A NEW MALE SEXUALITY

THE PROBLEM

The energy of men is kept suppressed by narrow definitions of male sexuality. One result is that it breaks out of this containment violently like a volcano blowing its top. With the challenging of the male supremacist values which define men and male sexuality under patriarchy, the amount of violence to women and gay men is dramatically increasing as men struggle to retain their power. This violence runs all the way through society and ends up in the home. Many couples live in an emotional quagmire that threatens to draw them down at any moment. They only manage to get by through denial and repression.

A friend of mine argues that this situation has arisen because of the mismatch between the narrow way society says relationships should happen and the way they actually do. We are all supposed to date, become engaged, marry, settle down, have children, and live happily ever after. With, of course, the husband in control and the wife in submission.

In fact, modern men and women are responding to and being driven by a far greater diversity of imperatives, passions, ideals, and principles. Many of us are gay or bisexual, are uninterested in the nine to five routine, are uninterested in marriage or children, and, when wanting to love and care for someone, are perhaps interested in doing this by not living with them or committing our whole life to them. Women may want a career and men may want to raise children. We are responding to a different pattern than the one currently laid down by society and, at present, the new pattern is unclear.

One of the first points to be made is that the patriarchal society which is now ubiquitous in the world, and has been in most places for three or four millennia, is deeply alienated from the body and fosters a pathological attitude toward sexuality. Most of its legal and spiritual codes were drawn up with the specific intention of controlling female sexuality, given the uncertainty of the role of the male in reproduction. As a result, sex, especially rape, has become a means of asserting the patriarchal ideology. "Fucking" means intercourse and exploitation. The latter is the characteristic and normally accepted criterion for the "power-over-others" mode of patriarchal society.

According to the government-funded National Women's Study, 683,000 women in the United States were raped in 1990. Even if this is inaccurate, many more rapes go unrecorded. At least one man in a group of ten has raped women and at least one woman in a group of eight has been raped. The figures of child molestation are only just emerging, as men and women have the courage to speak up or even to remember a repressed part of their lives. It is reckoned that sixty-one per cent of all reported rapes occurred before the woman reached the age of seventeen and thirty per cent of those were girls less than eleven years of age.[1]

In the patriarchal society, sex is used as a reward for correct behavior. A man can expect to be rewarded with sex if he competes for money, status, and power. In war, this reward is rarely made explicit, but it always has been implicitly considered as one of the spoils for the victor. As an incentive to work harder, the promise of sex is held out by the models who accompany advertisements for cars and other prestige objects. It is incredibly difficult for men to break out of the time-honored attitude of treating women as sex objects. Power-over-others, in this case women, is institutionalized into us as men.

In the city where I currently live, women who are employed by a large law firm quickly discover that they are expected to provide sex for the men. One of the senior partners in that company has recently become a federal judge, despite the fact that the F.B.I. team who examined his credentials knew of the practice. We may safely assume that such practice is widespread. The Clarence Thomas/Anita Hill hearings only reveal the tip of an iceberg of sexual exploitation in which men may genuinely consider themselves innocent, because we are all colluding in a huge, taken-for-granted institution.

Sexuality is a subject shied away from in schools, yet it is a vital ingredient of successful relationships and of procreation. Physical ecstasy is disapproved of and implicitly seen as "sinful" by the dominant Christian religion, especially for women. At the same time, the Church limits sexuality to heterosexual intercourse and insists on the implanting of the semen in the vagina. The capacity for the pleasure of the body is a largely untapped resource and surrounding it are layers of pressure, guilt, shame, and their converse, passivity and violence. Men still have the dualistic attitude of "good girls don't and bad girls do"—the archetype of the virgin or the whore. The "Sexual Revolution" may have helped release many inhibitions, but it also put the pressure on women to have sex even on the first date. Male activity in sex is largely confined to intercourse and achieving orgasm, at which point all further pleasure for women stops—if it ever began.

Gynecological health is largely in the hands of a male-dominated medical establishment whose practice is rooted in values which do not treat women as equals. It attempts to decide for them on the issue of abortion, relies excessively on surgery, and lacks adequate skills based upon real experience in counseling, if any is offered at all. Genital mutilation of young girls is practiced in many Muslim and African nations and is refused as a topic for debate at the United Nations on the grounds of "interfering with national customs." In "female circumcision," not only is the clitoris removed, but so is the labia, and the area sewn up tightly to increase the man's sexual pleasure. If the equivalent was practiced on the man, circumcision would amount to removal of the head of the penis. As it is, male circumcision is unnecessary genital mutilation and can be shown to seriously diminish sensitivity and impede masturbation and intercourse.[2]

Healthy themes of sexuality have become eliminated from our mythology, especially those of the *paganus*—the country-dwelling people who maintained the pre-patriarchal traditions. The tradition now drawn upon, mostly the Greek, supports rape and what amounts to the ideology of a closed men's club, because women were not seen as the equals of men politically or sexually in that society. Such themes dominate elitist education in the most wealthy and powerful Western countries.

The nuclear family is still favored by society because it forms the perfect working and consumer unit and no allowance is made for any other form. Homophobia keeps men apart and the man dependent upon the woman for his emotional needs. The monogamous heterosexual couple is the only sexual relationship approved of by society; all others have to go against the mainstream or are marginalized. The patrilineal institution of marriage is still popular, yet a society in which seventy-two percent of men married for two years or more are not monogamous and seventy percent of women married for more than five years seek sex outside of the marriage shows that something is not working.[3]

Finally, we hardly know what love is, so thoroughly have our values been muddled by the dualistic and Christian world view. However much Christianity tries to reform itself, the world, the body, sexuality, impulsive romantic love, homosexuality, the genetic principle, and women are all "evil"—to be transcended; while celibacy, abstinence, frugality, hierarchy, ordained and vicarious spirituality, and so on fall into the category of being "good." Christianity has killed tens of thousands—some say millions—during the time of the Inquisition for what it called "heresy." We can be sure this category included those who had a view of spirituality which was rooted in the somatic, sexual, pagan, and ecstatic experience of the body.

Plato, in the *Symposium*, has his characters speak of a state existing in the world where each person has been divided into two and must always seek their lost other half. This notion of the "divided self" has continued throughout the history of the Western world. It is expressed in concepts like "soul mate" and "my better half." The result of this dualism has been the creation of a view of love based upon the absence and, more rarely, the presence of the "lost other." This has several strands to it.

In religious practice, this view encourages the yearning for God to take on an almost sexual character—kept pure because never requited. If requited in actual physical experience, road-to-Damascus style, then it poses the Church with an enormous difficulty. The Church does not wish people to have direct experience of God. Only the Bible describes the "true" experience. Such a dilemma does not occur in Eastern religion, which by and large encourages the direct physical experience of the divine and does not make category distinctions of heresy and orthodoxy.

In the Middle Ages, this view generated the idea of "courtly love." Here a man pledged himself to a distant and sexually unavailable lady. What was gained in terms of being able to follow inner feelings of love without the restrictions of marriage was lost as a result of the denial of the physical context of love—sexuality. Courtly love can be understood in this context of denial, as can the semi-erotic yearning for an absent God. But in general terms of the wider mass of people and men in particular, denied and repressed somatic experience has resulted in the consciousness of the "other" as always being perfect, distant, and unobtainable. The self in this world view can never be whole.

In terms of the psyche, repressed inner contents will inevitably find their outlet in archetypal imagery, and this, for men, as a result of the mind/body dualism, manifests in feminine form. Jungians would call this the anima. The search for the anima has contributed to the identification of the "lost other" with the divine woman—which the Church incorporated as Mary—and the identification of the soul and the inner world with the feminine as a whole. All the time this was going on, actual, sexual women were being denied, dominated, and burned. Only abstract, distant, or vicarious experiences of God and of women (e.g., in courtly love) were socially acceptable.

Today, as a product of these strands, we are at the effect of ideas about love which focus on "getting" as the other side of denial. More often than not, we idealize the other and unrealistically adore them when they are "got." Love in this have/don't-have mode becomes an obsession. It is not really concerned with the partner at all but with fulfilling the inner psyche's demands for possession. The urge is to bind, to ensure loss cannot happen again when the other is found, to consume the other, orally, mentally, emotionally, and to endure times apart dramatically—sustaining a pathological preoccupation with pain. Eventually, when partners split up, it is felt as the end of the world. It is felt as loss of self. The pattern therefore is one of yearning, pain, desperation, then relief when the other is found, then fear of loss, jealousy, commitment/marriage, exclusivity, the split up, and around again. Any genuine caring and love has a difficult time emerging in this cycle.

What is the way out of this quandary—this terrible tangle of deception which lies around sexuality? What is the way to a joyful and healthy form of sexuality which will provide us with what we know to be one of the greatest pleasures of life? What is the way to a healthy form of loving that is not based upon the divisions and power issues of hierarchical dualism? I will go directly to what I feel to be a solution, define it, and then work backward from there to show how the archetype of the masculine being re-created in all the themes of this book finds its expression in this form of sexuality.

THE NEW MALE SEXUALITY

The new male sexuality is an expression of a man's power from within. As the teaching of the Grail and the Green Knight showed how to retain power and direct it inwardly—not project it out onto the world, onto women or men—so this form of sexuality will enable a man to connect with his inner self. It is a means of using every part of the body so that a man experiences himself as whole.

It is a man becoming ecstatic, understanding that his whole body—not just the penis—is an organ for pleasuring his partner and himself. It is knowing that it is possible to enjoy a much broader range of physical experiences than what is currently on offer. It is remaining in a state of ecstasy drawn from his own power, rather than dissipating it as quickly as possible either through ejaculation with a woman or in power moves with men.

1. The new male sexuality is semen-retaining. By this is meant that the purpose and the goal of sex is not just to pursue

intercourse and achieve orgasm, but to experience and give pleasure.

2. The new male sexuality is re-creative. By this is meant that sexuality is not only for procreation. It is also for the purpose of experiencing creative power and using it in practice. It is to go back into the "Dreamtime" when the world was being made and to feel archetypal power moving through us during ecstatic states of body and mind in lovemaking.

3. The new male sexuality is rejuvenative. By this is meant that through semen-retaining lovemaking and re-creative practice, the powers of sexuality can be directed toward self-creation. Rejuvenative sexuality produces a flow of regenerative energies that promote healing and development of a whole and healthy body and mind.

SEMEN-RETAINING SEXUALITY

The situation has arisen in the Western world where sex has become defined as foreplay (usually minimal) between a man and a woman, followed by intercourse leading to male orgasm. Most men reach orgasm and ejaculate within five minutes of entering the vagina. This is seen as healthy and as what "a man" should do. Religion sanctifies this. The woman is seen as providing for the man's orgasm, and in the process she should have hers. Most women do not achieve orgasm through penile thrusting—more than seventy per cent according to *The Hite Report*. When provision is made for them, this is considered as being "extra" and not related to the "main act" of intercourse. The pressure on both partners to perform is enormous, and this generates great anxiety.

The pressures on the man include: getting an erection, keeping it, having an orgasm, delaying it long enough for the woman to have hers, and being "man enough" to "score" in the eyes of his peers. Pressures on the woman include not being seen as too forward (a quality admired in the man) and helping the man get to orgasm while avoiding being raped. Often a woman saying "no" to sex is a result of her knowing it means intercourse, wanting to avoid pregnancy, and retaining a degree of control in an area of her life where she has any power left.

The simple solution to all these pressures is first of all to distinguish between sex and intercourse. Secondly, to have more goals in sexual activity than orgasm. Thirdly, to extend sexuality beyond coitus between heterosexuals. When it is realized that there exists a whole spectrum of experience previously ignored, then it is possible to move forward into all the joys of sexuality.

From this perspective, the matter of the retention of semen gains a context in which it can be understood. It is not a rigid dogma which has to be religiously adhered to. It is a way of redefining sexuality so that women are equally included in its definition, and it is based upon lovemaking with a partner with whom there is genuine friendship and love. The goal of ejaculation is replaced by intimate sharing with another of feelings, thoughts, and bodies along a huge continuum of possibilities. These can range from joint creative activity, to being held—which all authorities agree is the primary, basic need—to caressing, kissing, and mutual erotic stimulation. Included in this host of options can be intercourse and orgasm.[4]

There are, of course, times when it is appropriate to release semen; when the purpose and goal of sex, that of mutual pleasure, has been achieved. How often this release should be is open to debate. Most authorities on the subject agree that semen release in the above circumstances is appropriate for young men almost daily, for men in their thirties and forties a few times a week, for middle-aged men perhaps once a week, and for older men perhaps once a month depending on their health. But I will argue that it is dependent upon other factors that are central to the archetypal character of the masculine we are building in this book.

As for pleasure, the point is that there are no rules. The best guide is the body, both your own and your partner's. Set aside a whole afternoon, an evening, or a day for lovemaking. Let bathing, food sharing, massage, erotic costuming, dancing, gifting be a part of your lovemaking. And relax, an often difficult thing for us to do in a culture where we are taught it is better to give than to receive. Though it may take a while to learn, sex and intercourse in a relaxed and unhurried state will ultimately prove to be far more satisfying than the chase for an orgasm. Men will need to look closely at themselves during lovemaking to ensure compulsive wishes to ejaculate, dominate, perform, and be the "star" are not at work. Other hierarchical and patriarchal patterns such as unresponsiveness, silence, and noncommunication of feelings—the things most complained about by women—may also interfere.

The purpose of this kind of lovemaking is to feel pleasure. After a while of recurrently reaching high points of arousal, it is possible to experience intense pleasure upon retaining semen. In place of ejaculation and cessation, what may be called an "internal orgasm" occurs, where the phallus feels an orgasmic drawing in and up of vital energy. This state can last for hours, even days after lovemaking. In place of dissatisfaction from too-brief intercourse and one short spasm by the man, and quite likely none for the woman, the total satisfaction of being loved, held, and known by another begins to exist. Instead of feeling depleted, it is likely new energy will emerge which can then be carried over into other areas of life. The woman will also experience increased internal energy in this kind of lovemaking. Every climax can be different for a woman. They can build upon each other successively. Small climaxes, one on top of the other, may be far more satisfying for her and provide hours of lovemaking rather than one full orgasm attained quickly.

It is difficult for men, with their genital and orgasm-focused sexuality, to understand that women may be far more interested in non-vaginal sex. For many women, orgasm is not the goal of lovemaking. Instead the goal is what men call "foreplay"—that is, what occurs before the "real thing." Foreplay is continuous and expansive, whereas intercourse is focused and its usually rapid ejaculation brings sex to an end. It is reported from women's talking circles that, on average, foreplay lasts seven minutes and coitus perhaps one minute. Therefore in general women prefer "foreplay" and want it to last for hours because they know that soon after they take the man inside, the lovemaking will cease.

The socially sanctified goal of men—orgasm with ejaculation in the vagina—is the very thing many women try to avoid or prolong reaching. This is one of the roots of many women's "passivity" in sex. Hence the need for semen-retaining sexuality. Only if she knows the man will retain his semen and remain inside of her for a prolonged period of time in a relaxed and loving way can she begin to enjoy vaginal sex. The interior of the vagina is not as sensitive as the penis. The exact equivalent for women of the penis is the clitoris, which is often not stimulated by vaginal sex. Most women report being able to reach climax—when they want to—by stimulation of the clitoris, whereas only a small percentage are able to reach climax during coitus. It is important to remember that coitus or orgasm may not be the main thing for the woman at all.

A factor which may account for hard penile thrusting on the part of men is loss of sensitivity due to circumcision. The shaft and foreskin of the penis contain many nerves and the foreskin facilitates lovemaking with its rolling action. A goal of men today would be to stop their sons from being circumcised, a surgical operation currently being practiced on over half of all American males. Adequate hygienic instruction would more than outweigh any benefit the operation gains while avoiding its risks and, above all, allowing the retention of the full sensitivity of the penis.

I wrote above that the goal of men in sex is intercourse culminating in their orgasm, and though this may have been generally the case a few years ago, today there is an added goal which says a man should provide women with an orgasm too. A man would be selfish not to do this. A "real man" should be able to "give" his woman paroxysm after paroxysm of orgasmic ecstasy in intercourse. There are some broad misconceptions around this issue. As mentioned above, the woman's equivalent to the penis is not the vagina, it is the clitoris, which is not directly stimulated in coitus. Aiming for better and better technique in coitus is more likely to cause anxiety in a man than it is to provide an orgasm for a woman.

Orgasm is a state of mind, not a physical spasm. The full experience of orgasm comes from relaxation and release of anxiety, fear, and performance goals. Orgasm can only be provided for by oneself, not one's partner. We are not responsible for another's orgasm.

In my own sex life, I felt I was driven by two pressures. The first was, "I've gotta have an orgasm" (provided by the vagina of a woman). The second was, "I've gotta sustain my erection as long as possible, while moving as much as possible, so she can have an orgasm." The two pressures were incompatible. I usually ejaculated without much pleasure for myself or my partner. Sometimes the woman would be mad at me for coming, or I would succeed in pleasuring her only to have a barely felt climax for myself. It seemed I was either running toward orgasm or away from it. I was never remaining in the present where pleasure was available. I was actually afraid of my own orgasm. It was either too quick or too slow or too little or too late. The times when orgasm was wonderful was when I stopped worrying about my performance, moved into a full experience of my and my partner's total energy, relaxed, sensed with my whole being, and released in utter abandonment of self. I was having to deal with very deeply ingrained social values.

Here lies the rub—if I can use the phrase. Orgasm for the man means the cessation of his penis-focused sexuality. With the discharge of a teaspoonful of chemicals, the blood which sustains his erection departs, and he becomes limp, flaccid, and drained of sexual energy. With so much of his self-definition as a man dependent upon his virility, the collapse of his penis in the vagina of a very likely still aroused woman comes as a death to self. An annihilation in the oozing maw of the Great Goddess. Fear is a perfectly understandable response in these circumstances. So is domination and control of sexuality. So is preoccupation with performance, but it doesn't get us very far.

What is being proposed in the pages of this book is that a man celebrates his "little death" at the hands of the Goddess, learns to totally release to her, and dies to self. Only in this way can his linearity and transcendental focus let go into the flux and transformation of life. Only through total relaxation in sex, the removal of all goals, the removal of all which defines sex as being limited to certain acts, and the moving into a total experience of self as body, mind, and emotions, can release in orgasm be satisfying, fulfilling, and cosmically integrating.

TANTRA

It is to what has been called tantra that we must turn if we are to escape from the demands of having (heterosexual) intercourse and achieving an orgasm currently imposed upon us by patriarchal definitions of sexuality. In the Old Testament it is clearly stated that anything other than heterosexuality is wrong and a man is admonished for "spilling his seed upon the ground"—he must do it in women. The Catholic Church totally endorses this view. At

the same time, due to the spirit-matter dualism of patriarchal consciousness, sex is devoid of any holiness.

Tantra is not control of ejaculation but the establishment of a
state of being which allows the full round of pleasure. In tantra,
the continuum of experience that is available ranges from delight
and warmth and closeness—similar to hugging—through excitement and joy and arousal—similar to petting—to peaks of ecstasy
far beyond the brief spasm of orgasm. The culturally conditioned
drive to attain the known and brief experience of orgasm is far
superseded by going into the unknown territory of conscious
semen-retaining sex.

Tantra may begin with simply holding each other. This satis-
fies a deep and primary need. Breathing together, allowing every
part of the body to touch, and sensing the subtle currents of
energy moving through and over both partners' bodies, is as
enjoyable as intercourse. To really know and be known by the
other can satisfy something that no amount of "seven-minute
sex" can ever achieve.

Ride the wave of the sexual experience without any assumptions about what is going to take place. Relax and allow the holiness that waits to enter every facet of life to enter your being. How
easy this is in lovemaking! Resist any act that feels like pressure
and control. With sex defined as heterosexual intercourse—usually
initiated by the man—the woman had few choices but to go
through with it or say, "Not tonight, dear." But with sex defined as
an open-ended continuum of choices and possibilities without a
predetermined goal, then no participant will feel pressured to
"perform." Stroke each other, smell each other, explore, let the
deepest intermingling of every part take place. Extend your sexual
repertoire to include every part of the skin and every orifice. If the
wave of sexual feeling carries you to coitus, then a man needs to
retain climax until a totally different sensation of pleasure replaces
the traditional release. Eventually a distinction can be made
between climax in its many forms and the traditional male ejaculation. A total orgasm or "injaculation" generates pleasure on
many levels that altogether far exceeds the pleasure of ejaculation.

The main purpose for a man is to feel with the penis and
indeed with the whole body an experience of energy that is inter-

nal and ecstatic. After a while of practicing this kind of lovemaking, it is possible to feel subtle energies circulating between the partners. With his glans, the extraordinarily sensitive head of the penis, a man may feel drawn into a woman when she is at her peak times of arousal. And a woman can feel a man's internal energy far up inside of her as he reaches his heights of pleasure.

This is not possible if they are trying to provide for each other. It is not possible if they are trying to be responsible for the other's experience. The partners need to remain focused on themselves. Co-union occurs when the inner centers of the body are activated and generating energy and then interacting with those centers in another body on deep, psychosomatic levels of awareness. Partners can help each other do this through communication. Visualizing a circuit of energy going down the penis, up within the man's body, and down within the woman's body may help. Other visualizations are possible and are suggested in the books on this subject mentioned in the notes. These books are good on the physical side of lovemaking, with some reservations, as for example when they rigidly insist on no ejaculation. But they are weak on the re-creative side of sexuality, which is discussed next, and indeed constitutes the heart of tantra and the renaissance of the tradition being dealt with by this book.[5]

RE-CREATIVE SEXUALITY

At this stage in our journey toward a new male sexuality, it will be helpful to recall the pattern of the calendrical cycle of the year, the cycle of the elements, and the four talismans of the Tuatha de Danaan which became the objects of the Grail quest. This information, together with the symbol of the Tree of Life and the qualities of the Green Man, can now be addressed in the context of the initiation process into the Horned God. Figure 4 on page 159 will be most helpful in keeping all these themes and cycles in mind. It is now that these themes can be brought to a single focus.

Since it has not been possible or desirable to keep the sexual content of the masculine archetype out of the different patterns and cosmologies drawn from the ancient tradition in the preceding material, the reader is probably aware that the root or the Source frequently referred to is extremely sexual in its nature.

Every mythological character or god has contributed in their way toward portraying the directing of the masculine sexual energy and the ecstatic and creative state of a true sexuality. Gawain and Cu Chulainn literally "keep their heads" in the tale of the Green Knight, even though in Gawain's case a beautiful lady comes and offers him everything. Cernunnos sits upon the earth drawing on its deep chthonian subterranean energy. His daemonic sexual energy, though always suggested, is never shown outwardly, but as an internal and balanced force depicted by horns, the torc, and in some cases, as on the Gundestrup Cauldron, by his grasping of a ram-headed serpent.

The head in Celtic mythology is the repository of power. When libidinal power is drawn upward from the roots and directed through the body, as in the case of the Green Man, consciousness is flooded with energy. The head then becomes the source of poetic inspiration, music, intellect, art, and science. This is represented by the twigs, foliage, and fruit of the Tree of Knowledge gushing from the mouth of the Green Man.

William Irwin Thompson brilliantly develops the theme of the close connection between language and sexuality—between the head and the sexual organs.[6] In the ancient traditions, language was seen as the supreme ability of consciousness. Since the brain and the tongue are connected through the spinal column to the penis, communication during sex can raise a person's consciousness to the highest levels. The oral and genital areas are mediated by the spinal column, all of which may then be seen to contain one identical substance. In the words of Norman O. Brown, "The soul-substance is the seminal substance; the genius is the genital in the head. We would then all be carrying our seed in our head, like flowers."[7] This points to the use of language in lovemaking that will tap into the deepest potential of a man. Though eloquence may not always be appropriate, a man's love talk during sex may resolve one of women's greatest laments about men—lack of communication. At the same time, desire for physical action and orgasm will be transformed through tantra into an aesthetic—which can then be creatively expressed. Love talk is a means of connecting every faculty of a man, intensifying his passion and his concentration, allowing the expression of his emotions and of the

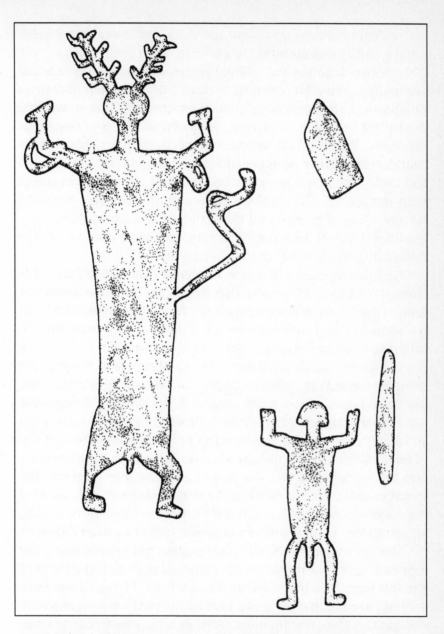

This petroglyph from Val Camonica in northern Italy lies in a context which dates from as early as the third millennium B.C.E. to as late as the fourth century B.C.E. The "god" and his "worshipper" have attributes in common with later portrayals of Cernunnos: horns, torc, and a serpent. There is no mistaking the phallic, fertile, and sacred nature of the scene.

sacred. These in turn may allow the visionary power of the arche-typal realm to emerge either in sex or in other creative acts.

The circulation of the internal energies of the body, visualized as moving around the calendar cycle of the year, whether done in one breath or as a year-long ritual re-enactment, attunes us to the dual rhythm that is so deeply imbedded in our psychosomatic processes. When this is joined together with the symbol of the World Tree, further power is added to the internal experience of the cycle. The tree's roots provide a visual metaphor for union with the Source. The trunk provides the internal focus necessary for the rising of energy, and the branches and crown express the abundance of the in-turned sexuality, so vividly depicted in the foliage-disgorging heads of the Green Man.

Finally, the theme is made explicit in the initiation of the Horned God. Here the phallus rises within, up the spine, and mani-fests as the horns of wisdom upon the head. The cycle of the year, the elements, and the Grail symbols lend their weight to this pat-tern. The Stone or the element of earth at midwinter is the source of power and the seat of sovereignty. The Grail cup or air at the spring equinox blends the different currents of energy arising from the Source and directs them to the spear or fire at summer solstice—the place of the highest manifestation of sovereign power. Over the autumnal equinox and Samhain the powers are released and dis-persed, transmuted by the sword or water and die to themselves, and are reintegrated into the psyche as renewable re-source. The spinal column, like the trunk of the tree, mediates the polarities of the cosmos, where the "...word is master of the elements of fire and air...(and) the sperm is master of the elements of earth and water."[8]

Now let us apply the archetypal pattern to the male body. The root or Source is at the penis. The trunk of the tree is the trunk of a man's body. The branches are his mouth and head. Those read-ers who are familiar with the idea of internal energy centers or chakras can elaborate upon this idea greatly. This archetypal pat-tern for the masculine, when incorporated into the activities of lovemaking, is an invaluable means to ecstasy. The energy and pleasure generated at the Source, then circulated through the body, out through the mouth and the crown of the head, and back down outside the body, or visualized as passing through the body of the partner, will make this cycle dynamic and immensely creative. The woman, attuned to the transformative qualities of the feminine, will assist in the flowing of the linear energies of the masculine while gaining from the focus and direction that he brings. Having ejaculation as the goal would only obscure this process. But precisely because a man must release, must let go and die to himself, orgasmic ejaculation at the point in the cycle represented by Samhain/winter solstice is necessary. This is not the release of a man's desire, nor the expression of his power over another. Neither is it the release represented in the cycle by Beltane/summer solstice for procreative purpose. It is the release of a man's attachment to his linear mode and his submission to the inner, fluid unknown in order that the cycle of transformation can go on. It is his "little death" to self.

The next stage in the re-creative process is possibly the most dynamic and exacting. We are ready to connect to the creative force of the world itself. I understand sexual energy as capable of this by virtue of its capacity to create new life. When a man and a woman come together to make a child, the biochemical fusion of egg and sperm which results is not simply a reproduction of themselves; it is a whole new life. In procreational sex they touch into a tremendous primeaval source of raw generative power. It is as though they touch into the Dreamtime, the time of creation itself, when the ancestors walked upon the earth and made the first things and the first people.

In semen retaining lovemaking, this power of creation is once again made accessible; only instead of using it for making babies, the main purpose at hand is that of re-creating the inner world. This is what is meant in the discussion on the archetypes as having the vehicle and the means to enter into their centers of potentially overwhelming power. Through connecting with their energies, we may re-establish the world order and re-create the archetypal powers within ourselves.

Sexuality is the most easily available means at our disposal for entering into the archetypal realms and thus tapping and directing sources of inner power. Many of us do this already with what we call "fantasy," but when this creative potential is consciously directed through verbal communication and in-turned sexual energy, the potential for transformation becomes enormous. I am certain this capacity of sexuality for re-creation is at the root of the truest and fullest meaning of the word tantra.

REJUVENATIVE SEXUALITY

In many Oriental books on sexuality the practice of semen-retaining lovemaking is greatly commended for its rejuvenative qualities. Strictly speaking, "rejuvenative" means restoring youth, but a more accurate definition of this I feel would be the maintaining of youthful health and vigor. I believe frequent lovemaking can contribute to this especially when, as the books suggest, it is combined with exercise, a good diet, and freedom from stress. However, as has been stated before, it is not so much absolute semen-retention that rejuvenates, but the practice of tantric sexuality where the focus is on re-creating wholeness within the psyche. In my view semen release is absolutely necessary at times in order for a man to experience letting go to the full power of transformation. This practice integrates repressed and disempowering unconscious contents with a profoundly harmonious cosmology. By tapping ancient and living traditions of power with their roots in archetypal forces and in the world, this practice, by virtue of its wholeness, creates a healthy and vigorous state of body and mind.

Robert Lawlor in his book *Earth Honoring: The New Male Sexuality,* suggests a threefold view of sexuality. The first stage he calls "romantic." The object of this kind of sexuality is not orgasmic control but the frequent and full release of ejaculation. Through its high currents of emotion, there is the positive passion of youth, but also anguish and idealization. The second stage is the "ritualization" of sexuality. Here emotional energies are developed and lovemaking is concerned with the "aesthetic pursuit of beauty." The lovers develop ritual patterns which are elegant, graceful and pleasurable to them. Lawlor suggests that at this stage the archetypal world can be participated in by contacting mythical characters that are "personifications of our own inner moods."

The third stage is "regenerative" sexuality, which is concerned with health, awareness, longevity, and a deep understanding of the body and its currents of energy. Spermatic retention is central to this. Lawlor recommends Dr. S. T. Chang's books for their knowledge of the body's meridians, subtle centers, reflexology points, and the role of sexuality in vitalizing and stimulating all parts of the psyche. It is what Lawlor has to say about regenerative sex that is closest to our theme.

He writes of the principle that draws all things together into relationship. He calls this the "logos." He suggests that "analogical wisdom" which sees connection and relationship is a feminine mode of thought, in contrast to the separatist and reductionist logic of masculine modes of thought. He writes:

> The goal of regenerative sexuality is to understand the ebb and flow of the universal emotive force as it moves from planetary, solar and lunar levels and through the principle of logos connects to the corresponding energy qualities in plants, animals, and minerals and the organs and nerves of our bodies. Through regenerative sex we can learn to constructively balance and direct these forces for the maintenance and pleasure of our bodies. More importantly, these sexual disciplines become great teachers for understanding the laws of nature.[9]

Here we arrive at the full constellation of forces that I refer to as archetypal and which have their origin in the process of physical evolution and the continuity of ancient tradition upon the planet. Here archetypes are more than mere "personifications of our own inner moods"; they are powerful, collectively created forces which provide us with the means of participating within the cosmic drama.

The energy of the plants, animals, and minerals comes to us through the presence within us of archetypal forces such as the Green Man, the Bachlach, Cernunnos, and the elemental beings known as the giants, fairies, and spirits of place. These are as much a product of our mythological tradition as they are of the bio-chemical, genetically created molecules that form our bodies.

Both creative expression in its cultural mother lode, and our biochemical, somatic makeup has interacted together through all the stages of our evolution and so has molded the dominant archetypal traditions with their own distinctive cosmologies upon the planet. Through physical acts we may make these known to ourselves, and through spiritual, mental, or other acts of consciousness we may also make these known to ourselves. But it is through the sexual act that we stir the deepest biochemical memories or cellular encodings. This combined with archetypal remembering or mythical re-telling locates us in the center of a congruent cosmos where the re-establishment of harmony and wholeness can only lead to health and rejuvenation.

SEXUAL MYTHOLOGIZING OR SEX IN PREHISTORY

When our Paleolithic ancestors went into the caves and painted the animals on walls and ceilings, they were also entering the yoni—the sexual opening of the Great Mother. The paintings they made were archetypal expressions of the physical powers they actually encountered in life. These were created not so much as conscious design but by the force of the archetype manifesting through the artists. They painted their experience of the unity of life.

When our Neolithic ancestors selected a piece of ground for the construction of a long barrow or a chambered mound, they too were responding to somatic imperatives from the archetypal realm. The opening of the land for a circle of stones, for the raising of a huge mound, was not so much a planned, designed, and conscious process but was rather a physical response to an upwelling of enormous archetypal force. As these people laid out ground with geometrical precision or carved stones into polyhedrons that contained universal mathematical formulae, they were enacting the messages of the inner archetypal realm which—as was shown in Chapters 6 and 10—contain precise spatial and temporal criteria.

The druidic people of the European tradition turned away from the technical accomplishments of the earlier age and went "back to nature" for their inspiration. This flowed into tremendous achievements in the poetic, musical, linguistic, mythical, metaphorical, and theatrical realms. They were theatrical in the sense of combining costume, dance, and movement with poetry, myth, and ritual on ceremonial occasions. Perhaps they turned to the springs and sacred groves and abandoned the megalithic sites because these were too rigid in form and had lost their original truth. We do not know. But we can be sure the druidic impulse was to follow the inner world of archetypal form, the chthonic world of continuity shaped by ancient tradition.

Many of these ancient practices were sexual in their nature. Sexuality as a means of connecting to the power of the archetypal realm was recognized and encouraged. The psychic literature (and even some of the archaeological literature) about Avebury, the huge stone circle in central-southern Britain, with its serpentine avenues and sacred mountain at Silbury, speaks of it as being a place where the vast reservoir of sexual energy was tapped into on ceremonial occasions. Through sexual enactment and mythologizing, the archetypal realm awoke in the world and renewed the sacred order of life.[10]

Prehistorical—or, as I prefer, pre-patriarchal—sexuality turned upon a spiritual as well as a procreative purpose. It is likely the association between intercourse and pregnancy was not firmly known—at least by men—until about 8,000 B.C.E. (See the section "Matriarchy and Settlement" in Chapter 3.) After that, social codes and legal structures were drawn up to place control of property, women, and their offspring into the hands of men. Judaic law admonished men not to "spill their seed" and promoted vaginal intercourse. The Catholic Church keeps the control of reproduction in the hands of men, denies birth control to women, denies a woman's right to chose whether she wishes to carry a child or not, and allows the man the right to have intercourse upon demand. The concept of "illegitimacy" was created under patriarchy because a child's status is determined by inheritance in the male line.

Intercourse, as it is now defined, symbolizes the male domination of women. As the woman lies below the thrusting man, she is reminded of her subservience. The act provides for his orgasm but not for one of her own and tells her, moreover, that her need for clitoral stimulation is not "normal." There is no questioning that perhaps the way the act is performed is what is not normal. It is certainly not spiritual.

Before the encoding of patriarchal sexuality, a man's orgasm provided by the woman was probably not the norm. It was far more likely to have been provided by himself or by other men. Masturbation, for example, is precisely where most men report the best purely physical pleasure is to be found. After all, sexual pleasure is a very delicate thing, and stimulation by oneself or by someone of the same sex is likely to be of a more sensitive nature. We know this was the preference of the Greeks and early Romans, and some vestiges of an honored homosexuality exist in Celtic sources.

It is likely that pre-patriarchal tribes or clans were structured to form a nucleus of women and children with men on the periphery. Social relationships were essentially defined by matrifocal and friendship bonds rather than by the actions of competing males. As we saw in Chapter 2 with the example of baboons, this is the case for primates. The men were probably organized into age groups who went through initiation together. Each group, male and female, had its own songs, myths, stories, dances, and symbols which constituted their "mysteries." Although men did compete, sometimes violently, their definition of self was not tied to values of sexual "conquest" and "performance" as it is today. Concepts of virginity, monogamy, heterosexuality, homophobia, widowhood, and marriage were unheard of. "Illegitimacy" was entirely unknown because children automatically became members of the clan. Men provided sexuality for themselves in the context of the men's circle. Women provided sexuality for themselves in the intimacy of the women's circle. Children were sexually intimate with each other, and were encouraged to be so.

Sexual relations between men and women may have taken place as mutual enjoyment of each other on a very free basis. Pressure to be a virgin, to be heterosexual, to marry, to provide orgasm, or to be monogamous did not exist. But most importantly, sexual relations between men and women were intrinsically filled with spiritual significance. It is probable that intercourse at certain times was a group religious activity, perhaps—for some groups— the only time men and women ever made love. Women, it appears, were the first timekeepers, keeping tally of menstrual phases and of pregnancy—and noticing their correlations with the moon—so it would seem likely they also prescribed the time of rituals and thus of coitus. It makes more sense that women were in charge of reproduction. If collectively enacted, the cycles of birth and the year could fuse into meaningful correspondence and thus be a part of the sacred order.

Such collective reenactment is a long way from us at this time. It may not even be desirable. However, we as couples, through tantric sexual practice, can enter into the mythical, symbolic, and archetypal worlds and by so doing renew the sacred order of our own lives. This can take many forms. The archetypes encountered need not be great or appear deeply spiritual. They may be our child within, the little boy or girl in need of re-creating a safe space where sharing is possible. On the other hand, they may go deep into the pre-patriarchal memory and provide an alternative cosmology. Through "remembering" the older traditions, we free ourselves of cultural expectations and of power relationships with which we oppress each other.

One tradition of relevance here is the Celtic practice of handfasting. A couple agree to be "hearth mates" for a fixed period of time. This is usually a year, from one celebration of a cross-quarter day such as Beltane to the next. The agreement could then be renewed. Women had considerable rights in this system, not least of which was the right to remain unmarried. She could also hold her own property and decide inheritance if she did choose to marry. An idea gaining acceptance quite widely now is that the nuclear family and its partner, marriage, is a relatively recent institution. As was suggested above, the basic unit of pre-patriarchal society was the clan, not the family. At the center of the clan were women and children with men on the periphery. The custom of handfasting, or something like it, may have originated in that time.[11]

Through clearing our minds of limiting beliefs in the area of sexuality, a whole range of legitimate choices become available: physical contact without sexual intimacy with men; masturbation, with oneself or with other men or women; full sexual relationships with other men; physical intimacy with women; full sexual relations with women; bisexual relations; sexual activity for personal growth and spiritual development. I would like to comment a little more on the latter here.

Pursuing the connection between the oral and the genital, an extremely valuable way of working a path into the archetypal realm is through myth. The characters in myth are the archetypes within ourselves—the giant figures of the past abiding in our unconsciousness. Through recounting a myth in lovemaking, perhaps each partner assuming roles they identify with, the archetypes come to life and can be directed by ourselves at the same time as they direct us. Certain mythical themes will speak more strongly to us than others, and this will relate to their relevance in the immediate situations of our own lives.

In my own experience, although I have my own favorite archetypal themes originating in distant historical contexts, the area I encounter most on inner journeys originates from my own genetic and geographical tradition. The ancient European tradition speaks to me most strongly. Its gods and goddesses, myths and symbols, language and monuments, provide me with the means to journey most deeply into the realms of meaning and power and locate me in an experience of an integrated cosmos. The entry into this world is not only made available through sexuality, but also through contemplation, meditation, and individual and shared ritual practice.

Since I adopted and owned my own genetic inheritance and moved over from a linear time standard to a "universal" one, I found my life turns around the cycle of the year, especially the cross-quarter days. I find myself living out its myth, or rather my myth: letting go and releasing at Samhain, renewing intention at Imbolc, celebrating at Beltane, harvesting at Lughnasad, and last but by no means least, transforming and growing through the dual rhythm of the Serpent Sons. These may be fantasies, but as fantasies of the creative imagination given life through observable periodicity and verbal communication and empowered by re-creative sexuality, they go far to establishing the kind of world I choose to live in.

THE DUAL RHYTHM OF MALE SEXUALITY

As was discussed in Chapters 4 and 7 and shown in figures 3 and 4, the god, in his form of the earth god—Cernunnos or Gwynn ap Nudd—or in his form of the sky god—Taranis or Gwythyr—revolves around the cycle of the year. The gods of the waxing year give way to the gods of the waning year at Samhain, and vice versa at Beltane. This creates a dual rhythm in the dynamic of the masculine archetype which needs to be carefully understood. In essence, the dual rhythm is constant. There is only a short period between the demise of the Star Son at Samhain and his re-emergence at winter solstice, and the demise of the Serpent Son at Beltane and his re-emergence at summer solstice. The god in his changing forms is always present. What does this dual rhythm mean in terms of male sexuality?

The task of the male is to reconcile and hold in balance a polarity which could at any time divide his psyche. This has happened in patriarchal consciousness with the division between tame and wild, Apollonian and Dionysian, city and country, men and women, slaves and free, and between light and dark or heaven and hell. These divisions continue on their way throughout the patriarchal cosmos, rendering all that is feminine, emotional, left-handed, lunar, earthy, of the shadow, etc., to the side of evil, and all that is masculine, intellectual, right-handed, solar, heavenly, of the light, etc., to the side of good. If the feminine archetype were to predominate—or to have equal weight—by virtue of its nature, consciousness would not make such categorical divisions. Connectedness, co-operation, relationship, continuum, shades of meaning would be more important than polarities. Distinctions would be capable of transforming one into the other, melding all together into a unified whole. This is not so for the masculine archetype.

The caduceus of the god Hermes or Mercury, who occupies the position between the worlds, represents the situation. In ancient Mediterranean symbolism, the central staff represents the pillar of the feminine, the omphalos or world egg or navel, and the two serpents entwined around its length represent the dual forces of the masculine. These have to be understood and balanced within the psyche before the man can reach wholeness and join with the woman in the *conjunctio* or the sacred marriage.

As a result of urban, transcendent religious thinking, the Serpent Son or the chthonian earth god has become a repressed aspect of the masculine archetype. He, as dragon, has been impaled on the lances of the shining solar god. He is identified with the "bad," demonic, irrational, chaotic, feminine, and shadowy aspects of the self. The male psyche needs to integrate him in order to become whole. This is the point of the dual rhythm. The male has to learn to walk in balance. He has to learn to walk in the Underworld as well as the Overworld. He has to consciously understand the dual rhythm in order for the powerful forces within his being to be balanced so he can become whole and creative once more.

As we have seen, a vital aspect of this is letting go. Without the release of his preoccupations, the male tendency to act in a linear and transcendental fashion is at odds with the changing forces of flux in the world. The man has to learn that he can hold on to nothing, that he can possess nothing. Ejaculation—the "little death"—in lovemaking expresses this. The Green Man expresses this with his cycle of dying and rising as the god of vegetation. The dual rhythm of the god is expressed by the fact that there are two forms of him, so each can die to the other, each giving way to the ascendancy of the other.

Here the basic form of the masculine archetype as outlined in the text can be very helpful because it provides for periods of disintegration and reintegration. It provides for a true orgasmic release in lovemaking, as a man is able to let go of every part of himself into the primeval womb of the Great Mother Goddess. In many ways this releasing aspect of the archetype is possibly the most important contribution to the awareness of masculinity as it currently exists; for at present there is no provision for circularity, for release, for surrender by men, for transformational definitions of masculinity, unless they are perceived as failure, loss, or weakness.

A man has a difficult time with this, especially when he becomes a fully sexual being. Despite his attempts to transcend or control the world, to dominate the cyclical principle, to produce harvests at his command, to force women into sex as he desires so his supremacy is never challenged, the changing nature of life always gets away from under him. The storms knock down his bridges and sink his ships, insects find ways to eat the harvest in his monocultural systems, his perfect geometric systems go awry, his penis falls, and women refuse to be tamed. This is in fact a blessing. For the rigidity a single serpent around the caduceus creates—as in patriarchy—would inevitably result in death through imbalance with the changing forces of life. The path back to unified consciousness through awareness of duality is a difficult one. Only through the holding of apparent paradox, through the integration of the Serpent Son and the Star Son, will we as men join with creation in its full dance.

So it is in the ancient tradition that a cosmology has arisen based upon the changing nature of day and night, of sun and moon, of the seasons, which locates the masculine within its cycle, requiring him to die to himself, to let go of his need to control, to release his single-minded, transcendental urge and be forever born anew. This cycle locates him within the cosmos, balances masculine and feminine within himself, integrates dark and light, above and below, ego and shadow—all the possible divisions of the psyche—to render him whole.

The symbol of the caduceus or the cosmic egg with its two entwining serpents depicts this balance of the masculine energies within the Great Round of life exactly. So does the cycle of the god as twins around the seasons of the year. Without this balance a man would suffer tremendously. He would see all he has ever built crumble around him. Without this he would learn nothing. He would be in a perpetually unchanging, rigid and lifeless state of morbidity. And yet it is hard to learn these lessons. The male has to learn to bring immanence, present-moment experience, transformation, and change into his life. Until he does so, he will find it difficult relating to the flux of the natural order and to other men and women in our society today.

LIVING TOGETHER AND MARRIAGE

Despite attempts to codify sexual relationships in marriage, the facts show that marriage as it is defined does not work. It is not because true social values are eroding that marriage does not work; marriage does not work because of the weakening of the false values of patrimony: the domination, subordination, exclusion, and possessiveness which have maintained the institution up until now. When people—mostly women—see the jealousy, rigidity, lack of freedom, control, exploitation, double standard, alienation, anger, and violence that marriage currently brings, it is no wonder that they want to get out from under it. Unfortunately, no societal models for marriage—or relationship—other than the obsessive-romantic or the patriarchal version exist. So if we do get out of them, we quickly fall into the next state of possession.

The perception by many that if marriage and the family falls apart, then society falls apart, is well founded. Women have long been the unacknowledged providers of comfort, support, and emotional security for men who otherwise have to exist in the harsh, homophobic, winner-take-all conditions of the political arena and the marketplace. Studies have shown that marriage benefits men emotionally far more than it does women. Most men over fifty remarry, but increasing numbers of women over fifty see no point in remarrying. In contemporary culture, the only opportunity given to men to express themselves emotionally is during intimacy with a woman. Women have been the center of the home for a long time, but now it is women who are pulling back from it.[12]

The hope is that through the collapse of the hierarchical family structure and because of the demand by women for new ways of relating, men will reassess for the better their attitudes toward women, other men, and the world. Men will be able to turn to each other for emotional sharing and intimacy. Unfortunately, this does not appear to be happening. In the absence of any thoughtful response to feminism or any attempts to analyze patriarchy, men are in a very weak position. Homophobia prevents bonding developing between men. Because competition and exploitation are the governing criteria of relationships in patriarchal society, men fear other men. Men feel they will be "fucked over" if they get close to and expose themselves to men.

Men project patriarchal values onto homosexual relationships and imagine the same kind of relationships of subordination and domination in them that exist in heterosexuality. The fear of being exploited by another man is frightening and abhorrent. The result is that many men feel, at one pole, that the only way they can get their emotional security is through a woman, and at the other pole that, without possessing her, she will leave. This is a basic insecurity. Add to that the insecurity created by the culturally imposed pressures on men to perform heroically in bed and we are in a very vulnerable position indeed.

Not surprisingly, this is the exact opposite of the predominant stereotypes in society, whereby women are supposed to be the ones who are insecure, demanding that their men create family and home. Women are the ones who are supposed to be afraid of being left without a partner. In fact, women have been shown to create their own security in the form of friends, family, and home wherever they go. It is men who resist change, don't make friends, and insist on marrying and living with their partners as their only means of emotional support. It is quite possible to argue that one of the reasons why patriarchal society (and men in particular) move work locations around is because it takes women out of the network of friends they have built up and pushes them back into the role of supportive wife. Through disempowering women and empowering men, society gets the kind of member it needs. Women know this subconsciously and resent it. How can sex be good when the life situation is only serving the husband's needs?

With this huge unwritten agenda at work in society, men need to look very carefully at themselves, especially when it comes to living with a woman. I am of the opinion that living with someone and then trying to make an indissoluble tie with them is on the same level of compulsion as is the drive for intercourse and orgasm. "Hi, well, we slept together last night. Do you wanna move in?" Alternatively, men, caught in the code of machismo, remain completely aloof and uncommitted. Men need to find the middle ground—all the possibilities of relating to women that lie between possessing someone and having no one. The essence of men's security has to derive from within.

Our developed schema of the masculine archetype shows why a redefinition of the psychology of sexuality and marriage is necessary. The male has to let go every time he makes a round of the cycle. Clearly, marriage as it stands today makes no provision for this. The man wants to know that the woman will be available for him the next time he wishes to sleep—emphasis, sleep—with her, and furthermore that she has not slept with anyone else while he has been away. To enforce this, their relationship is bound tightly together with promises, expectations, assumptions, rings, shared bed, property, and a host of other things which systematically eliminate the spontaneity, space, independent choice, freedom, and creativeness that lovemaking and a healthy relationship require. The only thing it does provide, security and apparent commitment from the man, are undermined by the issues mentioned above and by the man's socially engendered condescending, dominating, and controlling behavior as the relationship goes on. Such a situation clearly has to be addressed before there is any contemplation of having children.

The re-created scheme for the masculine archetype suggests a new pattern of sexual behavior for a man. The man learns to incorporate the dual rhythm of the archetype inside of himself. This requires a sensibility and a commitment to the development of the whole self. On the one hand he is being asked to direct his energies inwardly, to find and create his true self, and on the other hand he is being asked to consciously work upon himself to release attachments, dependencies, expectations, and the need to control and exploit the surrounding world. In sexually relating to another, these issues surface constantly. So it is here that either the most work gets done and the most growth occurs or the most pathology and inertia arising from the old patterns is perpetuated.

The key components of the new male sexuality in this situation are:

- Contacting and developing the whole masculine archetype with its connection to the ancient tradition

- Following the wisdom of the physical body and drawing on the inner power of the Source

- Retaining semen in order to sustain re-creative tantric sex

- Letting go of the aspects of sexually relating to women or men that remove consciousness from the present-moment experience

An example of the latter would be accessing the unconscious conditioning which denies men physical and emotional contact with other men. This would amount to a total reconstruction of our philosophy and a post-patriarchal definition of our psychological makeup.

As an exercise, a man may examine all the sexual responses that he has toward women during the day. He may ask himself, "Why am I looking at this woman as a sex object?" "Is this sexual assessment appropriate right now?" "How is this sexual feeling affecting my responses in the situation?" Men are having to deal with an immensely long-standing and ingrained attitude which exploits women as sex objects and inferior beings. This is not a situation which will change overnight or in the seventy-plus years since women won the vote. It will be very hard to change. In the same way as we needed to exert the moral muscle to understand that slavery was wrong, so do men today need to make the effort not to allow these attitudes to override more appropriate responses. It is not that sexual appreciation of women is wrong; women sexually appreciate men, but we are faced with having to recognize that we are in an unequal situation where we have power that women do not have. This makes it all the more imperative that men make the conscious effort to keep sexual feelings out of daily affairs, and, in effect, to positively discriminate in favor of women in appropriate situations such as the workplace and politics, until the situation is addressed and attitudes have changed.

Another exercise is where a man imagines (or practices) sharing lovemaking with a woman with another man. Alternatively he explores sexuality across rigid hetero-, bi-, or homosexual boundaries. There are many possibilities. This will enable him to face his fear of male intimacy. It means he cannot hold onto a woman or a partner and has to constantly work against homophobia, control, domination, and possessiveness—all the issues of patriarchy. It means moving to a transpersonal level of sexuality which challenges deeply held definitions of masculinity, a state difficult to reach from where most of us are now.

The results of exploring every implication of these exercises in an ongoing way are potentially very rewarding. The man has to let go of distancing himself from men. He has to let go of control over women, possessiveness, and other ingrained dominating values. He is thus able to stay in the present-moment experience, know himself better, relate better to men and women, and consequently be a better lover. Perhaps above all, through creating new forms of sexuality which cross rigid patriarchal definitions of gender that are tied up with masculine identity, a man can discover and become secure in a self-definition which does not have as its basis sexism, fear, exploitation, and inequality. However, as the world situation is unlikely to change overnight, men are going to continue to be afraid of intimacy with other men and will continue to draw upon women for their security and attempt to maintain their dominance and control over them. Until this changes and, to put it simply, until men learn to cooperate instead of compete, then women will keep walking away from marriage and relationship in ever increasing numbers.

RELATIONSHIPS OF POWER

In a society which requires a man to be tough, competitive, on top, and in control, a woman using her power in initiating sex and stimulating a man to orgasm will provoke feelings of powerlessness or impotence in him. He loses his erection as his virility is consumed in the devouring maw of the Great Mother. A man should always take the woman, proving his power, not vice-versa. In a patriarchal society, every act of coitus amounts to an act of rape, and ideally the woman should be a virgin. Many young men admit their motives in having intercourse were to prove that they were "men" in the eyes of their peers and to demonstrate that they were "straight." If a woman initiates sex and he is not ready, then he loses face in the eyes of his peers. She is a whore. He may accuse her of making him impotent, of taking his power, and turn to a younger "virginal" woman with whom he can always initiate sex. Even after many years of marriage, a woman should not be forward. She should remain subordinate. But if sex can only happen when he's ready, it leads to the universal complaint of men that women are too cold. Women in this double bind are damned if they do and damned if they don't.

The difficulty lies in the complex daemonic and chthonian nature of female sexuality as opposed to the simpler, external surface nature of male sexuality. Women are hidden, inner, soft, dark, secret, pulsating, labial, moist, fluid, consuming, possessed by limitless internal procreative forces, while men are all external, outward, firm, hard, obvious, and procreatively limited by erection or non-erection. One solution to the struggle of power between the sexes lies in the celebration of homoeroticism rather than homophobia on the part of men. Instead of being constantly challenged by women's sexuality and needing to dominate it in the narrow confines of the male-initiated, on top, penetration to orgasm, safe, clean-edged, heterosexual mode, a man willing to explore the murky depths of his own inner daemonic nature will leave behind the power struggles, one-upmanship, and control created by patriarchal values and be able to relax into a huge realm of erotica. In the current atmosphere of homophobia, men do not know what they are missing.

I am not suggesting homosexual affairs for all men but an appreciation of other forms of sexuality. An extending of sensual appreciation beyond its current limited repertoire into areas where same-sex love and emotional sharing can emerge, where men can care for each other and not compete. This will relieve the enormous pressure on women to provide sex and intimacy for men as subordinates at the same time as it relieves the pressure on intimacy to always end up in sex. As an illustration of the wealth of this realm, think for a moment where male homoeroticism and homosexuality has contributed to culture: in literature, sculpture, art, theater, cuisine, fashion, cinema, decor. Any repression of homoeroticism through fear and accusation of homosexuality is an indication of the impoverishment of society.

The problem of modern society is not homosexuality. It is runaway homophobia and heterosexuality. Human sexuality is distinctive in that sexual preference is not only innate but is also culturally engendered. Every facet of human sexuality is directed and controlled, if not created, by social attitudes. Narrow cultural definitions of sexuality foster fundamental heterosexual pathologies and equally unhealthy homosexual responses. We need to be free of all gender stereotyping and allow the changing emotional and physical needs of our bodies their full play. We can be anything we want to be.

For a full discussion of homophobia, see the section so titled in Chapter 12.

TRANSCENDENCE AND IMMANENCE

One of the key distinctions made between the nature of the masculine and feminine in this book has been one where immanence has been ascribed to the feminine and transcendence to the masculine. Much of the blame for actions that have resulted in harm to the earth has been attributed to the transcendental world view. I call this "hierarchical transcendence." It is the theme of patriarchy with its vertical power structure where everything good is projected "upward" and everything bad "downward." This book counters this ascent emphasis with a cyclical schema for the masculine archetype. Over and over again, the preference for an immanent and transformational world view has been expressed.

What exactly is meant by immanence, especially as it appears to bring the feminine mode into preeminence? And what is so bad about transcendence, the attempt to get beyond the world? The transcendental urge has been present in men and women all over the world and has not invariably led to denial and exploitation of the earth. Indeed, the ascetic practice of yogis in India, though aimed to transcend the world, has brought them into lifestyles that are very harmonious with it. Striving to go beyond one's present condition or seeking a nonattachment to the whirling flow of much human life would seem to be a beneficent and positive quality. It reminds me of the adage, "Be in the world but not of it."

In the part of England where I was born, there is a similar saying that has a different emphasis—which I prefer: "Live as though you were going to die tomorrow, but farm as though you were going to live forever." This combines a more explicit immanence with a transcendent quality which seeks to improve the present not only for oneself but for others. "Trans," after all, does not mean "beyond" or "above," but "across." And it is this idea of transcendence which I have attempted to bring into the cycle of the dual rhythm of the masculine archetype. The Apollonian transcendental urge is not wrong. It is merely an aspect of the masculine that, while invaluable for the creative impulse, the overview, and the depth it can bring, needs to be incorporated into the everpresent and changing nature of life on earth. I call this "positive transcendence."

Everything we do and everything we are will change and pass away. Transcendence cannot be set in opposition to this. If it is, it will create rigidity and dogmas that will oppress and exploit life. If heaven is in the future and beyond the world, then we may as well really make the world hell, right? Transcendence must be set in complementarity to change. If it is not, then it will create the very things that will make the human lot unbearable and engender the wish to truly escape from life. This is not transcendence, but the denial of life. This is the basic attitude behind the current concept of suffering or even dying for another. Suffering has become glorified as an agent of transcendence when in fact it is the denial of life. At the same time, it has implicitly or even explicitly sanctioned the infliction of suffering upon others and has created other forms of deadly hierarchical transcendence which have legitimated the domination and exploitation of the entire planet.

The solution to these cosmological dilemmas is the incorporation of the positive urge to transcendence within the pagan experience of immanence: the blending of earth and sky gods and goddesses. In the Celtic cosmos, the sun and moon are both masculine and feminine, the earth god is as significant as the earth goddess, the heavenly goddess as significant as the sky god. It is only as a result of vested interest by authorities that sex has been ascribed to cosmic powers in order to justify the authorities' own secular power. Immanence may be defined as the constant coming into being or ever-present manifestation of the self-creative and reflexive universe. Another way of putting it may be the perpetual discovery of one's self in the world and the world's discovery of itself in us. Each needs the other to fulfill life's purpose—the anthropic principle. Immanence suggests no theory, no paradigm, no sexual hierarchy, no cosmology, and no religion, simply the inherent experience of life.

The aspect of immanence which I call reflexiveness I defined elsewhere as the capacity of the infinite universe to accommodate any theory projected onto it and so provide evidence for itself in its own manifestations. The robes of the emperor prove him to be the emperor when, in fact, he is only enrobed as a result of the accommodating nature of the universe. In this case, the reflex of the universe manifests through the people, with or without their agreement—to provide him with the trappings that it can also take away. In fact or in idea the result is the same: See! He has no clothes.

As can be realized with only a little research, the most oppressive regimes are supported by the most hierarchical of transcendental cosmologies. They define themselves by projecting all that is good upon their leaders and draw legitimation for their power from a reified and absolutely rarified source—no source at all. At the same time, they project all that is bad upon an enemy either without or within their midst. They declare as heresy the idea that power is immanent and therefore present in everything equally, because that would encourage—heaven forbid—people to think for themselves. In fact, power comes from nowhere but the people. And the world changes because people want it to change, not because of some external, godlike mechanism.

Concepts of immanence and transcendence are directly involved with power, the nature of it, and where it comes from. Starhawk's contribution to understanding the different modes of power was simply and eloquently expressed as immanence being "power from within" and transcendence as being "power over."[13] Later, she added a third position that enables a synthesis of the positive aspects of transcendence with immanence, and this was "power with." This is power manifesting from within everyone, recognized by everyone, and shared with all.[14] Here the positive, achievement-oriented, clean-edged aspects of the masculine mode of transcendence, an expression of his power from within, may be incorporated into a cosmology of shared power. When men are willing to move from the "ascendent" aspect to the "trans" aspect of their archetypal mode of operation, then men will feel connected to each other, to the planet, and to women.

This is possible provided the transcendental urge of the masculine does not run to fix its manifestations in the world, but releases its creations into the ongoing flux of the transformative character of immanence. Men need to create, to go beyond limits, to transcend, to express themselves externally. But they also need to let go of their creations and honor the cooperative, egalitarian, and empathetic—if miasmic, chaotic, and fluid—nature of the feminine mode. The establishment of such a cosmology will have huge political implications and effectively stop the empowerment of those who, in terms of energy, status, prestige, and wealth, climb the ranking ladder of the hierarchical model of power.

All ideologies, whether coming from a masculine or a feminine perspective, tend to appeal to nature, to the "natural order," for the legitimation of their power. Men draw support for their dominant social position from television programs which show males of an animal species competing for domination over other males and females. A huge amount of time and attention is given to male animals locked in combat. The universe seems content to accommodate all theories, but we, however, already view the world through acculturated eyes. Instead of always seeing competition and hierarchy in nature, why do we not focus on the complex systems of friendship, reciprocity, and cooperation that exist within nature? Indeed, as we saw with the baboons, these qualities are far more prevalent and are far more important to the continuation and life of the tribe than a few aggressive males. If domination is the "natural order," then war, terrorism, rape, murder, and ecological destruction are inevitable. We may as well all give up now. Fortunately, the earth does appear to favor the support of life, so our present behavior does seem to be—well, manmade.

Women, especially, need to be wary of adopting the forms of masculine power, for once achieved these will be seen to be hollow. No state-of-the-art office in any high tower in New York can fill the present powerlessness felt in those who live by the rules of the patriarchal culture. No amount of power can obviate the fact that guns and rockets, media attention, and titles are nothing compared to the true power that comes from within—the power which comes from gnosis, from immanence, from the present moment, from the body—from the Source.

The Source. From deep within. From the roots of the Tree of Life. From the World Tree—the *axis mundi*—the gnomon set in the earth connecting the worlds. From the stone, the cave, the throne, the Lia Fail—the source of sovereignty—the place of winter solstice. From the place of the dark, the Serpent Son, the earthy rainbow serpent, the goddess of the underworld. From the place of the dark waters and of midnight. Consider this time deeply in our crude charts of the archetypal realms of the masculine and the feminine. Consider what it meant to generation upon generation of our ancestors. What formed in their minds about this time—and in so forming, made them? What made them enter the cave, the opening into the Mother, and paint their dreams?

What imperative drove them to build such earthworks as Newgrange or the long barrows oriented to winter solstice rising sun? What drove them to spend so many years constructing such vast edifices to withstand the passage of time and be such precise markers of it? What archetypal power was lending its force to such effort? There is no hint of anything but joy in this power at these places. There are no overseers, no whips, no weapons of war, no chiefs, no prestigious burials. There was only a great communal effort that moved stone and earth, shaped it, and carved it. An effort which moved in response to an overwhelming feeling. A response that revealed the universe to itself. A response to the outpouring of power from within the earth itself. A celebration of the power of the Source. Immanence—power from within—finding its transcendental expression through power shared with others. A time of union of masculine and feminine in their deepest, most interior embrace.

The expression. Consider now summer solstice. The peak of solar power. The cloaking of earth in a garment of green. The longest day, the warmest time. The time of the rainbow serpent of the sky, the Star Son, the Solar Goddess, and the Burning Spear. Consider the Green Man, foliage gushing from his mouth. The trees preparing their fruit. Consider the sprigs of wisdom, of poetry, language, intellect. The Tree of Knowledge preparing its garlands to drape around the inspired. Midday, noon, midsummer, light. The beneficent Mother pouring her abundance over the earth.

What this meant to our ancestors is not hard to imagine. What formed in their minds and moved in their limbs is easy to know. They danced around the oak tree. Its crown blazed with fire. They, ecstatic, moved through its smoke. The sun overhead, the earth below, the two rising to meet each other—abundance flooding the land. The Star Son rode in the chariot of the Solar Goddess. The Earth Goddess dreamt of her sky-god lover. Everything was possible. Everything was, and there was more to give: the creature to the spear of the hunter, the design to the woven cloth, the shapes to the vessels of clay. The dreaming of the earth soared. Her ecstasy surrounded her lover in their most outer, most exterior embrace.

And between these times? The equinoxes of equal day and night? It's hard to say. The times of balance, of meeting as equals. The springtime rush of inspired energy after the long dark of winter. The autumn of disintegration, of release after the fullness of summer. The promise of the spring—the cauldron, the chalice beginning to fill. The time for plowing, for preparing the seed, the time of quickening. The young woman's time, Imbolc. The lovemaking of Beltane. The shoots on the new plants. The blossom on the trees. The earth dreaming a song of awakening. Then the fulfillment of autumn. The bringing in from the fields, the turning in of the waste, the full storage bins. The labor of Lughnasad, the harvest moons and Samhain. The old woman's time. The time of the sword, of cutting off, of separation. The seed in the store. The dissolving of old ties. The flowing downward into the sleep of the earth. The rains washing away the ribbons from the dancing floors. The dream returning—to winter—to be dreamt once more.

These are the times of emergence for the archetypes. And still, every year can be a day and every day an hour and every hour a minute and every minute a breath. And our power is immanent and ready to fly. Ready to imagine, to create, to write these words, revealing ourselves to ourselves, here and now, yet away. And if I were to be asked which is preeminent, the masculine or the feminine? Earth or sea, sea or sky? Or where does sovereignty lie? I would answer in each other's arms is equality, and in my knowledge of her and her knowledge of me I come to know my own and see her sovereignty.

THE NEW MASCULINE

Through aligning himself with the cycle of the year, by acknowledging and working with unconscious contents, by emotionally going through the cycle of death and rebirth, a man can literally "come to his senses" rather than trying to get out of his body and wander in the wastelands of abstract thought and dualistic hierarchical projection. This is the situation we are trying to address. It is through male willingness to open to the full cycle of the masculine archetype that we can journey consciously to the greater circles of experience and not remain in the essentially linear and bounded modes of existence. Unconsciousness, instead of being a standby for whenever change threatens, then can become a depth in which the sources of our fear and of our ecstasy can be experienced. Instead of living in the bounded role model of masculinity given to us by our social conditioning—a man is tough, in control, dominant, heterosexual, unafraid—we can live in acceptance and allowance of the entire continuum of the contents of our feeling, inner world. A MAN is: sensitive, fierce, despairing, intuitive, doubting, courageous, fearful, nurturing, playful, empathetic, loving, strong, soft, sexually open, able to cry, be wrong, be angry, wonder, and enjoy.

It is within and through the transformative, watery feminine archetypal character that the masculine can journey the Great Round of existence. His powerful ego and sense of separate self with all of its transcendental and willful urges finds its movement upon the arms of the universe, but he also needs to remember that he is held by them. In the same way as the loving mother allows her young child to run free and play, so the universe allows every freedom. Yet, to continue the analogy, as the mother's arms are never far away and are determining the extent of the possibilities that the child can play in, so the universe—while infinitely giving—is also finitely constraining. Its apparent freedom should never be confused for a lack of the responsibility—moral, ethical, and ecological—that goes with it.

The right to split the atom, breed genes, synthesize a chemical, build a space station, accrue power, climb a mountain, clear-cut a forest, or conquer a country is not given simply because "it is there." No, the fact it is there highlights the incredible gifts and the freedom we have been given by the universe. These have to be considered alongside the responsibility and the intelligence of the order that goes with them. Just because we can see dominance in some of the relationships of nature, or because we can dominate something, doesn't mean it is right.

By intelligent order I mean the finely balanced and reciprocal sets of relationships which maintain the existence of the cosmos. This order is not based upon consciousness, nor upon matter, but upon the cooperating intelligence which underlies both of them and all relationships. It is the synthesis of the transcendental, clean, bright, and ordered Apollonian world and the daemonic, chaotic, and murky Dionysian. Put in another way, the structure of our incredibly complex bodies was not accidentally created by the chance joining together of different atoms in the swampy primeval soup. Intelligence, energy, and matter unfold and enfold each other as one. None of the finely reciprocal relationships of life on earth arose by chance.

There is a dynamic at work in this which quantum physics describes as consisting of interconnections. These derive from what the scientist David Bohm describes as a source and generating matrix he calls "the implicate order." Here, the "explicate order" of the world makes no sense as sets of isolated, consuming, and consumed entities, but understood as sets of intelligently ordered relationships to the whole, the world makes perfect sense.[15]

Ultimately, in my view, this intelligent order of the universe becomes our intelligence—the relationship between things as apparently diverse as matter and consciousness becoming as significant as the things themselves. This implies a profound harmony with life, a profound care and love, a profound way of living upon the earth and relating to others. This surely is the message of the Green Man with his head among the trees.

To sum up this chapter and pull everything into a whole would be difficult were it not for one fact. This is, that the body remembers and possesses the wisdom to enact the fundamental themes which are in harmony with the cosmos. In comparison to our true chthonian wildness, the ancient kinesthetic memory of the body and the coding of the universal intelligence, the tame and puritanical ideology of contemporary culture is shallow and hollow.

In school, we were told that what distinguished us from animals was our ability to create civilization through our faculty of reason. Without culture, we would all be savages at the mercy of our tyrannical hormones. Yes, culture is indispensable; it must and always will be created by humans. Culture is the vehicle in which our daemonic drives find expression as ideas and are thus rendered safe. Culture should never be censored; it would defeat its own purpose. But what of a culture that is itself tyrannous and constrains sexuality, for example, to a fraction of its total expression? And what of a reason whose evident goals are a permanent state of political aggression and the economic dominion over and destruction of nature?

No! Humans cannot be distinguished from animals, from wildness, from nature, from the unconscious realms. We cannot be distinguished from the intense communion our bodies share with these things. Our distinction is self-made, and if continued will lead to our own demise. Through our bodies, our somatic processes, and especially through sexuality, we awaken to awareness of the interconnections, not the separations between things.

We awaken to all the nuances of life. Sexuality possibly holds the most powerful key for our return, for our re-creation of ourselves. Sexuality is the nature of the body itself, and through it we celebrate our unity with all the elements of life on earth.

NOTES

1. The 1992 study by the Crime Victims Research and Treatment Center gives the number of women raped in the U.S. as 683,000 per year.

2. The purpose of circumcision according to Moses Maimonodes was "...to limit sexual intercourse...and thus cause a man to be moderate..." (*Guide for the Perplexed* 3:49). "There are no medical indications for undertaking routine circumcision on newborn male infants, as the hazards of the operation outweigh any possible advantages" (Australian National Health and Medical Research Council). Both quotes from "The Loss" by Billy Ray Boyd, in *Men and Intimacy*, ed. Franklin Abbot (Crossing Press, 1990).

3. Shere Hite, *Women and Love* (Alfred A. Knopf, 1987), 395–6.

4. It is possible to make the case that the reason why humans lost their body hair during the evolutionary process and developed extremely thin and sensitive skin was to allow their erogenous areas to extend over the entire surface of the body. No other creature has such a large and sensitive pleasure-giving organ as the human skin. The pleasure provided by the sense of touch over the total area of the skin far exceeds that provided by any other sense or physical organ. It would seem foolish to neglect this unique capacity of the body whose only evolutionary adaptation seems to be for the enhancement of pleasure. If this were not the case, then it would make far more sense for us to have retained body hair and thick and insensitive skin for the purposes of protection. The argument that we lost our body hair during the aquatic stage of our evolution is not borne out by creatures like the sea otter, who as a tool-using mammal comes fairly close to the primate, yet shows no sign of ever losing its fur.

5. Jolan Chang, (1) *The Tao of Love and Sex*, (2) *The Tao of the Loving Couple* (E. P. Dutton, 1983); Stephen Chang, *The Tao of Sexuality: The Book of Infinite Wisdom* (San Francisco, 1986); Mantak Chia and Michael Winn, *Taoist Secrets of Love: Cultivating Male Sexual Energy* (New York,

1986); Margo Anand, *The Art of Sexual Ecstasy* (Jeremy P. Tarcher, 1989); Gedün Chöpel, *Tibetan Arts of Love* (Ithaca: Snow Lion, 1992).

6. William Irwin Thompson, *The Time Falling Bodies Take to Light* (1981), 15–27.

7. Norman O. Brown, *Love's Body* (Vintage, 1968), 136.

8. Thompson, 17.

9. Robert Lawlor, *Earth Honouring: The New Male Sexuality* (Park Street Press, 1989), 133–5.

10. Michael Dames, *The Silbury Treasure* (London: Thames & Hudson, 1976) and *The Avebury Cycle* (London: Thames & Hudson, 1977).

11. Jean Markdale, *Women of the Celts* (Rochester: Inner Traditions, 1975), 30–40.

12. Hite, 532–7.

13. Starhawk, *Dreaming the Dark* (1982).

14 Starhawk, *Truth or Dare* (1987), 8–10.

15. David Bohm, *Wholeness and the Implicate Order* (London: Routledge & Kegan Paul, 1980).

10

GEOMANCY AND GEOMEN

INTRODUCTION

In the early 1980s I was taught to dowse by Sig Lonegren. We visited an area of Britain called Dartmoor, famous for its mists, bogs, ancient ruins, and prison, and there he taught me many aspects of dowsing. Investigating late Neolithic dwelling sites we found no, what he would call, "earth energies," but we found plenty at the sites those people constructed for ceremonial purposes. Invariably these mysterious telluric forces were tied to the presence of underground water. This led into the diverse and much explored field of water divining. It was all very new and interesting.

One of the things Sig said to me right at the beginning was that the dowsing tools, the angle rods, pendulum, forked stick, wand, and so on, were only there as instruments to verify the dowser's own responses. Eventually they could be dispensed with. I wondered what he meant by this. After a while of dowsing on my own, I began to realize that the answers I received were only as good as the questions I asked. The answers available were given not by the instruments but by the perceptive abilities of my own being which the instruments had attuned me to. I was able to dispense with the dowsing tools from that point on and use my whole body as a sensory instrument. Dowsing also showed me that what I had always done on the land was attune to its subtle qualities. From my subsequent reading I realized that there was a name for this—geomancy.

Principles and systems of geomancy are ideally practiced within a framework which recognizes the interaction between the outer world and the inner dimensions of consciousness. In this sense, geomancy is a holistic practice. It is as much based upon principles derived from observation of the natural world as it is upon awareness of the perceptual and cognitive frameworks—the beliefs, world views, and cosmologies held in the mind of the observer. If this subjective-objective interaction is not recognized, then personal caprice tends to predominate in any given situation. It is usually the case when watching more than one dowser at work that they will arrive at conclusions, which, while not necessarily exclusive, will differ according to the favorite cosmology of the individual. Geomancy, like science or art, is as much an investigative practice into the ordering intelligence of the inner and outer worlds as it is a creative one. But by admitting from the outset that it can be both rational and intuitive, based on observation and on the nature of consciousness, it at least has a good chance of becoming a skill appropriate for the requirements of an integrated and holistic world.

My feeling is that it is a skill essential for men to develop. Geomancy puts us in touch with the little-used and often-denied senses in our body and so balances our transcendental urge. It locates us within and attunes us to the landscape. Geomancy confronts the issue of modern men as we make our home in anonymous urban sprawls where we are no longer part of any tribe, tradition, or even community.

As men are predominantly the manifestors, builders, and achievers of the human race, geomancy helps us determine the results of our world-shaping behavior. Is the house I'm building integrated into and contributing to the local ecology, or is it diminishing it? Is it placed in a way that will create an order in the landscape which is attuned to universal patterns, or is it placed haphazardly without reference to elements that will be positive and integrating? What can I incorporate into the design that will facilitate creativity in the office, relaxation in the lounge, sleep and lovemaking in the bedroom, and harmony in the kitchen? Where and how shall the sacred space be? The questions go on and on. The answers are only as good as our refinement of the questions. Many of them can be answered with sound common sense. But I thought it appropriate to outline some principles that have been used in geomantic practice throughout the world, as they are especially relevant to us as aspiring geomen.

Geomancy, furthermore, as a practice has left considerable evidence of itself. Many cultures around the world had or still have a geomantic tradition. Archaeology, currently the only method of studying the past where nothing has been written, is not sufficient of itself to deal with the cognitive and symbolic aspects of human existence. But through repetition or enactment of fundamental geomantic principles, it is possible to empathize with the actions of our predecessors to so great an extent that it is as though we see through their eyes, act through their senses, experience through their view of the cosmos. In this way we may understand our story upon the earth without recourse to intrusive compartmentalizing analytic and reductionist tools. Yet, wherever we begin, we begin with knowledge of the self, with gnosis of ourselves as geomen.

GNOSIS AND GNOMONS

The fundamental geomantic act of gnosis—self-knowledge—is the establishment of the center and the circumference. Which comes first is impossible to say. Without the surround there cannot be a center and vice-versa. Immediately upon this, some traditions might say even before the circumference is established, there is the axis around which the world turns. This would seem to generate the logical progression of unity, center, line, and plane, or the numerical steps of (1) corresponding to unity and center, (2) the axis dividing the above and the below, (3) the middle plane, and, in some cases, (4) the cardinal directions. Every cosmology and its manifest expression, the temple, invariably begins with these fundamental spatial acts. Whether the temple is large or small, a simple altar or a stone, its establishment creates the area within, the area without, and the gateways between them. This temple is the sacred space defined by its *temenos* or boundary, and it is the "template" for all sacred space and time (Latin for time = *tempus*).

The *axis mundi* at the center of the sacred space generates the symmetry of the above and the below. We have seen how the symbol of the World Tree in Celtic and Nordic mythology creates an Underworld, Annwn or Utgard, at least as great as Asgard, the heavens, with humans dwelling in the realm between—Mitgard. In Christian cosmology this threefold division would be represented by the realms of heaven, earth, and hell. The repression of the latter gives it on the one hand great power in the unconscious, and on the other hand unbalances the sacred order, making it top heavy.

Establishing the sacred template is the essential purpose of mythology, ritual, and ceremony. Through the retelling of myth, especially the myths of creation, Mircea Eliade suggests the order of the cosmos is renewed, while ritual ensures participation within it.[1] Through the re-enactment of the sacred drama of creation, the cosmos is restored to its perfect form and humans can participate in every part of it. Details such as the placement of ritual objects in certain directions, the counting out of precise numbers whether in measures, movements, or objects, the construction of sacred space according to the cosmic template, ensures that all the universal elements and patterns are maintained in their rightful order.

Mimi Lobell puts forward the case that in the earliest societies the cosmos was not divided in any way. Even before the "Great Round" society (which she sees as describing the Neolithic period in Europe) with its circular structures and cyclical views of space, there existed a stage she calls the "Sensitive Chaos." Here space is "an immediate flowing topological continuum with little geometric order." The landscape is a living "organism with lines and nodes of energy depending on human care for vitality." The predominant symbol is the spiral.

This is a useful idea and certainly applies to undifferentiated human experience. But I feel the Paleolithic cave artists and shamans would still have drawn upon basic spatial concepts such as center, above, and below.[2] It is important to keep in mind that the combination of eye and brain works geometrically. Long before there was geometry and number, primates could swing in trees and human intelligence could calculate the niceties of the trajectory through space of an arrow, spear, or stone toward a moving target.

Returning to the geomantic act, it is probable that the simple gnomon—an upright post or pillar—provided the first step in establishing the sacred template. Placed in the center, it entered the earth below and reached to the sky above. Around it turned a shadow forming a circumference and from whose movement could be determined daily and seasonal time, direction, and measure. Many traditions have myths to illustrate this. I have chosen one from the Yavapai of Arizona.

Hanyiko said, "Build me a shelter." The people went and cut four posts and put a roof on it. He said, "No, not like that." So they leant three posts together, and he said, "No, not like that." He showed them how to do it. Then they went and got a cottonwood and stripped it and set it up in the middle of the camp. Then Hanyiko said, "Yes, that's the way to do it." He went and sat in its shade and every time the sun moved round, he moved with it. In each place he sat, he told the people about that place. He told them the time to plant the corn and when to harvest it. He told them when to go south to pick the saguaro fruit, and when it was good to get the agave. He told them the names of each direction and the star that went with them. He told them which things were good to do and which were not. Hanyiko was the first elder or shaman. When he died and the first flood came, it was the corn, growing from his heart in the place where he was buried, on which the people climbed up to the next world. He showed the Yavapai—the People of the Sun—many good things.[3]

The gnomon is a singularly appropriate symbol for the archetypal masculine that we are attempting to re-create. In our gnosis as geomen, the gnomon not only stands for the phallus, but for the "I." It stands for the sense of self we have closely identified with the *axis mundi* and the cyclical nature of the World Tree.

If a simple spatial differentiation were to be made between the archetypal feminine and the archetypal masculine it would be one where the former was concerned with horizontal space, with the center to the circumference, and the latter with vertical space, the axis connecting the center with the above and the below. Men are concerned with vertical paradigms, ascent structures, and linear

movements. Women are concerned with paradigms which emphasize lateral movement, localized power, and relationships. While
men are the creators of hierarchy, they also have the power to connect with every part of the cosmos they create and not maintain
dualities of which they refuse to recognize half. Men can reconnect the daemonic to the transcendental, heaven to hell, earth to
spirit, if they so choose.

Such a simple principle would seem to hold true to the vision
of the cave given in Chapter 8. The vertical movements in the
journey correspond closely to the nature of masculine energy,
while the horizontal movements are more concerned with the
feminine—movement through the trees, into the cave, and out
again. The spatial archetypal relationships, however, become more
interesting if we were to conceive of the feminine as being spheri-
cal or even spiral and the masculine as being a continuum of the
vertical movement of the gnomon outward and back around to
coalesce again at its root (see figure 1). This would make the points
of connection between the archetypes especially pronounced at
the solstices and in a more diffuse way at the equinoxes. Precisely
what our schema for the masculine archetype informs us—figure
4, page 159. It is also obvious why, in a male-defined world, vertical options: hierarchy, transcendental religion, high-rise construction are preferred, and horizontal, feminine options: integration,
connectedness, low cluster-style dwellings, are devalued and
ignored. It is the extension of the gnomon into the dispersing and
coalescing cycle of the archetypal scheme that brings the masculine tendencies into a harmonious relationship with the feminine.

There is also a phenomenon the Greeks called "gnomonic
expansion" which was a type of growth that left the emergent figures similar to the original. Horns and seashells display this kind
of growth. A characteristic of this is that spirals can be drawn on
figures which grow in this way. These forms are everywhere in
nature. Robert Lawlor provides excellent examples and exercises in
geometrically and numerically understanding this principle.[4] But
for our purposes it is to the form of the spiral as it has appeared in
Neolithic contexts as carvings on stone and in later contexts as the
labyrinth that I wish to turn.

LABYRINTHS

It was while journeying in Ireland and examining the symbols carved on the stones of the zs of the Sidhe, especially at Loughcrew and the Boyne Valley, that I arrived at the understanding that one of the functions of the underground chambers was for male initiation. This was essentially a process that brought the potentially destructive energies of men into the sacred space—the time of creation—and impressed upon them the sacred template of the cosmos. This primary order was expressed by the structure of the chambered mounds themselves and by the carvings engraved upon them. Spatially, the initiates entered the rounded interior chambers through a long, straight passageway which formed one arm of a quadrature. The other three directions were represented by side chambers. This was entry into sacred space. It was probably a very subduing experience for the young men undergoing initiation. The fact that, at equinox at Loughcrew and at winter solstice at Newgrange, the interior chambers were penetrated by a shaft of light further served to impress upon them the order of the cosmos.

What of the carvings? These are many and varied, from circular to spiral, from floriate to rectangular, and from wavy to zig-zagged and checkered. Martin Brennan has done invaluable work with these forms, demonstrating their function as light markers and probably as calendars for the lunar and solar cycles.[5] However, the patterns intrigued me as spatial archetypes. I began following them in my mind's eye until they took on three dimensionality. One of the things I realized was that in this way of perceiving them, a wavy line and a spiral might be functions of the same movement expressed along a different axis within the limitations of a flat surface of representation.

As most of the designs would have been concealed in the darkness of the chamber and as most of our young men would be undergoing an inner transformation—a ritual journey to contact the archetypal realms, facilitated by elders and enhanced by fasting and other ritual practice—it is likely that the designs when perceived (by the light of the dawning sun?) would have taken on a preternatural quality. They would correspond with the archetypal patterns encountered within. The designs would have been understood, not mentally, but directly as symbol. They would have been understood as dynamic, as the pattern of movement of the form of the cosmic template. For the point of the ancient tradition, in contrast to the modern, is that it understood the world to be in constant flux. The world order was change, not a fixed, idealistic scheme. In this way the inner and the outer worlds would achieve congruence and the young men—with their potentially dangerous hormonal energy—would have been brought into the structure of society as cosmos.

Little or nothing remains today of such a process of initiation. But it was in negotiating the twists and the turns of the spirals and the other patterns on the stones in my mind's eye that I realized similar properties lie in the labyrinths that exist in many places and traditions of the world. They are, in all likelihood, of ancient origin. Labyrinths, furthermore, laid out upon the ground, can be participated in. They provide an experience and an enactment of a process that has existed for millennia and so give us a means of integrating ourselves, as men, into a meaningful cosmos.

In the ancient Greek and the pre-Greek, Mycenean, and Minoan traditions, there exists the earliest description of a labyrinth that we have in written form. Constructed by the craftsman Daedalus for Minos, the ruler of Crete, it housed the half-man, half-beast that was the result of Queen Pasiphae's union with a bull. Daedalus is akin to Hephaistos, who forges items for the goddess in the realm of earth. The goddess appears here as queen expressing what is clearly a chthonic origin for men. The hero Theseus, through the help of the goddess's daughter Ariadne, the weaver and spider, is able to negotiate the labyrinth and so integrate the splendid but destructive potential of the Minotaur, the wild man, at its center. The world order is thus restored.

Ariadne, who provided the "clue," the thread that guided Theseus through the labyrinth, later instigates the Crane Dance. This dance, still alive in Greece today, imitates the movement of the long-legged crane with its steps forward and backward. Translated into the meander pattern—the spiral—the labyrinth finds resonance with the dance, with the footsteps of the crane. And as the labyrinth researcher Jeff Saward has shown, the meander extended generates the full form of the traditional labyrinth.

Petroglyph in an Irish chambered mound associated with the Sidhe.

This is depicted on Mycenean coins.[6] As a final synchronicity it is of course the bag made from crane skin that contains the mysteries of language and script in Irish mythology. Here we come close once again to the symbols carved on the stones of the Neolithic megaliths which facilitate movement between the worlds and integration of ourselves, as men, into an ordered but changing cosmos.

In his invaluable book on labyrinthine lore, Sig Lonegren has suggested that by threading the labyrinth, preferably by running a large one laid out on the ground, we lose the constraints which normally maintain separation between the right and left hemispheres of the brain. We come into a whole brain state of cognition, the right brain being concerned with intuitive processes and the left brain with rational, analytical processes.[7] The integration of earth and sky god, the chthonic Dionysian with the heavenly Apollonian. It will be useful to mention here that the labyrinth, by a generally agreed-upon definition, is unicursal, a single path leading to a center and out again. A maze is a puzzle with many options. The former clearly tells you where to go while the latter tries to get you lost—a big difference.

The form of the classical labyrinth shown in the diagram on the opposite page is found in contexts as far apart as Arizona, northern and southern Europe, India, and Java. Everywhere it is the symbol for initiation, death, and rebirth. As far as I know, it is only in the Northern European context that the form was laid out in large patterns upon the ground, usually made of stone or turf. They were also incorporated into the floors of the Gothic cathedrals, a famous example being at Chartres. One tradition accompanying the labyrinth, that of young men pursuing a young woman around its circuits, may relate to the theme of balancing the analytical-masculine with the intuitive-feminine aspects of the psyche.

Whatever the personal experience of threading the labyrinth, it is a powerful archetypal symbol with special relevance to masculine mysteries. Constructing a labyrinth and then using it in a variety of ways brings us closer to re-enacting the traditions of our ancestors. By entering into the sets of relationships with which their minds worked, we re-create the tradition within ourselves. Who or what is the man-beast at its core? That the labyrinth has been used in such diverse geographical and historical contexts shows, as with the gnomon, that we are approaching the center of a universal mystery. It remains for us to use it, not consign it to the category of just being another curiosity, if we wish for its meaning to enter our lives.

Classical labyrinth

THE VISION OF GEOMANCY

In workshops I have included a visualization encouraging each person to see the world as they would like it to be and as if there were no restraint upon their ability to make it possible. I ask them to visualize what each aspect of life would look like. Where would energy come from? How and where would people live? What kind of transportation would exist? What kind of agriculture? What would the landscape of the earth look like? And the extraordinary thing, at any rate extraordinary to me, is that in essence, the vision of the world people would like to live in is more or less the same. To give a few details: generally there are no cities, no roads, no big industry or agriculture, and no centralized government or economy. There are, however, small scale, low, cluster-like dwellings set among a tree-dominated "agriculture," ease of communication and transport, and an abundance of energy through technologies, often psychokinetic, that we have yet to develop.

What I find interesting about these visions is that they are often similar to the ideas and perceptions arising in people when they study the ancient megalithic sites. They conclude that the Neolithic people must have had a way of working with the land that enhanced the flow of subtle natural forces to ensure the abundance and well-being of life. In *The New View Over Atlantis*, John Michell gives the classic vision of such an ecologically and cosmically integrated people. They construct stone circles, earthworks, ley lines, and other temples in the landscape in geometrical and numerical accord with the harmonious principles of life. John Michell:

> A great scientific instrument lies sprawled over the entire surface of the globe. At some period, thousands of years ago, almost every corner of the world was visited by people with a particular task to accomplish. With the help of some remarkable power...these men [sic] created vast astronomical instruments, circles of erect pillars, pyramids, underground tunnels, cyclopean stone platforms, all linked together by a network of tracks and alignments, whose course from horizon to horizon was marked by stones, mounds and earthworks.[8]

Well, this is geomancy, and although it may be a moot point to argue that the megalith builders were working on such a huge scale with the universal powers—in ways that we do not understand and would call magic—it is unquestionable that we have in our hands now the means to create the vision we have of a perfect planet. Furthermore, as the writer Tom Graves loves to point out, we would call those means at our disposal "technology," but the megalithic builders would call our technological means "magic."[9]

It's up to us to draw upon the magical technologies we impute to the past—including ritual, music, and myth-telling. It's up to us to make them our own, so the vision we have of the future can be a blend of what is the best from the creative-intuitive-magical and the rational-technological sides of the brain. This is what I mean by geomancy being a holistic practice. And so, for us as geomen, as men of the earth, practicing gnosis—self-knowledge—around our gnomons, uniting above, below, and center in our dance, it is vitally important that we have a clear vision of the future, however distant, that draws upon the past, in order to direct and empower our actions in the present.

From a perspective such as this, where power is seen as arising out of the earth—through the continuity of our lineages—into ourselves, we, as geomen in a geocentric universe practicing geomancy, do not need to fall into any "ism" or take any position regarding the appearance of the mysterious upon the earth. There is no extraterrestrial agency working upon the earth that has not already come out of it. There are no autonomous agents of good or evil. There is only ourselves—containing the infinite, manifesting immanence—and the apparently inexplicable mysteries of the earth serve to demonstrate the capacity of the reflexive universe to reveal ourselves back to ourselves.

This is not to deny the apparently autonomous archetypal realm, inhabited by daemonic or enspiriting forces, the *anima mundi*—the animating spirit of the world. But these powers are also us. We interact—that might be the best word—with them, using our magical and material technologies to make them what they are. This is "geomythics." It is the process where, through imaginative and creative action stimulated by and given back to the earth, we animate the world with forms and forces, which then have life as spirits of place—*genius loci*—reinforced by further processes of myth making.

GEO-PHILOSOPHY

The application of design to nature to foster self-maintaining and self-increasing local ecosystems, which sustain ecological diversity through providing for every species in the food chain as a component of the system, is an aspect of geomancy. See Bill Mollison's books on permaculture for a full development of this view.[10] This replaces the old hierarchical, pyramidal, and exploitative system of agriculture that sees humanity as the worthy recipient of all resources and in the process destroys the fertility of the soil and pollutes the total biosphere.

As Green Men, as geomen, it is necessary to create a philosophy based upon the land, better still, upon the total ecology of local bio-regions and ultimately of the planet. Present philosophy, ethics, theology, metaphysics, physics, and secular codes of practice focus either upon a transcendental, externalized moral source or mechanical models or place humanity in the supreme position of value and worth. The life of one human being is adjudged to be more important in contemporary society than the enormous amount of mineral matter, micro-bacteria, plant and animal material which sustains them. Such a model of destructive consumption contains within it its own demise. This now should be obvious to all. As the creatures immediately below us in the pyramidal food-chain model are being poisoned and destroyed, it follows that we will be next. The only life that does thrive in such a model is that which eats the output of the system, in this case the rats, cockroaches, carrion birds, and other scavengers.

The animals mentioned above are city dwellers or feeders on the "garbage" produced by the cities. We are what we create. The city and the consciousness it creates is probably the greatest obstacle to geo-man-tic development. It seems that the word for those who did not live in the city in Latin was *paganus,* and it also applied to those who maintained the old fertility festivals. The glory of the city to the Greek and Latin mind was precisely that it separated men—and their attendant women and slaves—from the countryside. The city allowed them to live in the realm of pure mind, to develop belief in a world run by perfect unchanging laws of mathematics and geometry, and to denigrate and despise the pagan in the fields.

Living in New York, London, or Chicago, or any other metropolis, provides sets of cognition or symbols which shape our lives. These are enacted in our psyche through our physical participation within them, and they make certain archetypal contents available. The dominant themes of the city include the following dichotomies: centers of power—suburbs of powerlessness; concentrations of wealth—widespread poverty; specific places of art and beauty—general ugliness; many small cliques—general lack of community. Such patterns reinforce the impression the universe is naturally divided into haves and have nots.

Then there are the themes of systemization: the efficient grid lines of roads, architecture, office space, computer screens, pavements, city clothes, documents, and papers. These reinforce the impression that the universe is mechanistically organized, only requiring study and application to manipulate. Then there are the themes of chaos: the ready availability of breakdown, gridlock, mugging, violence, murder, rape, pornography, and drugs. These reinforce the impression of a crude universal dualism: the controlling and the controlled, the good and the evil, the virgin or the whore.

In the city the available archetypal and symbolic content is not conducive to understanding the role of what it means to be a man. Especially if we want to be a man in a world of power from within, cosmological holism, and ecological harmony. At the same time, the city experience spills out into the countryside, blending all towns into an indistinguishable uniformity and perpetuating the division between culture and nature. In the anonymity of the city we experience most intensely the feeling of not belonging to any tribe or tradition.

It is unfortunate that where nature is still claimed as wild, such as in advertisements for the Marlboro man, the western ranching, rodeo reality actually has as its aim the total annihilation of the truly wild creatures and the total control of land and resources. Last week I picked up a newspaper to read that the first cougar to be seen in an area of Utah for more than thirty years had been shot. The fact the cougar had returned to its natural habitat was not the theme of the story, but the triumph of the hunter and the pleasure of the local ranchers at the death of the animal was the only message. In fact, unless one is of an extremely rare isolationist kind, the range of city experience available is probably more conducive to discovering useful masculine roles than is the present destructive and blinkered human experience of the country. My argument is not with culture but with the kind of culture that we have.

It is possible the inner archetypal realm, rather than the external physical world, is the area we need to work with, as men, at this stage of our existence. Contacted through our bodies, and above all, through our sexuality, the archetypes carry the deep memories, the ancestral encodings that our tamed woods, decimated wildernesses, and animals can no longer carry, or only carry in a rarely attained remoteness. Through re-membering our ancient knowledge from within we will move into a world view which once again locates us as a part of all things.

Eventually, as the inner world of deep memory comes alive in us, so we will act to leave the wild places alone, act to allow the world to have its repositories of wildness that are more valuable to us than any treasure contained in a bank vault. And we are already acting, slowly, sometimes clumsily, allowing birds to have their migration stations here, the forests to have a haven there, to stop the use of species-destroying chemicals. In many cases it is already a generation too late, and only through genetic and archetypal memory can we carry on the presence of extinct species and departed ecological niches.

Geomantic power, women's power, people power, nature's power, and the ancient tradition of male power always rested on and in the land, outside of urban concentrations. The history of patriarchy and its material development has been to separate culture from the land and to concentrate power in its urban centers. Gradually, churches, divorced from the countryside and the natural shrines at grove or spring, were built in every village. Gradually, cities grew, taxing the surrounding land and using pseudo-geomantic techniques to concentrate power. The ancient image of the cosmos as changing flux in the womb of the Great Goddess, was replaced by a rigid world view of perfect, unchanging, mechanical, and geometrical order. The pyramid and the government house replaced the sacred mountain; the obelisk replaced the World Tree; the tax office replaced the sacred spring; and avenues focusing lines of sight on important buildings replaced the wandering lines of ridges, hills, and rivers.

The city defines humanity as a political animal outside of natural law. The urban cosmology, with its reified and deified Apollonian gods, allows all that is natural to be exploited, controlled, and repressed. So long as urban culture remains in its present state, so long as science remains focused on physics and not on organic biology, and so long as philosophy and religion remain transcendentally oriented, things are likely to remain as they are. Indeed, as resources dry up and the ecological limits of the present system are reached, things are likely to become worse. Economic recession is taking place, and given present consciousness will require a scapegoat. With the devolvement of power in the former U.S.S.R., who will the West blame? The "enemy" in its own midst? The nonconformists? The Muslims? The pagans? Most likely it will continue to set itself against nature and promote industrial, materialist, urban-consumer consciousness.

On a more positive note, what would a geocentric, earth or Gaia-centered philosophy look like?

Despite the work of enlightened churches like St. John the Divine in New York, the failure of Christianity to provide a cos-

mology which is life-affirming, pluralistic, egalitarian, earth honoring, and body positive is inevitably the triumph of paganism.
Ancient paganism with its pantheistic views; its emphasis on natural cycles of fertility and sexuality; its multigender orientation; its
honoring of biological diversity and every "spirit of place"; its tol-
erant, pluralistic, inclusive, non-proselytizing nature; its mythos of
immanence; and its capacity to provide the grammar of primitive
or phylogenetic experience allowing direct communication to the
realm of spirit, means that it inevitably becomes the cosmology of
relevance for people today.

Paganism, however, is too reactionary a word. "Pantheism"
might be better. "Ecocentric" sounds eccentric. Whatever word
geo-philosophy hits upon to describe itself it must be quite distinct from what has dominated for the past millennia. To be quite
clear, it is my opinion that no amount of revisioning from even
"liberation" scholars can shift the patriarchal destructiveness
inherent in Christianity.

A developed geo-philosophy would replace the linear, dualistic, mechanistic, and vertical pyramid world view with a horizontal, holistic, biological, and cyclical one. At the same time, it
would replace the hierarchical and destructive model of agriculture with an organic, sustainable, and creative one, hence "per-
manent-culture" or permaculture. In such a system, the goal is to
increase the turnover and the quality of the biomass in a way
which is appropriate for every part of the ecosystem. Forests
would become more like forests, marshlands more like marshlands. Bovids would run on plains not in cleared rain forests. The
earth would be understood as a self-stabilizing planet consisting
of organisms and environments which interact with each other to
maintain the total biosphere within limits favorable to all life,
humans not excluded.[11]

Intervention occurs to restore damaged zones to their natural
succession and to harvest food and materials that are a result of
the increased productivity of the ecosystem. The numbers of wild
animals would soar in such schemes. Cougars and other predators
are actually beneficial to agriculture. Wolves and coyotes force
herds to keep together, so churning the soil and stopping the
widespread grazing of all new shoots. The amount of human labor

and input of fossil energy would dramatically decrease. We can be sure that ancient festivals were geared to such a view of increase as their participants realized their dependency within a greater ecological sphere. Indeed, Australian Aboriginal geomythical practice is centered around visiting sites known as "places of increase" and recounting stories or performing actions there that will ensure abundance and fertility during the coming cycle.

A similar practice needs to prevail in contemporary food production. In place of fields being treated as chemical pans to float plants in, true fertility must be realized as lying in the quality of the life of the soil. This can be measured in humus content or in the numbers of living organisms, mostly microbacterial, that inhabit it. The living content of the soil is a true indicator of our wealth. It is contained in the top few inches of a relatively small area of the planet. And our longest lasting and possibly most enriching relationship in life—continuing even after we die—is that which we have to the soil. Our moral goal is to increase that storehouse of wealth, to enrich our relationship to the land, and hand it down to the coming generations in health and wholeness.

This is a philosophical and spiritual practice of great significance. There are few human goals of more importance than the restoration of the consciousness in which land and spirituality are seen as one. Culture cannot be set against nature; it must embrace and include it. There are few necessities more pressing or spiritual activities of more meaning than this. If these words are doubted, it is rewarding to observe the practice of one of the planet's oldest and still maintained living traditions.

The yearly cycle of the Hopi in northern Arizona turns upon the coming, the activity, and the departure of the spirits known as Kachinas. These take on many forms. Every plant and animal is represented by a Kachina, such as the corn, squash, crow, butterfly, and eagle. There are also other Kachinas, such as the Mudheads, the Ogres, and the Clowns. All dance at specific festivals for the time of year: the planting times, the harvest times, and for rain and the continuation of life. It is an inspiring and memorable thing to see the Kachinas emerge from the roofs of the clan kivas (partially underground ceremonial lodges) enter the village plazas, and dance for the cycle of life, for the health and well-being—not of the individual—but for the life of the soil and with it the tribe. In comparison, the rites for individuals, of birth, marriage, and death, though accompanied by costumes and dance, are, to quote Hopi, "just a social dance," to "have a good time," and to facilitate personal transformation, a totally different quality to the dances of the Kachinas. In the words of Grandfather David Monongye from his address sent to the Dalai Lama in 1982:

> ...each ceremony fits into an annual cycle according to the seasons. All activities, songs and dance movements involved in this cycle help keep the earth in balance, especially the weather conditions necessary for each season.... The Hopi speak of living at the spiritual center of the earth. They describe the earth as a spotted fawn, each spot having a certain power.... We know that Hopi land is not the only spiritual center in the world. Other places were set aside *in other lands* to serve as sanctuaries during a time of great world change in the future. Their roots will be found *through ancient knowledge* leading to those places.[12]

Grandfather David's words also contained a warning that the use of advanced technology to achieve greater wealth and control over nature "would bring great harm to both land and life." And he suggests that our "actions through prayer are so powerful that they decide the future of life on earth." It is up to us to "choose whether the great cycles of nature will bring forth prosperity or disaster. This power was practiced long ago, when our spiritual thoughts were one."

The words emphasized are mine to show that it is through the re-membering and re-creation of our own ancient native traditions, specific to the geographical locations of our arising and the formation of our own cognitive and expressive powers, that we can contribute to the life and well-being of the "spotted fawn," the vibrant body which is the skin and the soil of the earth.

NOTES

1. Mircea Eliade, *Myth and Reality*, 5–6.

2. Mimi Lobell; see note 3, ch. 6.

3. Adapted from E. W. Gifford, "Northeastern and Western Yavapai Myths," *Journal of American Folklore* 46 (1943).

4. Robert Lawlor, *Sacred Geometry* (Thames & Hudson, 1982), 32–7 and 65 ff.

5. Martin Brennan, *The Stars and Stones;* also, *The Boyne Valley Vision* (Dolmen Press, 1980).

6. Jeff and Debbie Saward produce a periodical, *Caerdroia,* for those interested in labyrinthine lore. For information, telephone (U.K.) 0268-751915.

7. Sig Lonegren, *Labyrinths: Ancient Myths and Modern Uses* (Gothic Image, 1991).

8. John Michell, *The New View Over Atlantis,* 83.

9. Tom Graves, *Magic and Technology* (Gothic Image).

10. For example, Bill Mollison, *Permaculture* (Covelo, Calif.: Island Press, 1990) and *Permaculture: A Designers Manual* (Davis, Calif.: AG Access Corp., 1988).

11. James Lovelock developed these ideas in his books on the Gaia theory (*Gaia: A New Look at Life on Earth,* Oxford University Press, 1979, and *The Ages of Gaia,* Norton, 1988). An excellent introduction to the subject is Elisabet Sahtouris, *Gaia: The Human Journey from Chaos to Cosmos* (Simon and Schuster, 1989).

12. Quoted from Robert Boissiere, *The Return of Bahana* (1989). The full compilation of these texts can be found in *Cross-Cultural Exchange and Prophetic Tradition: The Hopi and Tibetan Dialogue* by Joan Price.

11

REDEFINING
THE ROLES

THE PSYCHOSOMATIC MEMORY

Pursuing the conclusion arrived at in the chapter on the new male sexuality—that it is within our bodies we will find the answers to the question of what it means to be a man—it is time to examine the dominant archetypes of masculinity and attempt to reach some new definitions of the familiar roles of father, warrior, king, boy, magician, priest, god, and wise old man. The meaning of the roles lies in the dynamic between the individual and the collective on the one hand—which gives rise to a myriad of possible definitions—and, on the other hand, in the dynamic between the physical world and the archetypal realm.

This book has proposed a continuity of psychosomatic knowledge from the ancient past as a result of this latter dynamic and has suggested that both sides of the dynamic maintain this knowledge. On the physical side, it has been suggested that the strata for the transfer of ancestral and genetic information lies in the body, possibly in the biochemical code contained in the DNA and RNA molecules. And on the archetypal side, we have resorted to ideas drawn from holistic approaches and quantum physics, where the existence of an autonomous collective unconscious is suggested by the field generated by the relationship between entities.

According to Stanislav Grof, the "holonomic" approach emphasizes information rather than substance. It is the science of "vibratory patterns rather than of mechanical interactions." It can be used to understand why consciousness is able to be "invaded with unusual power by various archetypal entities or mythological sequences that according to mechanistic science should have no independent existence."[1]

Quantum physics has led to such ideas as the "morphogenetic fields" of Rupert Sheldrake, or the "implicate order" of David Bohm. These suggest that the explicate patterns of the universe are to be found in ordering principles from which both matter and consciousness derive and are the source of archetypal and mythological phenomena as well as the collective unconscious and historical events.[2] Reality is the sum of energy, meaning, information, and substance constantly involved in an interactive process of enfolding and unfolding. Stanislav Grof adds to this that archetypal phenomena "must be seen as ordering principles supraordinated to and preceding material reality, rather than its derivatives." But in my view, this is going too far. It is too determinative, and ignores the role of the individual's biochemical reality. The genetic principle is as inherent to life as the archetypal, and although the "ordering principles" of both may be finally revealed to be the ultimate information, it is only through their interaction that these principles can be known.

We cannot escape from the fact that raw, complex, chthonian immanence is the working principle of the universe, not a simple, ideal, and fixed transcendental order. My cup of tea beside me now is as important to my vitally subjective frame of reference as any quantum leap to holistic intelligence and an illusory transcendental objectivity. Indeed, without my cup of tea, there would be no comfortable and ordinary state of being—no respite from being "invaded" by extraordinary transcendental, ecstatic, or archetypal experiences. Although immanence can be ecstatic, I think it is only as a result of patriarchal conditioning that we think spiritual experience has to be always like that, when in fact the sacred way of life could appear to be quite ordinary.

In the end, whether the source I am referring to is inherent in the genetic coding, the body, the archetypal realm, the intelligence of the universe, some quantum level of matter, or any combination of them, is largely irrelevant. It only remains to be experienced for its interactive, congruent, holonomic, or holistic nature to be made instantly apparent. Where it is relevant is in avoiding false sources, be they of the latest, popular scientific kind, or of a religious kind, or of any kind of belief described by a word ending in "ism." That includes masculism, feminism, paganism, animism, and so on. The universe responds to all these things—it always has—but it does not respond to them kindly, preferring creativity and meaning anytime over dogma and explanation. And meaning today is definitely in short supply amid the host of explanations offered and the alienation from the creative world of nature. Right now, we can leave the theorists by saying that as long as they subscribe to the dominant paradigm of modern culture—a vertical hierarchy with its attendant dualism dominated by reductionist concepts of salvation, evolution, or progress to future economic, political, and spiritual goals—the experience of life will pass them by.

Hierarchical evolutionism pervades the writing of even the most provocative and enlightened of thinkers. It is as though to simply take the step to allow present-moment immanent experience and phylogenetic ancestral continuity were the most forbidden and heinous of crimes.

So, let it be spelled out: Right now, in this moment, without mediation or special technique to access it, there is the experience of your being that is directly connected to a source of immanent power which has its continuity through the psycho-genetic lineage of your ancestors. This experience, while usually quite ordinary, has unlimited access to different aspects of reality beyond our normal mechanistic view of time and space, and its only requirement is that you are breathing. Through letting go of the limiting notions of self with its cosmological separativeness and linear time, it is possible to enter a dynamic world of ever-changing creative flux and limitless energy. The preternatural aspects of reality come to us through the synchronistic and sympathetic nature of the archetypal realm, and only in our culture with its spiritual-material dualism are these "otherworldly" realms seen as

being in any way unusual. We are amazing, and we don't have to
be commodified and repackaged and presented back to ourselves
by church or media to know it.

THE HOUSE OF THE FOUR ROOMS

Returning to the journey I made with my two friends, Diana and
Theo, to Ireland, it is appropriate at this point to tell another story
about the process I underwent in my encounters with the archetypal masculine. This experience precedes the account given in
Chapter 8, "The Initiation of the Horned God."

That morning as I stared out over the lawns of the quiet retreat
house where we were guests—it was a very civilized old house with
marble floors and columns—and watched the hares playing in the
fields, Theo came into the room in a very excited state. Diana and
I teased her for a moment about her excitement before she took
some deep breaths, calmed down, and explained that she had
found a most interesting building and would we come and look.

"It's the room with the four doors!" she said.

The hard cobbles of the courtyard shone with the morning
dew as we walked across them. We came up before a heavy
wooden door. It looked as though it could have taken a coach and
four horses. Theo swung open the door, and we paused as our eyes
adjusted to the gloomy interior of the empty building. The room
before us was square and high-walled. We had entered through a
door that was set across a corner. High overhead, set upon
squinches supported by round arches, was a dome and rotunda
with four windows—the only source of light. There was no ornament, just a few old hay bales and some moldy horse harness. It
seemed strange that such an architectural feat should have been
accomplished for a stable.

The sun must have emerged from behind a cloud, for a single
shaft of light entered through one of the windows. It shone
through the shifting dust particles and formed a square of gold on
the opposite wall. In the center of each wall was a large doorway.
Theo, now somber, said they led to rooms that were all exactly the

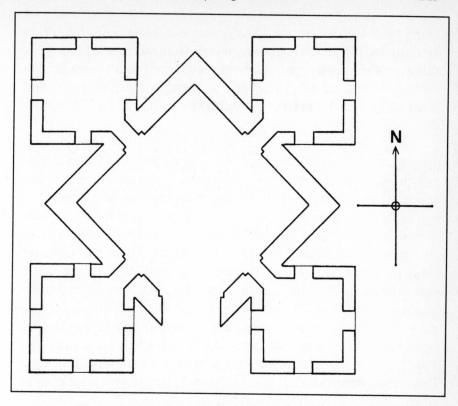

The house of the four rooms in Ireland, used as the site of a ritual

same and equally empty. I wanted to look, but she said to wait because she had an idea.

"We could make a ceremony out of this," she said, walking to the center of the room. "It's very simple. We reflect on what we would like the four rooms to represent. Then enter each one in turn. Each room has four stations, set out to the compass points, which we could work our way around honoring each one in whatever way we please. West is over there." Theo gestured toward one of the corners.

I thought I saw an incongruency. "You must mean the corners point to the compass directions in the rooms then. Their walls are set northeast, southeast, and so on. The stations will be in the corners."

"No. You see, in the same way as we entered through the corner of this room, you will enter by the corners of the other rooms. Each room has a window central to each of its walls in the same way as this one has doors. It's very unusual." Theo counted off on her fingers, "Four doors to four rooms. Four rooms with four windows—north, south, east and west. Four times four is sixteen. We can enter each room as part of a fourfold cycle, make our ceremonies, or whatever, then return to the center. Okay?" We nodded. " Let's meet in half an hour."

I went away in awe at the strange construction of the building. I went up the stairs at the back of the main house. I found a window to look down upon the "stables" and began to understand the geometry of the design. I made the accompanying diagram.

Each of the four rooms was topped by a small dome partly concealed by a parapet. The center room had a dome set upon a rotunda at least twice the size of the others. There was nothing opulent about the design. The craftsmanship of the gray stone determined the building, as though solid Irish masons had been given an unusual plan and solved the problems of the construction with the basic traditions that they were familiar with. An Arab, an Indian, or an Italian would have made it look quite different. As they were, the stables blended in with everything else. Once they were noticed, they appeared strange and a little contrived. They were also very compelling.

As I reflected on what the four rooms could represent for me, I became confused. What did Theo want or expect from me? I felt emotionally tangled and resisted being controlled. But the rooms drew me. After about forty minutes, I was ready to go, confused and unknowing.

I crossed the slippery yard to the large wooden door. I entered and stood inside. On the floor was a feather, which I picked up. It felt like a gift. I became aware that Diana and Theo had already begun their fourfold cycle. I could hear and sometimes see them through the open doors.

It then struck me that I knew what I had to do. I immediately crossed to the northwest door and entered. I walked furiously around the room, beating the air with my feather. At the center of the room I paused, opened my mouth, drew in a large lungful of air, and yelled.

It shook the wooden rafters above. Some large particles fell. Dust slowly filtered downward through the ray of sunlight that slanted in from the south window. I felt so angry. I felt so much pain and despair. I was at the beginning of a wonderful journey. A journey into the world, and I wanted the world to know it was a terrifying place.

What made it so bad was that it was getting hard to breathe in there. There was pollution in the atmosphere that no one seemed to notice. The seas were being poisoned, the forests felled. I was being skinned. I was terrified and afraid and I wanted to tell the world about it. Why, soon there might not even be air to breathe, or pure water to drink.

I did not care who heard. I filled my lungs and yelled again. I was very angry and afraid, yet it was a release of a burden I had been carrying for years. I did not have to feel guilty at protesting about that which was truly terrifying. I did not mind who saw my fear and terror. I felt like a little boy. I left the room and went back to the one at the center. From there I went through the door in the southwest wall.

It was sunnier in here. The atmosphere was charged with energy. I felt that my body was painted with bright swirling designs, and I could feel the power of my limbs. I felt that I wanted to leap, to run, to dance, to sing, to throw things. I worked my way around the four windows—north, south, east, and west—honoring the flow of this energy. I felt constrained by the four walls. They hindered my movements. But through the window to the south I could see the hares in the fields, and my spirit ran and leapt with them. I was totally energized to do whatever I needed to do, to fight the world if necessary to get my point across. I returned to the center room, entirely oblivious to whatever Diana and Theo were doing. I did not want to be constrained by their perception of me.

From there, the door to the southeast felt like the right one to enter next. I walked in, and a soft light bathed the walls. There was no direct light. The room with its four windows felt balanced. It seemed to be saying, "Your energy is good, but temper it with wisdom." My skin felt it was covered by a light but amazingly warm, feathered cloak. The four directions each seemed to represent an art or a science. There was a direction devoted to the knowledge of the plants, of medicine; a direction devoted to mathematics, geometry, chemistry, and physics; a direction devoted to crafts and beauty; and a direction devoted to music that seemed to fuse the others together in a new alchemy of spirit. I shook my feather and left a prayer at each station that they would come to life.

Back under the large dome of the central room I wondered what aspect of myself the remaining northeast door contained. I had been a boy, a warrior, and a wise man. What could remain? I crossed the floor and came to the door of the room. It creaked on its hinges as I pushed it open. I hesitated for a moment. Then I knew I entered the room of the father.

All of my anger came welling up like a flood. The anger I had felt at the beginning of the cycle of the rooms and which had been stirring for months. It brought tears to my eyes—hot, stinging tears—through which I could not see. I tried to ignore the feeling and whisked around the quarters honoring each, hoping the feeling would go away.

Finally, I came to stand in the last quarter of the room. The sixteenth station in the cycle. On the wall beside the window I could see a shape in the rough plaster that resembled the outline of the head of a dignified man with a proud nose.

I became furious. I cursed the outline of the man. I insulted it. I accused it. I knocked down in my mind's eye the men: priests, politicians, bishops, lords, managing directors, saints, judges, kings, and finally the gods, who seemed to stretch away in rows behind it.

I realized one of the root causes of my anger. The people who had exploited the world, bringing death and slavery to whole nations of people and to whole species of animals, who were destroying the environment and who were using political, economic, technological. and spiritual power to maintain that domination and control over others, were almost always men.

I knew this was irrational. I did not know that women were any better. All I knew was that this was how it was in the world, now. Those in power were men, had been men, and I was one of them. I began to feel ashamed. I felt pushed into a mold I did not like, that made me one of those figures on the wall. I resented what that made me, especially in my relationships to women. I again felt overwhelmingly, incredibly angry.

The next thing I knew was that I was tearing out of the building. I ran across the yard, into the gardens and over to one of the magnificent weeping beech trees that stood there. I felt safe in the enclosing arms of the tree. The tree knew my pain and could absorb it. I dug a hole with a stick. Visualizing it as decomposing as food for the tree, I dumped my anger into the ground.

It took a long time. I was angry with my own father. I was angry with the images of the male that I had been fed from birth. I was angry with the men who were using power for their own ends. And I was angry with myself.

Later, going inside, I felt tired but much better. I felt I had accepted my pain, anger, and despair—the fears I had always carried but had never been able to express. I felt I had taken an important step.

"Wow!" Diana said, "that shout of yours. I thought you were such a quiet, gentle man."

I thought I was too. But now that I had accepted other parts of myself, the trouble was that I no longer knew what kind of man I was supposed to be.

ARCHETYPES OF POWER

One idea emerging from this story is that it perfectly illustrates the synchronicity of archetypal and physical enactment. Without my vigorous actions—the yelling, the striding, the beating of the air with the feather, the spatial movement around the rooms, the running outside, and the digging of the hole—the archetypal realm would not have become available. And without the informing power of the unconscious content—the boy, the warrior, the wise old man, the father, the god, the tyrant, and so on—the physical elements on their own would have remained meaningless. Throughout the interaction the serendipity of the symbols provided was extraordinary: the feather, the hares, the sun, the rooms themselves, the plaster patterns on the wall, the tree. Naturally, they were selected by me, but they amply illustrate the capacity of the reflexive universe to provide *sui generis,* the outer reality to confirm the inner. There is a symmetry in the relations between mind and matter. This is an important point. When approached in the right way the universe is user-friendly.

Carl Jung searched for synchronicity as a principle unifying the inner and the outer worlds. Werner Heisenberg, the creator of quantum theory, suggested that elementary particles were simply the material realizations of a fundamental but abstract realm of symmetry. Einstein showed once and for all that energy and matter were different aspects of the same generative order. Time is now accepted as a relative function of perception. All this points out that science is moving into an area which was previously the domain of native peoples and mystics.

THE BOY

The young child in us needs to play. In order to play, he needs to create a safe space around him. Some psychologists may say he is attempting to recreate the security of the mother's womb. However that may be, when we feel safe enough, we, as men, like to play. The bedroom is a possible safe space where that side of us can emerge, but there are perils here. There are cross-cutting masculine definitions at work which deny and annihilate the little boy. When the little boy opens without safety, he becomes wounded. He may feel betrayed by opening to others who should be safe, but then violate him. He retreats to an inner world which, although innocent, by being blocked off, will impede his further growth.

Initiation into manhood in patriarchal society was designed to dispel vulnerability and allow the boy to enter the world of men. This was a time when the boy should no longer feel the gentle touch of women but the hardness and toughness of men. Through initiation into adulthood at the hands of men, the boy became "thick-skinned," able to hide his inner self from the male world he was entering. Studies have shown that the firm, boisterous touch of men is as important to the development of a child as the gentler touch of women. Children love to be tossed and carried by men. But too often patriarchal society has not only severely restricted contact between men and children but has restricted the natural homoeroticism that boys share between themselves. To be taken by men at adolescence into a world of homophobia, masculine invulnerability, and competition, when in fact by virtue of his maturity he should be entering the world of women, the boy is entirely suppressed. Patriarchal society has it completely back-to-front.

THE YOUNG MAN OR THE WARRIOR

This is a time of vitality, of energy. The young man now needs the initiation that will focus and direct his energy. In traditional patriarchal societies, this involved separation from the mother, sometimes achieved in a mock-battle, ritual way. Then an introduction into the men's lodge or men's society. To impress upon him the importance of the occasion, some kind of ordeal was involved; for example, bodily scarification—the testing of the thickness of his skin. This has become the blind sadism of men's fraternities where pain is inflicted not for growth, but for the pleasure of making another suffer like the members did. This kind of tradition is maintained in the armed forces. Here the abuse suffered in the name of "making a man out of you," is calculated to instill repressed rage which can only be released upon the "enemy."

In pre-patriarchal society, war could not be conducted in anger, or for any other reason than personal honor. The prowess of a warrior was measured by the self-control and conduct he displayed when confronting his opponent. War created honor for its participants from face to face ritual combat between equals. It was important that the opponent had honor and was not treated with the contempt created by dualistic "God and the enemy" consciousness. There can be little honor for a man blindly obeying the hierarchical command structure—in his mechanical space, the controls of an airplane, or encased in a tank, supported by long- range artillery and rockets—bombing or rolling over an unequally armed and unknown foe. In fact, warfare as it has become, let alone its reasons, is a disgrace to all of us in society. It has betrayed the warrior in men.

Initiation in pre-patriarchal society included initiation into sexuality. This would have been explicit. As much courage is needed in the bedroom as is needed in war. Far from being removed from the company of women, initiation took the young men into it. Older women frequently took on the role of teaching the right use of the body for sexual procreation and pleasure.

Through the awakening sexuality the young man learned how to remain "thin-skinned" and retain his playfulness and sensitivity while also becoming aware of his responsibilities as a grown man. In Australian Aboriginal society today, older women are seen as being the most attractive and have no difficulty in finding husbands or lovers into old age.

The adolescent stage for a man is an extremely critical time, when he is in need of most teaching on how to focus his energies. Teenagers, it will be observed, have lost the spontaneity of childhood, the true rebelliousness of the little boy, and almost invariably have a compulsion to conform, to belong to some group that provides identity. The armed forces recognize this and have always provided a powerful form of identity. Initiation into the warrior groups, the regiment, shapes the man, but at the same time, it fosters the "enemy" consciousness, homophobia, misogyny, and other values inimical to self-realization. It takes a very special group of men to cultivate the warrior and temper him with wisdom.

Outside of the military, the warrior in the young man finds its initiation in gangs, in daredevil exploits, in shared substance abuse, in fashions of clothing, music, and sport, some of which can lead to results of a severely inhibitory kind—self- or socially inflicted. Others may choose to conform to the status quo, which, because it is currently militaristically dominated and economically, socially, and ecologically leading to a dead end, amounts to the same thing. It is a rare individual who can find his way between the Scylla of mainstream society and the Charybdis of the alternative, and find his warrior nature still intact.

Once again, I think the solution lies in the ancient tradition of the warrior archetype. The role of the soldier has to be assimilated back into the culture that gave it birth, and rethought, re-created in a way which restores honor to the role. Some cultures have maintained vestiges of this. There are initiatory traditions among tribal peoples in Africa and North America which look useful. But these are all under threat. It's up to us to re-create from our own ancestral lineage and psychosomatic memory forms of male initiation that focus the powerful energies of the warrior in the man. It's up to us to create that which helps it avoid compulsively falling into conformity and provide it with a context in which self-realization is possible and through which all the values of a man can be cultivated. After all, even in patriarchy, when the killing is over and the dead are buried, it is known that the cooperation and support the battlefield required was far more important to the making of the man than the ruthlessness and competition.

Much work needs to be done in this area. Current male initiation practices are appalling. It is each man's own coming to self-knowledge in a supportive context provided more by the sheer physical presence of other men, rather than by anything they can say or do, that makes the man.

THE FATHER

I almost feel like omitting this section altogether, for as I approach it, my own personal experiences color my thoughts and suggest only negative descriptions and images of fatherhood. There must be, however, contained within the archetypal realm, many positive images of the father that will greatly enhance its role within our lives. As initiator and guide into manhood, his role is vital to us. This is probably the area most in need of redemption and re-creation from the archetypal realm as a result of patriarchal overlays.

As I suffered continuous abuse from my father—in whatever form he took, biological, educational, spiritual, social—and never experienced a positive, "surrogate" father, I, as a result, have never wished to be a father. This is partly also because the world my child would have come into was controlled by men to the point of systemic family, social, economic, and political pathology. I never learned the language of intimacy that I feel fathering requires. This probably discounts anything further I have to say upon the subject. I am still angry at the Father. I hate the way his image is used in patriarchal society and in religion today. I can only state that a goal of mine in writing this book was to come to terms with that aspect within me, and to arrive at a point where I, as a man, can reach out and find a communion with men about what having a father and fathering means. This is a work in progress.

In the Celtic tradition, the Irish Father God, the Daghda, possessed a cauldron from which such abundance poured that no company, it was said, could ever leave its presence unthankful. And yet, the image presented of the Daghda in the mythologies is curious. Sometimes he is wise, sometimes he appears as a glutinous and scurrilous fool. He is a sensitive, skilled, and noble harpist and a clumsy, club-carrying, lusty peasant. Perhaps these paradoxes will provide a foundation upon which a healthy understanding of the archetypal father can be built.

A recent book, *Iron John: A Book About Men,* by Robert Bly, focuses upon what Bly describes as lack of the father in men's lives, and this would appear to be useful. But closer inspection limited its value for me. In the first place, the work struck me as being against women. The model of fathering which Bly upholds bases itself upon such profoundly misogynistic archetypes as the Greek father god Zeus. In Bly's key tale, that of Iron John, the hero lives happily ever after upon being given the king's daughter as his wife. The woman in the tale passes from father to husband in the best patriarchal fashion.

In the second place, according to Bly, men who listen to women and specifically to what feminist women are saying become "soft." Men have to leave the realm of the feminine. They have to take the key from under their mother's pillow and depart from her. This is too limiting. Lack of the father is not addressed by removal from the mother. Men can extend themselves to being "soft," feminine, and sensitive without losing anything. Bly manages to overlook the fact that the established social order by its nature is patriarchal ("ruled by fathers") and includes in its values power over, abuse, and violence against women. If the statistics are anything to go by, the problem is not "soft" men, but the alarming increase in violence against women by "hard" men who are acting out the implicit values of patriarchy in order to conform to its masculist mores.

Men are being initiated by their fathers into the wrong things. Women, especially feminist women, are our allies in ending the abuses of patriarchy. If we set ourselves against them, then norms of dominance and supremacy continue unchallenged. My intuition suggests that much of Bly's and other male writer's anti-feminist stance is a reaction to the anti-male component of the women's movement. It does not understand the necessary anger many women (and men) feel about patriarchy.

Although it is time for men to come up with their own analysis of patriarchy and a new definition of masculinity, this will not be achieved through any further denial of "feminine" values. If the men's movement is to grow, then feminist thought will be vital to it. Only there have systematic attempts been made to describe and challenge patriarchy. We must always remember that it is not men or women who are the problem, it is the system of patriarchy in which we all collude, which we all support, whose values we adopt, and which we are all the victims of in the long term. When finally men define their "new masculinity," then it is likely that a major area of action will be the rectification of the results of male power, privilege, and violence in our relationships to women. These are important issues which Bly does not address.

THE KING

The king as an archetype within ourselves is, I feel, in much the same position as the warrior and the father—misunderstood, malaligned, and exploited by patriarchal ideas. This is partly the result of the vertical and ascent oriented model of power that has predominated in our thinking for several thousand years. In place of sovereignty being in the hands of the king, the pharaoh, the solar god, the deity at the head of the pantheon—distributing power downward to lesser beings—we need a concept of kingship which restores sovereignty to the self. This is very difficult to achieve because we have become so accustomed to giving away our power to those who promise or appear to protect us. That the only thing we need protection from are those in whom we have invested power, the conquerors, really shows up the irony of the whole hierarchical system!

The social order of hierarchy, with its kings at the top, has also created the obedient servant mentality. We don't feel we deserve or are able to receive anything. Our duty is to serve, even die, for the master. This self-negation provides as great an obstacle to self-realization of sovereignty as does the present concept of kingship. They are two sides of the same coin.

Contemporary monarchy for the most part debases the inner power of what I would prefer to call the archetype of sovereignty. Perhaps one way to restore the symbol would be a period of time spent pursuing a way of life which relied on no one else—was totally self-sufficient. Sovereignty may then be realized to lie nowhere but in one's own resources and in the nature of the land itself. Once this was known, it may then be possible to begin moving toward a society where the sovereign role was ritually enacted—probably through a cycle of deposition and renewal—and collectively perceived as being vital for the prosperity and fertility of the land and all who lived upon it. We are a long way from realizing such a spiritual vision. The legends of the Grail and the mythology of the Wounded (Fisher) King appear to be at the heart of the restoration of the archetype of sovereignty.

THE MAGICIAN

> And while they were talking, they saw a clown coming towards them, old striped clothes he had, and puddle water splashing in his shoes...and his ears through the old cloak that was over his head...
>
> "Let the gate-keeper be brought to me," said O'Donnell. And when the gate-keeper came, he asked was it he let in this man, and the gate-keeper said he did not, and that he never saw him before. "Let him off, O'Donnell," said the stranger, "for it was as easy for me to come in, as it will be to me to go out again."[3]

So enters Manannan ap Lir, shape-shifter, trickster, sorcerer, and ever-youthful sea god of the Tuatha de Danaan, into the house of Aodh Dubh O'Donnell. Manannan has several more tricks up his sleeve, including one where he makes boats from pea pods and little sticks and so magnifies them that his land, the Isle of Man, appears well defended from any hostile fleet. That is, if his island can be found at all from behind the mantle of mist he has conjured to conceal it.

Manannan emerges here and there in the Celtic literature as a humorous, powerful, but always benign being. He shares much in common with Merlin, including the power of metamorphosis and the musical and linguistic skills of the Bards. He is the maker of the Crane Bag which contains the secrets of language, which:

> When the sea was full
> its treasures were visible in its middle;
> when the fierce sea was in ebb, the Crane Bag
> in turn was empty.[4]

From accounts like these we can begin to understand the otherworldly power of the magician archetype. The Celts loved this power. Their legends reveal their readiness to slip over at any time into the bright and sublimely beautiful Otherworld. This is not a world to visit in order to escape the harshness of "reality." The Celts had no concept of bodily imprisonment or of sin requiring purgatory, rather it is a parallel world easily entered and, taken together with this one, constitutes the whole of reality.

Reclaiming the power of the magician, or of the shaman, gives us the ability to create a new world with our thoughts, dreams, and actions and then enter into it with our imagination. It is a fantastic world, but not a transcendent one. It shares in the immanent properties of this world, including humor. Maybe it's time to allow the magician's power to play a little more in our lives.

> "I could do another trick for you," he [Manannan] said; "I could wag the ear on one side of my head and the ear on the other side would stay still." "Do it then," said O'Cealaigh. So the man of tricks took hold of one of his ears and wagged it up and down. "That is a good trick indeed," said O'Cealaigh. "I will show you another one now," he said.[5]

THE PRIEST

We are fortunate in retaining some knowledge of the druid in what little remains of Celtic history. It provides some vital and healthy clues for re-creating the archetype of the priest. Putting aside the romantic notions of a white-robed, venerable patriarch standing atop a dolmen with his golden sickle and mistletoe—for here the current conception of a priest is being perpetuated—and returning to the ancient past, we find the Druid played a fulfilling role in the life of the people.

Most significantly perhaps, the Druid was not separate from the people. He (or she) did not mediate between a "higher" realm and the world. He was very much of the world and served as the memory and carrier of knowledge of the people. The Druid committed to memory family genealogies, poems, stories, songs, and legends. He learned and taught medical, biological, and astronomical skills. He settled claims, advised and arbitrated in disputes. He was the authority in spiritual matters.

As a shaman, the druid had personal power. This power came from visions and could be used in situations where healing was required. To gain power required considerable effort, often over many years. It could not be won by learning alone. An old Irish poem runs:

> Seven years your right,
> Under a flagstone in a quagmire,
> Without food, without taste,
> But the thirst you ever torturing,
> The law of the judges your lesson,
> And prayer your language;
> And if you live to return
> You will be, for a time, a druid, perhaps.

For this power to be kept a druid had to demonstrate his skills in his own right. There was no tenure of office, no divine right, no priestly establishment to maintain him. The classical and Christian writers could not understand the druids. To them, the archetype of the priest could not be disassociated from the temple or the church. But the druids practiced in nature, in the sacred groves, and were dismissed as fools who listened to "the twittering of birds."

Restoring a sense of the sacred to masculinity could be greatly enhanced by re-creating the archetype of the priest. The archetype has been severely harmed by several millennia of patriarchy and, as a result, the priest's functions in the psyche are almost totally in abeyance. He may deliver oracular insights, focus spiritual practice, create sacred space, conduct ceremony, provide music and healing and, although this may be moving toward another archetypal sphere, be a source of what was for the Celts the greatest gift, poetry.

To use the role of the priest for what it has become, a tool of power over others, denigrates and destroys the archetype. In some ways the priest must be the humblest of men. The priestly power has been used to create male elites, to claim impossible abilities, to extort wealth and services, and thus demonstrates the extreme delicacy that is needed in handling this archetypal energy. The druid, in eschewing external forms, in maintaining only the natural world as his temple, gives us clues for the path of reclamation.

THE GOD

The god speaks to us of hunting, of acting with reciprocation to all animal species. The god wears horns, telling us that, like the antlers of the stag, our power ebbs and flows and will fall to be renewed again. The god wears green and bears foliage, echoing the same mystery of transformation. The god sits on the throne, drawing up his power from the earth. The god aspires, seeks, goes on the quest, descends to the underworld, journeys the round of existence, and so becomes whole. The god is sexual, phallic. His rites are ones of pleasure and joy. The god honors the goddess. He learns to pleasure her, receive pleasure, and listen to her requests. The god brings her things that gleam, that shine, that glow, that exude, that are numinous with the intelligence of the universe. The god oils and paints himself for the goddess. He softens the hard edges of his body so that he may be a fit offering for her sacred place, her soft, formless, holy cave. The god takes care of the children, initiates them, passes on the knowing. The god hangs vulnerable on the World Tree, crying to know more. The god puts his head on the chopping block of the Bachlach and waits for the blow. The god ejaculates for his pleasure and for his death. The god dies to his boyhood, dies to his old selves. He dies to his knowing and so becomes wise.

The god does all these things ritually. He walks the circle of the law, enacts the ritual cycle of the year, and in so doing he becomes his whole self. The god is born, nourished, nourishes, makes love with, dies, and is mourned by women. Each stage of our roles in life can be measured by the health of their relationship to women. The god is nourished, parented, nourishes, parents, initiates, and is mourned by men. The richness of our roles can again be estimated by the health of our relationships to other men. These are the criteria of the god, before which the role of masculinity in contemporary culture can be evaluated. These are the roles by which our ancestors measured themselves and devoted their time and energy. How much time do we give to the children of today? How much is that worth to us? How much time do we give to our fathers? How much time spent questing for a vision? Or, if time is the wrong criterion, how much of our psychosomatic substance?

THE WISE OLD MAN

It's fairly easy for us as men to arrive at a place where we can be comfortable with the archetype of the Wise Old Man. But I think this is not to be trusted and relates to an aspect of the father that has become misused for the purpose of extolling men and giving them positions of authority. To get an idea of the true power of the archetype, it may be necessary to look at the equivalent in the archetypal feminine and see that there is a hollow place in the masculine for which no words exist. The Wise Old Woman in the feminine archetype is rarely called such. The words which are applied are usually ones such as crone, hag, witch, harridan, nag, even spinster or widow, with their attendant derogatory values. What are the equivalent words for old men? I can't think of any.

The Wise Old Man for me is not made in the image our social upbringing wants him to be: serene, kind, happy, generous, and understanding. He is actually furious with most of what he sees. He is more likely to beat it with a stick than smilingly nod his approval. He is grumpy, mean, and cantankerous, unpredictable and critical. He suffers from the hot flashes of the spermo-pause. He is as much a trickster as he is given to creating embarrassing social situations or revelling in crude body functions—the Dirty Old Man?

He does, however, let us know exactly what he feels and laughs and cries with us, egging us on. Perhaps above all, he does not pretend to know that he knows what he is talking about. He has given up on the certainties of youth and the teachings of adulthood. He has become a child again. He rests on the throne of the earth, on the continuity of life through the ebb and flow of its transformations. He is one with the mother again. Continuity from within is his focus, the maintenance of the knowledge of life in its immanent manifestations—not as transcendental or abstract theorizing. This is surprising, because it is he who draws ever closer to death. But confronted with that greatest of mysteries, the circle of absolute unknowingness—the dissolving in the final cycle—he can only say that right here and now, life goes on.

As we learn, as men, to sit in our circles again, around our council fires, we will find the need for elders. Their power is precisely of the kind we need to re-create our lives. Like the green man, wisdom as substance gushes from their head. Like the stag men in the Cave of the Horned God, they do not need to speak. To shake their medicine bag of secrets is enough. Yet, when they do speak, we must listen and take heed; not to the words, but to the way they are holding them; not to what is on their mind, but how it is held there. We must listen to their development of wisdom in the head through the indrawing of the seed into the body. As we come to honor the wise green men, so we honor the part of ourselves which is of the continually renewing ancient tradition that shapes our lives on earth.

NOTES

1. Stanislav Grof, *Beyond the Brain* (New York, 1985), 75 and 343–4.

2. Rupert Sheldrake, *A New Science of Life* (Los Angeles, 1981).

3. Lady Gregory, *Gods and Fighting Men*, 99.

4. E. Macneill, *Duanaire Finn* (Irish Texts Society, 1908); quoted from John Matthews, *Taliesin*, 81.

5. Lady Gregory, 102.

12

THE WAY AHEAD

The emphasis of this book has been theoretical, philosophical, even mystical. It has emphasized being rather than doing. It has been about establishing a spiritual foundation for ourselves as men based upon the innate wisdom of our own inner tradition. A tradition based upon the experience of our bodies and focused sexuality. Much in the way of action has been omitted. Practical issues of fatherhood, family, gay male rights, political activism, and the daily details of struggle against abuse of all kinds have not been covered here. It would be enough material for another book. Yet inner spiritual work and outer political work are ultimately the same thing—one always translates into the other. "The personal is political." And from the strength we create within, we can support each other to go out and make a difference in the world.

It has not been my intention to write a "how-to-do-it" book, though. To create another fashionable cult of weekly meetings or workshops for a predominantly white, middle-aged, comparatively wealthy few. The intention has been to cross all contextual boundaries and place the attention back on the individual. The intention has been to place attention on the immanent source of personal power.

For too long we have had the scientists, the patriarchs, and the spiritual leaders selling their cosmology and their "only way" to truth and salvation. For too long we've had business and the media converting energy and repackaging ideas into "trends," commodities, and concessions. These "experts" end up standing between us and our creative source, not as a means of access to it. For this reason I have written down some suggestions that I feel elucidate the nature of the way ahead for men and that will allow us to discern what is a part of it and what is not. From a true sense of our personal power, we can act. From a true sense of our personal power, we can join together to find solutions to real current political problems. I will be quite dogmatic, itself a fault, but please understand that this is no bible; it is only my opinion.

RE-CREATIVE MASCULINITY

In place of analytical thinking and dogmatic theologizing, paradigmatic shifts, and mechanical reductionist cosmologies, our present-moment immanent connection to our own source of power, rooted in the continuity of lineage over the hundreds of thousands of years of our arising, will be re-creative. Creative in the sense of energetic, perpetually ongoing, imaginative, open, and positively transcendent. Re-creative in our own direct building upon the source established in our psyches and bodies by those who have gone before. Acknowledging the archetypal power and context from the past, being able to find our way through it, and not merely be at the effect of it, we re-create ourselves anew.

DIRECT EXPERIENCE

For men to move into the re-creative state of their own masculinity and discover its contents, they must experience it for themselves. No vicarious assistance provided. No shortcuts. The discovery of power from within can never become a mass movement. It is about individuation, self-knowledge, or gnosis. Archetypal energies rooted in ancient tradition, mythology, and somatic experience are tools for individual growth. If they were to become exteriorized, induced into awareness through the hands of a charismatic leader or a mass movement, they would have the power to engender atrocities on the scale of the Inquisition.

The Nazi movement in Germany appealed to blood, land, and the pre-Christian Germanic tradition—Jung called it "possession by Wotan." The archetypal forces unleashed gave rise to a racism and a world view which caused the torture and death of millions of Jews. Similar atavistic forces with their mass appeal are at work in many places in the world today. They take measures to exterminate the "impure," to provide "ethnic cleansing," to ensure the preservation of the "faithful." As H. G. Baynes wrote in 1941 in his work *Germany Possessed,* "A truth that is germane to the problem of individuation may lead to disaster if shouted through loudspeakers to the multitude."[1]

Archetypes have power. Ancient ones provide tyrants with a perfect source of legitimation. Plato's ideal forms become fascist when translated into the laws of the perfect state.

CONSCIOUS RECEPTIVITY

To begin the experience of re-creative masculinity, especially when archetypal contents are being encouraged to emerge from the unconscious, it is necessary to increase conscious receptivity. In the first place, it is necessary to be open. By this is meant that it is necessary to be able to listen to every point of view, every perspective, and not believe that certain beliefs are the right ones. In the second place, it helps to relax into the perceptive mode of the body rather than that of the presuppositions of the mind. It helps to meditate, to be quiet, or only vocal as a means of assisting imaginative re-creation; e.g., song and mythical storytelling. In the third place, it helps to physically enact ritual processes such as the calendrical cycle. Talking about it and doing it divide us like the anthropologist and his subjects. Talking about it takes us out of our bodies, out of the present moment experience, and dissolves unconscious contents before they can even emerge. The goal is to know oneself, not to get others to know you.

The goal is to know that we hunger for truth, not to know what truth is. The goal is to know that we are whole, not to prove wholeness or otherwise achieve it, master it, or even to have it as our goal. The process is one of individual awakening to the world of immanence, change, and nature, not translating it into fixed, mental, exterior forms which are then open to misinterpretation and manipulation.

Re-creative masculine sexuality is best served by a clear mind and a healthy body. There is no direct evidence that drugs were used, except for medicinal purposes, by our European ancestors. If any hallucinogen was employed, it was probably the psilocybin mushroom, which covers damp meadows in great quantity in summer. Compared to the powerful hallucinogens of other cultures, this mushroom is mild and fairly nontoxic. The way drugs are used in other cultures should also give us a good indication of appropriate ways to use them in our own. Until a careful and sacred context for their use can be re-established, it is best to forego them altogether.

DISCRIMINATION

Once the re-creative energies are tapped through sexuality, ritual, or other practice, it does not mean every archetypal manifestation is necessarily of the essence. By this is meant that inner dynamics have long been overlaid with theories and interpretations. It may take a while to get the feel of deep ancestral, mythological, and archetypal powers. There is no mistaking them when they come; but still, do not give any of them the reality they would not otherwise have. They are, for all their power, subjective interior forces. They require a certain psychic distance or discrimination in their subsequent contemplation and use. Their quality will be realized in the effect they have in changing your life. Some experiences may take years to assimilate, let alone ever understand or act upon. Some may never emerge to consciousness and remain informing us from the unconscious depths. Some of them may be very ordinary, and not at all the "peak" experiences transcendent spirituality says we should have.

An encounter with the archetypal powers as described in this book is an encounter with what we immediately know to be our true selves. They are powers we already have, not something we have to try to achieve. When Plato said we live in a cave and perceive only shadows of the true reality, he opened the way for one of the greatest falsehoods to which the planet has ever been subjected. The archetypal powers are not real principles underlying the world and which one day, if we strive to obey the right laws, will manifest, for instance, as the perfect city on earth—the New Jerusalem of St. John. There is no simple, fixed, geometrical, underlying, and transcendant truth. There is organic, complex, and "chaotic" nature. And in the process of our growing within nature, there are synchronistic forces at work which will guide us, inspire us, fill us with visions that enable us to take our part in the play of life on earth.

INTEGRITY

The re-creative state of masculinity implies absolute honesty and integrity. The lies told to cover up the lack of integrity are lies to oneself, maintaining the old values of the patriarchal conditioning. Sexuality holds the clues, for within it, imbalances will be evident. Tantric sex with a partner who is held in love, esteem, respect, equality, and trust is one of the most powerful ways for every aspect of ourselves to be mirrored back to us. It takes a very rare group of peers to achieve a similar level of honesty.

MALE SUPPORT

Archetypal re-enactment is an intensely personal thing. The archetypes constellate themselves uniquely for each one of us. Yet there is also an intense desire to share and communicate the meaningful experience of them with others. It would be advantageous for men to try to come together to share these experiences with each other. Only in this way will we get beyond the competitiveness inculcated into us by the requirements of this society to keep us separate, unorganized as workers, available as consumers, and murderous in times of war.

This will be very difficult for us to do. We will have a great deal of resistance and judgment about this. Guilt may overwhelm us. We are trained not to support each other and to actually constantly undermine each other. Power over others is institutionalized in us. We are trained to talk but not to listen. We are trained to override emotional responses—let alone emerging unconscious ones—and to always appear in control, dominant, clever, witty, and courageous. Well, it's time to let go of all that. We have to do it. Informal times where feelings can be expressed as well as formal times with masks, costumes, movement, and darkness etc. will be of great help. Planning a ritual which involves these elements will establish an archetypal common ground where a transpersonal quality can be present. Men sitting down and talking has the potential to accomplish for our recovery what twelve-step programs have done for the recovery of millions of alcoholics, children of alcoholics, incest survivors, overeaters, codependents, and others with whom we share a common disease.

BROTHERHOOD

In re-creating our masculinity, we will need to move toward a new definition of male friendship or brotherhood. Not the old mutual back-scratching society with its machismo and locker-room language and humor, but one based upon an awareness of the inner and the emotional worlds. Feeling, caring, touching, and sensitivity will be of the essence here. The old men's clubs are in fact characterized by insensitivity—especially to emotional, mental, and physical pain. They are also characterized by their accompanying desensitizing activities: drinking, smoking, physical endurance and competitiveness, plus verbal foulness and abuse of those outside the club. There is also the emotional and physical distance fostered by homophobia.

In place of the old male image, tough on the outside and empty within, we need to be courageous explorers within and able to express the full range of who we are without. This means expressing feelings of hurt, of fear, of despair, of sadness, of anger, of jealousy, of inadequacy, of doubt and shame—all the things that are contrary to what we were told made "a man" when we were children and teenagers. This may be easier for most men in the one-on-one situation, between friends, out on a hike or in some other informal setting. But, although it may involve the greatest risks, the greatest gains are to be found by pushing against our resistance and exposing ourselves in a group of men. This will have to happen anyway if inner transformations are to be translated into outer change.

Feminists are assessing the backlash that's going on against the women's movement right now and we can be sure that a similar backlash will take place against the incipient men's movement. Any attempt by men to return to their inner tradition will be met by derision, because it directly counters the images and drives of contemporary masculinity. Men pursuing their roots will be portrayed as chest-thumping savages, or as self-centered sissies. Men seeking to define themselves in flexible, changing, gender-crossing, feeling ways will be portrayed as weak, feminine wimps, even by feminists. Anything which threatens the "business as usual" mentality of the patriarchal world will be severely attacked. However, a good indication of exactly how well we are doing will be the numbers of nerves we are touching—the ridicule we are invoking in the media.

MONEY AND EQUALITY

In re-creating our masculinity, the state of mutual sensitivity which is necessary will require us to be equals. Only as equals can we communicate with each other and offer support to each other. Only as equals can we empower each other. Only from a context of equality can we really respect each other's contribution to the whole. One of the things I believe this means is that money should not change hands for any event involved with men's activity, apart from general considerations of expenses, transport, equipment, etc. Courses, talks, workshops, rituals need to be offered free. If it is felt that a man's skill could be of benefit to a group, then money could be pooled to cover his expenses, provided these were not excessive. What is at stake is too important to allow the creation of another group of celebrities that will maintain the general social activity of giving away our power.

We all participate in this giving away of power because of the old patriarchal paradigm. In this vertical model of the cosmos, we want to believe that someone else is taking care of things, and consequently someone does. As a result, powerful impulses arising from within the people—the manifestation of archetypal contents, the urge for greater ecological harmony, for spiritual experience, for egalitarian political forms and so on—become co-opted or contextualized by powerful individuals or corporations. They then sell them back to the people in a form that enables them to profit from them in terms of wealth and power. This makes the impulse "safe." It brings it into the established hierarchical model of the world where everything is separate. This giving away of power must be vigorously resisted—even when it is to the "stars" of the psychological, literary, artistic, musical, and theatrical worlds. We must learn to support each other as equals, communicating directly with each other and exploring forms that are new, unfixed, unsafe, collective, and not the property of "experts."

Ultimately, such a heretical view will lead us away from the centralized economy altogether. It will lead us to one where goods, information, and services are shared on a huge decentralized network according to human need. It is my opinion that the only global economy worth running is one based upon community and compassion. It is clear that the present one is plunging each nation into irredeemable debt and destructive codependency.

HOMOPHOBIA

At present, relationships between men operate within a tiny range of physical and emotional intimacy, a range much smaller than that enjoyed by women or children. The vehemence which accompanies the denunciation of homosexuality—"disgusting," "dirty," "they deserve to be diseased," and so on—is an indication of the strength of the conflict between the long-denied yearning men have to share deeply with each other and the values of patriarchy which say such sharing is not "masculine."

Society demands that men do not make physical contact with each other, that they are "tough" and competitive. The vehemence of the response to homosexual relations in which men are able to contact each other and not be competitive is because it challenges the core of the patriarchal definition of what it means to be a "man." As human sexual preference is not only innate but also a cultural choice, men who have been "successfully" socialized into the heterosexual norm and feel homosexual attraction may manifest extremely violent behavior. In the same way as believers may need to convert others to assuage their own lack of faith, heterosexuals need to persecute gays to assuage their own contradictory impulses. In the attempt to conform to "masculinity," they are likely to beat up or even kill gay men, sometimes after coming on to them. I have been told this behavior can be observed in schoolyards and is common in the military.

Young men form bonds and prove themselves in attacking those who society labels as the "other." Identity is provided by attacking the stranger, the "outgroup" within society. It seems that deep emotional sharing between heterosexual men is also possible in conditions of extreme stress. The bonding which many men experience when in combat reveals what should be possible between men in normal circumstances were this not denied. Under fire, men sometimes find the courage not only to face the enemy but to reveal and share with their comrades the fearful, vulnerable, and tender parts of themselves. It is ironic that the contempt generated for the "enemy" by the military in order to create the kind of bonding between men which it needs for the achieving of its goals should backfire in this way. For in conditions of extreme stress, a man's need for emotional and physical contact will sometimes create exactly those values of heart and soul which will not kill, nor hold contempt for and manufacture the "other" or an "enemy." The result, in some cases, may be a poor soldier; but the man may have discovered what love for others and his country really means.

In patriarchal society, masculinity is defined by its capacity to compete with and beat others and have power over them. "Masculinity" means being stronger, sharper, tougher, more forceful, able to have one's way with women, and be less vulnerable than other men. Above all, a man should not expose his feelings to other men and especially not touch them in an affectionate manner. There is the very real fear that opening up to a man or showing any sign of "weakness" will mean exploitation—rape—and domination. Things a man in patriarchal society cannot tolerate, but which women have to contend with every day.

The homophobia present within us is an indication of the degree of exploitation of women by us. The degree of the inculcation of patriarchal values of dominance and exploitation of women within us is indicated by our projection of these values onto homosexual relationships between men.[2]

The limits to the area of physical contact between men appear to be set by a man's quick sexual response. If, for example, physical contact goes beyond a slap on the back or a quick handshake and lasts, let us say, three seconds, then fear of homosexuality with a man or the entry of sexual connotations with a woman will end the contact. In the latter case contact will usually end with the woman's withdrawal.

Cut off from emotion and the enjoyment of touching and being touched, men inhabit a land of wasted potential. In the truly "liberated" society where the full range of adult sexual preferences are accepted, men would be able to go further with each other into the realms of emotional and physical contact short of sexual intimacy than they would with women. Men, after all, share the same bodies, know them well and have the potential for intense physical pleasure through touching each other before sexual boundaries are reached. How would it be possible for men to experience a much broader spectrum of intimacy between themselves and women before the present narrow, three-second limit of homophobia and sexual come-ons cuts in?

In the first place, the answer lies in sexual responsibility. When I am being responsible for my sexual energy, those around me, men and women, know that if we open up to intimacy then I will not sexually come on to them. Conversely, if I know they will take sexual responsibility for themselves, then I can open up to greater intimacy and physical contact. So far so good. But the problem seems to be that men are always ready for sex and have no choice in the matter. A man's sex drive is "natural." It is a product of his testosterone, and being touched would trigger it in a way he cannot be held responsible for.

Contrary to this popular belief, a man's off-on instant sexual response is not a "natural," instinctive thing. It is a socially defined response that men always have the ability to exercise choice and response-ability over. If men are "always ready for sex," then why is impotence so common? "Impotence" is the fear of not being able to perform in the sexually correct way as defined by the patriarchal society. That is, to immediately get it up, get it in, and have an orgasm. In a society where a much wider range of experiences were possible in physical and sexual intimacy, I believe that men would have a huge variety of responses and preferences apart from the above norm, so opening potentials for wide-reaching loving relationships. Furthermore, men will be seen to need a length of time for arousal that is equal to that of women. A man's instant sexual readiness is a construct of patriarchal society where the conditioning says he must get it off as many times and in as quick and big a way as possible. Yet a man does have choices, and foremost among these is responsibility for his sexual energy.

In the second place, men need to explore the boundaries between men. Homophobia is a powerful force on the planet today for aggression, violence, and destruction. It operates in the military to keep men apart from each other and deprived of emotional comfort. Without touch, a crying child will become angry, destructive, and abusive; the chances are that when it is picked up and simply held it will calm down. By denying their emotional needs and sustaining their competitive drive, the military keeps men in a state where they will kill. As it is, a huge contradiction exists between military values and homosexual values. The men in the military today are right; open homosexuality would undermine its effectiveness. The question for the United States is not should homosexuality preclude admission to the military, but does the kind of military we have reflect the way we now want our world to go?

A recent debate has focused on whether sexual preference is culturally determined or innate. The consensus is that either one or the other is too simplistic. While for some people, sexual preference may be genetically cast in concrete, for most people the combination of society and biology determine sexual preference. In this context, a homosexual preference can be seen as a healthy response to the narrow confines of heterosexual indoctrination. The latter's behavior is constantly being typified for people by socially sanctified forms of behavior. A homosexual walks the ground unexplored by socially normative behavior and thus expands the realm of human experience. Native American cultures have honored this role with the *berdache* tradition.

The problem in modern society is not homosexuality, but the homophobia created by narrow sexual definitions. These lead to violent behavior, self-hatred, and bigotry. It is not the sexual drive itself which is violent, but it is the action taken by a man to prove that he is not a "deviant" from the patriarchal, heterosexual norm that is violent.

This point cannot be stressed too strongly. It is not a man's sexual nature that is being held accountable here, but the nature of the system which provides him with his self-definition. Violence and power over others allow a man to prove that according to the values of patriarchy he is a "real man." Until men learn to enjoy the pleasures of connecting with each other in sensitive, emotional, and caring ways, then the fear and distance which exist between us will continue to wreak havoc on the earth. The constant attempts to prove that we are "men" will result in ever-worsening displays of oppression, bigotry, and sexual abuse that will destroy the bonds of love and caring which maintain us and our continued presence upon the planet.

Communication and physical contact between men does not necessarily mean sexual contact. All men can exercise their responsibility and define their own boundaries. But it is possible for men to experience with each other a huge area of intimacy which is actually vital for our emotional, mental, and physical well-being before sexual boundaries are reached. The focus on an exclusive heterosexuality has severely limited gender identity and multiple sexual orientation.

As was presented in the chapter entitled "Toward a New Male Sexuality," a man's emotional and sexual dependence upon a woman is a historical construct of patriarchy, and over a broader area of time and space, sexuality between men and sexuality between women were far more likely to have been commonplace. In sexual history, human bisexuality is the common ground. In having the courage to explore emotional, physical, and sexual areas with the same sex, men will encounter the patterns which lead to exploitation and inequality. If these patterns are dealt with, men will find their relationships with women will improve and deepen as exploitation ceases and the pressure on women to be the sole satisfier of emotional and sexual needs will be relieved. At the same time, relationships with men will move into a vast and unexplored territory. When men are willing to step beyond the homophobic taboos of patriarchy, they will find opening up a rich land of physical and emotional intimacy and contact which will usher in a new era for the planet.

THE SACRED

In re-creating our masculinity from roots embedded in our own native tradition, there is a certain element at work which I call the sacred. Examine for a moment the ritual practices of other living native traditions and you will see they are treated with the greatest respect. Respect does not exclude lightheartedness, parody, joking, or candor. Such exclusions from sacred life are more or less a product of the Church—it is hard to imagine a Hopi clown dancing down the isle of a Protestant church—but it does include an immense awareness of what is important and what is not questioned, challenged, or intentionally interfered with. The Hopi example is a good one. It shows that while children and visitors are not excluded from the Kachina dances, and informal life goes on around them, the masks, costumes, rattles, and other instruments of the Kachinas are sacred objects, kept in the clan kivas, and the dropping of a single feather never goes unnoticed.[3] Likewise, the songs, the movements, the patterns of the dance have been handed down over many generations and are treated as sacred.

In our tradition, we are not so fortunate as to have an unbroken material continuity. But we can guess that the masks, costumes, and instruments of our ancestors were considered as possessing power and were treated accordingly. As we access the knowledge of our tradition through ritual reenactment and archetypal journeying, we may see things we wish to re-create. These need to be held in a sacred way. We cannot expect others to know this, or even to know what to do around our spaces, power objects, or rituals. But we ourselves need to hold them in a certain, respectful way. This will be seen and be the best teaching we can possibly provide.

There is a further aspect of the sacred that arises once immanence is accepted into our lives. This could be expressed as, "To whom do we pray if there are no intermediaries between us and god, no vertical structure of ascent, no heaven—nor hell—and indeed, no god?" For prayerfulness is necessary and, according to the Hopi and many other traditional people, "maintains the balance of the world." Yet it is difficult for us to pray when the object of our prayers has been either personalized, reified to nonexistence, or otherwise made meaningless by a clearly human-created and hierarchically self-serving cosmology.

With respect to the Plains Indians of North America, their prayers are addressed to Wakan Tanka, which is usually translated as "Great Spirit." A more accurate translation would be "Great Mystery." Even so, this is too literal, and perhaps could be better understood as "that which is when standing on the edge of the unknown." Could we live with this in our lives? No god, no goddess, nor the certainty of faith, nor the comfort of any belief, nor the security of any world view or cosmology, but the nakedness and the openness of being unknowing. Such a position does not imply any separation from the life source. It does not imply a state of being in need of any redemption. Neither does it imply a world separate from the sacred. It does imply a certain humbleness—a sense of wonder—the ability to look out and say, "I don't know the answers. I do not know what will come. There is much beyond what I know. But I am here. I feel this life force and I am grateful for this. I am one with life. May all be the best it can be for all beings."

RITUAL

Rituals are ceremonial occasions when rites are enacted to facilitate transition from one state to another. Rites of passage from boyhood to manhood, from one year to the next, from the close of one cycle to the beginning of another, or simply times of giving thanks for these transitions—all are examples of ritual. It is slightly unfortunate these words: "ritual," "rite," and "ceremony," like "myth," are beginning to lose their original meanings and have become, in the secular society, words that denote something false, too formal, or empty. In the face of this there may be a preference to use other words to describe ritual acts. I personally prefer "ceremony" or words that are particular for the occasion, like a dance or a festival, or a drumming circle, or a fire, or a sacred space, or an initiation, or a feast after a river trip, or a meditation. This last word comes out a little hesitantly, because most rituals I participate in are based upon action. In fact, ritual implies a determined mode of action.

What is gained from a ritual is proportionate to what is put in. To the extent the body can be involved, with movement, painting, costume, singing, and so on, the richer will be the experience. Sometimes the preparation for the ritual may take many times longer than the event itself. It is rewarding to prepare for it with the same consciousness that is held for the event. In my experience, if an individual turns up at a ritual and does not participate but remains an "observer," they will be a drain on the energy. Detachment itself is use of power, and in patriarchal society withholding is a classic means of control.

There is, of course, no reason why rituals cannot be individually enacted. But it is my sense that they only achieve positive transcendence and power when communally undertaken. Ritual provides a means through which it is possible to connect with archetypal and mythological contents that take us from the personal to the transpersonal or universal realms.

The rituals men can work with from the ancient tradition sketched out in this book are those which come from within. They are not therefore immediately shared communal events. It will take many years for our tribal experience to be re-created. Because of this, if rituals are attempted communally, it is a good idea to do some planning beforehand so there is a basic structure. It is a good idea for certain individuals to take responsibility for directing the form the ritual will take—possibly on a revolving basis—to prepare it and use their intuition as to what the group needs to be informed about and what can be left undescribed and spontaneous. There has to be great care in this. Control is an issue. Those in any position of responsibility need to be extremely sensitive to the power this automatically gives them.

I personally am not willing to undergo ritual under auspices I am unhappy with. Among tribal peoples, for example the Hopi, there is not one aspect of the ceremonial dances that is not explicitly prescribed—although of course the clowns may play around the edges. Some individuals may wish to eschew formal ritual altogether and take the group out to a show, to a fair, or on an adventure. These can be occasions generating great intimacy, but they may not touch the deep archetypal realms where transformations can be facilitated.

If there is not a directing core group working with the agreement of all involved, rituals tend to be dominated by a few controlling individuals or bog down in inertia. There may need to be scene creators, direction keepers, gatekeepers, firekeepers, and musicians. There may need to be dance leaders, specific "spirits" in costumes, or sweat-lodge water pourers and rock carriers. The responsibility of these people to perform these roles needs to be agreed upon beforehand. Certain roles need extensive initiation into them before they can be performed. There needs to be no drawing of personal power from these roles. They are services offered for no other purpose than to facilitate the whole group—in which the power lies.

Drumming and sweat lodges are becoming very popular among men's groups. Sweats are a ceremonial practice of purification in the native American tradition and need to be respected as such. They have very specific forms and honor the lineages through which the tradition comes. Only those with the authority invested by the lineage can conduct sweats in the tradition. I am of the opinion that it is preferable that those traditions be learned from but not practiced by those of European descent. However, sweats are also a northern European tradition, ranging from the saunas of Scandinavia to the beehive stone huts of the Irish Celts. It is possible to re-create ceremonies that draw upon these sources, including the native American, provided the sources are honored and the forms used are held in a sacred way. I would call this an eclectic sweat. It needs the agreement beforehand of all those involved about what their intentions are. Drumming, too, is not a prerogative of native Americans. It is a worldwide tradition. Care must be taken when drawing upon any of the sacred traditions of the world that they are honored. It is best to draw upon your own sacred tradition.

From the native tradition of Europe, it is possible to follow a ritual cycle around the year. The dual rhythm of the god and the field of the goddess (see Chapter 4) are marked by festivals of transition at the cross-quarter days, solstices, and equinoxes. This creates eight main festival times a year. These are key points around which generative themes can cluster. Details of each point can be picked out from the text for enactment. For example, my favorite Samhain ritual involves costuming, fire building, and selecting certain twigs that represent aspects of myself I wish to leave behind and throwing them on the fire. On top of this are personal rituals of transition which can be performed at any time, but male initiation, for example, would be enhanced by rites performed at Beltane. This cycle, though, is not the only cosmological scheme available, if we need one at all. Individuals might find an alternative mythical calendar more suited to their own archetypal experiences.

A SELF-INITIATORY TRADITION

No individual or group has unique access to the means of re-creating the archetypal masculine or any other aspect of our native tradition. Nobody can define the experience of another. This is what I call a self-initiatory tradition with no mediators between us and the source. Any saying theirs is the true tradition and all others are wrong should be ignored. Any attention given to them will further fuel their fires. Even so, we can take the work of those who are not claiming authority and test it through application to our own experience. At this stage everything is an offering to our re-creation and for the test.

Centralization and institutions are best avoided. Even something as apparently innocuous as a newsletter carries power for the individuals responsible for its production. The men's movement can only exist on the level of grassroots if patriarchal forms of power are to dissolve. Perhaps if a demand for a newsletter did exist, then a revolving editorship would be best.

THE FAMILY OF MEN

If there is to be a men's movement, then it requires a comprehensive and inclusive vision. It must include every minority or majority within it. If it does not, then it will perpetuate the competitive values of patriarchal society and some will be "in" and others will be "out." Powerful individuals, the mythopoeic branch, the gay branch, or the political branch may seek to define it and control struggles, and division will result. The men's movement can include all of these branches in its family tree. To that end, the focus needs to remain on the individual man in grassroots contexts. On that level every kind of group can exist: black, brown, white, yellow, red, green, blue. We are in an age of individuality and the sense of tribe, of belonging, will take time to be recreated. Whatever the case, we need to be aware to be positively for things rather than against them. We have to make the effort to allow every point of view. It will not do to be simply anti-patriarchy or anti-feminist or anti-anything. This will only distract us from making the changes that are necessary in ourselves.

We have a long way to go. Re-creative masculinity asks us to become many things. It asks us to step beyond ourselves and become each other's sons, brothers, fathers, and grandfathers. In caring for each other as well as in accessing the deep wisdom traditions of our inheritance and in providing re-enactment of ritual, myth, and initiation, it also asks us to learn about the mystery, which joins both male and female in the continuity of the cycle of life.

We must learn to be concerned with living on the edge of the mystery—for the living of life for no other reason than that which is its own reason. We must learn to allow every feeling, every diverse perception of our minds. We must learn to live in and enjoy the full range of sensuality, ecstasy, and capacity for intimacy of our own bodies. Within our body-mind lies the wisdom for the unfolding of our selves and thus the pattern of the future for our world. The mind is the body. The body is the mind. Spirit is the world. The world is spirit. All is involved in the one dance of life.

Wherever the next life takes us does not concern us until we are there. When we have undergone the radical metamorphosis necessary for existence in another dimension—by definition at present conceptually beyond ours, but nonetheless existing, as demonstrated by the effortlessness of the infinite universe in providing all possible worlds—then we will be concerned with a transcendent world, only to find that our experience of it will be right here and now.

And right here and now, at this end, there is a beginning. A new beginning for men as we claim our true source of energy, our true identity, and self-definition. This power accumulates for those of us who find the courage to journey within and find our own source of being. Power which then, starting with every man, helps to define his larger future—in his community, in his society, and in his story.

NOTES

1. Quoted from Morris Berman, *Coming to Our Senses*, 291.

2. Although on the surface homosexual relations between women may appear to be slightly more tolerated in patriarchal society, this is only so long as they remain subordinate. The moment a women in a position of authority reveals, or is thought to reveal, lesbian traits, the discrimination against her will be multiplied. Women in the military are caught between the masculine qualities demanded by the job and the accusations created by exhibiting those qualities. If they attempt to prove their femininity, they will not be considered suitable for promotion. If they show how tough they are, they will be considered lesbian and not fit for promotion. Women in this male-defined world are caught in a complex double bind.

3. In 1992, I learned that the Kachina dances at Hopi were now closed to visitors. This was due to the portrayal of Kachinas in a comic book.

SELECTED BIBLIOGRAPHY

Abbot, Franklin. *Men and Intimacy*. Freedom, Calif.: The Crossing Press, 1990.

Anand, Margo. *The Art of Sexual Ecstasy*. Los Angeles: Jeremy P. Tarcher, 1989.

Anderson, William. *Green Man*. London: Thames & Hudson, 1990.

Basford, Kathleen. *The Green Man*. Ipswich, Mass.: Ipswich Press, 1978.

Berman, Morris. *Coming to our Senses*. New York: Bantam, 1990.

———. *The Re-enchantment of the World*. New York: Bantam, 1984.

Bleakley, Alan. *Fruits of the Moon Tree*. San Rafael, Calif.: Gateway Books, 1984.

Boissiere, Robert. *The Return of Pahana: A Hopi Myth*. Santa Fe: Bear & Co., 1990.

Brennan, Martin. *The Stars and Stones: Ancient Art and Astronomy in Ireland*. London: Thames & Hudson, 1983.

Chang, Stephen. *The Tao of Sexuality*. San Francisco: Tao Publishing, 1986.

Chia, Mantak. *Taoist Secrets of Love*. Santa Fe: Aurora Press, 1984.

Condren, Mary. *The Serpent and the Goddess*. New York: Harper Collins, 1989.

Daly, Mary. *Gyn Ecology*. Boston: Beacon Press, 1978.

Eisler, Riane. *The Chalice and the Blade*. San Francisco: Harper & Row, 1987.

Faludi, Susan. *Backlash: the Undeclared War Against American Women*. New York: Crown Publishers. 1991.

Gimbutas. Maria. *The Goddesses and Gods of Old Europe*. London: Thames & Hudson, 1982.

Hite, Shere. *The Hite Report on Male Sexuality*. New York: Dell, 1981.

———. *Women and Love*. New York: Alfred A. Knopf, 1987.

Hutton, Ronald. *The Pagan Religions of the Ancient British Isles: their Nature and Legacy*. Oxford: Basil Blackwell, 1991.

Jung, Emma and Marie-Louise Von Franz. *The Grail Legend*. London: Hodder & Stoughton, 1971.

Keen, Sam. *Faces of the Enemy: Reflections of the Hostile Imagination*. New York: Harper Collins, 1986.

———. *Fire in the Belly: On Being a Man*. New York: Bantam, 1991.

Lawlor, Robert. *Earth Honoring: The New Male Sexuality*. Rochester, Vt.: Park Street Press, 1989.

———. *Sacred Geometry: Philosophy and Practice* London: Thames & Hudson, 1982.

Le Guin, Ursula K. *Always Coming Home*. San Francisco: Harper & Row, 1985.

Lonegren, Sig. *Labyrinths: Ancient Myths & Modern Uses*. Glastonbury: Gothic Image, 1991.

MacCana, Proinsias. *Celtic Mythology*. London: Hamlyn, 1970.

Matthews, John, ed. *Choirs of the God: Revisioning Masculinity*. London: Mandala, 1991.

———. *Taliesin: Shamanism and the Bardic Mysteries in Britain and Ireland*. Wellingborough: The Aquarian Press, 1991.

Michell, John. *The New View Over Atlantis*. London: Thames & Hudson, 1983 .

Morgan, Elaine. *The Descent of Woman*. New York: Bantam, 1973.

Paglia, Camille. *Sexual Personae, Art and Decadence from Nefertiti to Emily Dickens*. New York: Vintage, 1990.

Peat, F. David. *Synchronicity: The Bridge Between Matter and Mind*. New York: Bantam, 1987.

Ross, Anne. *Pagan Celtic Britain*. New York: Routledge, 1967.

Starhawk. *Dreaming the Dark*. Boston: Beacon Press, 1982.

———. *Truth or Dare*. San Francisco: Harper & Row, 1990.

Thompson, William Irwin. *The Time Falling Bodies Take to Light*. New York: St. Martins Press, 1981.

INDEX

On the following pages you will find listed, with their current prices, some of the books now available on related subjects. Your book dealer stocks most of these and will stock new titles in the Llewellyn series as they become available. We urge your patronage.

To Get a Free Catalog

You are invited to write for our bi-monthly news magazine/catalog, *Llewellyn's New Worlds of Mind and Spirit*. A sample copy is free, and it will continue coming to you at no cost as long as you are an active mail customer. Or you may subscribe for just $10 in the United States and Canada ($20 overseas, first class mail). Many bookstores also have *New Worlds* available to their customers. Ask for it.

In *New Worlds* you will find news and features about new books, tapes and services; announcements of meetings and seminars; helpful articles; author interviews and much more. Write to:

Llewellyn's New Worlds of Mind and Spirit
P.O. Box 64383-K458, St. Paul, MN 55164-0383, U.S.A.

TO ORDER BOOKS AND TAPES

If your book store does not carry the titles described on the following pages, you may order them directly from Llewellyn by sending the full price in U.S. funds, plus postage and handling (see below).

Credit Card Orders: VISA, MasterCard, American Express are accepted. Call us toll-free within the United States and Canada at 1-800-THE-MOON.

Special Group Discount: Because there is a great deal of interest in group discussion and study of the subject matter of this book, we offer a 20% quantity discount to group leaders or agents. Our Special Quantity Price for a minimum order of five copies of *His Story* is $59.80 cash-with-order. Include postage and handling charges noted below.

Postage and Handling: Include $4 postage and handling for orders $15 and under; $5 for orders *over* $15. There are no postage and handling charges for orders over $100. Postage and handling rates are subject to change. We ship UPS whenever possible within the continental United States; delivery is guaranteed. Please provide your street address as UPS does not deliver to P.O. boxes. Orders shipped to Alaska, Hawaii, Canada, Mexico and Puerto Rico will be sent via first class mail. Allow 4–6 weeks for delivery.

International Orders: Airmail – add retail price of each book and $5 for each non-book item (audiotapes, etc.); Surface mail – add $1 per item.

Minnesota residents add 7% sales tax.

Mail orders to:
Llewellyn Worldwide
P.O. Box 64383-K458, St. Paul, MN 55164-0383, U.S.A.

For customer service, call (612) 291-1970.

Prices subject to change without notice.

THE GRAIL CASTLE
Male Myths & Mysteries in the Celtic Tradition
by Kenneth Johnson & Marguerite Elsbeth

Explore the mysteries which lie at the core of being male when you take a quest into the most powerful myth of Western civilization: the Celtic-Teutonic-Christian myth of the Grail Castle.

The Pagan Celtic culture's world view—which stressed an intense involvement with the magical world of nature—strongly resonates for men today because it offers a direct experience with the spirit often lacking in their lives. This book describes the four primary male archetypes—the King or Father, the Hero or Warrior, the Magician or Wise Man and the Lover—which the authors exemplify with stories from the Welsh Mabinogion, the Ulster Cycle and other old Pagan sources. Exercises and meditations designed to activate these inner myths will awaken men to how myths—as they live on today in the collective unconscious and popular culture— shape their lives. Finally, men will learn how to heal the Fisher King—who lies at the heart of the Grail Castle myth—to achieve integration of the four archetypal paths.

1–56718–369–7, 6 x 9, 224 pp., illus., index $12.00

THE 21 LESSONS OF MERLYN
A Study in Druid Magic & Lore
by Douglas Monroe

For those with an inner drive to touch genuine Druidism—or who feel that the lore of King Arthur touches them personally—The 21 Lessons of Merlyn will come as an engrossing adventure and psychological journey into history and magic. This is a complete introductory course in Celtic Druidism, packaged within the framework of 21 authentic and expanded folk story/ lessons that read like a novel. These lessons, set in late Celtic Britain ca A.D. 500, depict the training and initiation of the real King Arthur at the hands of the real Merlyn-the-Druid: one of the last great champions of Paganism within the dawning age of Christianity. As you follow the boy Arthur's apprenticeship from his first encounter with Merlyn in the woods, you can study your own program of Druid apprentiship with the detailed practical ritual applications that follow each story. The 21 folk tales were collected by the author in Britain and Wales during a ten-year period; the Druidic teachings are based on the actual, never-before-published 16th-century manuscript entitled *The Book of Pheryllt*.

0–87542–496–1, 420 pgs., 6 x 9, illus., softcover $12.95

Prices subject to change without notice.

EARTH GOD RISING
The Return of the Male Mysteries
by Alan Richardson

Today, in an age that is witnessing the return of the Goddess in all ways and on all levels, the idea of one more male deity may appear to be a step backward. But along with looking toward the feminine powers as a cure for our personal and social ills, we must remember to invoke those forgotten and positive aspects of our most ancient God. The Horned God is just, never cruel; firm, but not vindictive. The Horned Gods loves women as equals. He provides the balance needed in this New Age, and he must be invoked as clearly and as ardently as the Goddess to whom he is twin.

The how-to section of this book shows how to make direct contact with your most ancient potentials, as exemplified by the Goddess and the Horned God. Using the simplest of techniques, available to everyone in any circumstance, Earth God Rising shows how we can create our own mystery and bring about real magical transformations without the need for groups, gurus, or elaborate ceremonies.

0–87542–672–7, 224 pgs., 5¼ x 8, illus., softcover   **$9.95**

NORTHERN MAGIC
Mysteries of the Norse, Germans & English
by Edred Thorsson

This in-depth primer of the magic of the Northern Way introduces the major concepts and practices of Gothic or Germanic magic. English, German, Dutch, Icelandic, Danish, Norwegian, and Swedish peoples are all directly descended from this ancient Germanic cultural stock. According to author Edred Thorsson, if you are interested in living a holistic life with unity of body-mind-spirit, a key to knowing your spiritual heritage is found in the heritage of your body—in the natural features which you have inherited from your distant ancestors. Most readers of this book already "speak the language" of the Teutonic tradition.

Northern Magic contains material that has never before been discussed in a practical way. This book outlines the ways of Northern magic and the character of the Northern magician. It explores the theories of traditional Northern psychology (or the lore of the soul) in some depth, as well as the religious tradition of the Troth and the whole Germanic theology. The remaining chapters make up a series of "mini-grimoires" on four basic magical techniques in the Northern Way: Younger Futhark rune magic, Icelandic galdor staves, Pennsylvania hex signs, and "seith" (or shamanism). This is an excellent overview of the Teutonic tradition that will interest neophytes as well as long-time travelers along the Northern Way.

0–87542–782–0, 224 pgs., mass market, illus.   **$4.95**

Prices subject to change without notice.

THE ANCIENT & SHINING ONES
World Myth, Magic & Religion
by D.J. Conway

The Ancient & Shining Ones is a handy, comprehensive reference guide to the myths and deities from ancient religions around the world. Now you can easily find the information you need to develop your own rituals and worship using the Gods/Goddesses with which you resonate most strongly. More than just a mythological dictionary, *The Ancient & Shining Ones* explains the magickal aspects of each deity and explores such practices as Witchcraft, Ceremonial Magick, Shamanism and the Qabala. It also discusses the importance of ritual and magick, and what makes magick work.

Most people are too vague in appealing for help from the Cosmic Beings—they either end up contacting the wrong energy source, or they are unable to make any contact at all, and their petitions go unanswered. In order to touch the power of the universe, we must re-educate ourselves about the Ancient Ones. The ancient pools of energy created and fed by centuries of belief and worship in the deities still exist. Today these energies can bring peace of mind, spiritual illumination and contentment. On a very earthy level, they can produce love, good health, money, protection, and success.

0–87542–170–9, 448 pgs., 7 x 10, 300 illus., softcover   **$17.95**

THE BOOK OF OGHAM
The Celtic Tree Oracle
by Edred Thorsson

Drink deeply from the very source of the Druids' traditional lore. The oghamic Celtic tradition represents an important breakthrough in the practical study of Celtic religion and magick. Within the pages of *The Book of Ogham* you will find the *complete and authentic* system of divination based on the letters of the Celtic ogham alphabet (commonly designated by tree names), and a whole world of experiential Celtic spirituality.

Come to understand the Celtic Way to new depths, discover methodological secrets shared by the Druids and Drightens of old, receive complete instructions for the practice of ogham divination, and find objective inner truths concealed deep within yourself.

The true and inner learning of oghams is a pathway to awakening the deeply rooted structural patterns of the Celtic psyche or soul. Read, study and work with the ogham oracle. . . open up the mysterious and hidden world within . . . and become part of the eternal stream of tradition that transcends the individual self. Come, and drink directly from the true cauldron of inspiration: the secret lore and practices of the ancient Celtic Druids.

0–87542–783–9, 224 pgs., 6 x 9, illus., glossary, softcover   **$12.95**

Prices subject to change without notice.

THE SACRED CAULDRON
Secrets of the Druids
by Tadhg MacCrossan

Here is a comprehensive course in the history and development of Celtic religious lore, the secrets taught by the Druids, and a guide to the modern performance of the rites and ceremonies as practiced by members of the "Druidactos," a spiritual organization devoted to the revival of this ancient way of life.

The Sacred Cauldron evolved out of MacCrossan's extensive research in comparative mythology and Indo-European linguistics, etymology and archaeology. He has gone beyond the stereotypical image of standing stones and white-robed priests to piece together the truth about Druidism.The reader will find detailed interpretations of the words, phrases and titles that are indigenous to this ancient religion. Here also are step-by-step instructions for ceremonial rites for modern-day practice.

0–87542–103–2, 302 pgs., 5¼ x 8, illus., softcover   **$10.95**

GREENFIRE
Making Love with the Goddess
by Sirona Knight

Now you and your partner can apply the vast amounts of energy generated by sexual union and orgasm to improve every facet of your life, spirituality and relationship!

Greenfire offers an innovative approach to the goddess tradition in the area of sexual expression and exploration by joining elements of traditional Celtic Gwyddonic ritual and symbolism with tasteful erotic passages and guided fantasy. This book offers straightforward instruction for the solitary practitioner focusing on creating a viable relationship with one partner by merging with the divine aspects that exist inside each of us. Journey through each of the eight Sabbats with the Goddess and her consort, exploring their different aspects along the way through concepts, rituals and guided imagery. Rapport with the goddess and her consort acts as an avenue to personal awareness and more fulfilling sexual experience. Deepen your metaphysical understanding while improving your ability to enjoy a more satisfying sexual experience. Greenfire is your guide to attaining the oneness you've longed for between woman and man, goddess and god—and within yourself.

1–56718–386–7, 6 x 9, 224 pp., index, softcover   **$14.95**

Prices subject to change without notice.

ANIMAL-SPEAK
The Spiritual & Magical Powers of Creatures Great & Small
by Ted Andrews

The animal world has much to teach us. Some are experts at survival and adaptation, some never get cancer, some embody strength and courage while others exude playfulness. Animals remind us of the potential we can unfold, but before we can learn from them, we must first be able to speak with them.

Now, for perhaps the first time ever, myth and fact are combined in a manner that will teach you how to speak and understand the language of the animals in your life. *Animal-Speak* helps you meet and work with animals as totems and spirits—by learning the language of their behaviors within the physical world. It provides techniques for reading signs and omens in nature so you can open to higher perceptions and even prophecy. It reveals the hidden, mythical and realistic roles of 45 animals, 60 birds, 8 insects and 6 reptiles.

Animals will become a part of you, revealing to you the majesty and divine in all life. They will restore your childlike wonder of the world and strengthen your belief in magic, dreams and possibilities.

0–87542–028–1, 400 pgs., 7 x 10, illus., photos, softcover $16.00

LEGEND
The Arthurian Tarot
by Anna-Marie Ferguson

Gallery artist and writer Anna-Marie Ferguson has paired the ancient divinatory system of the tarot with the Arthurian myth to create Legend: The Arthurian Tarot. The exquisitely beautiful watercolor paintings of this tarot deck illustrate characters, places and tales from the legends that blend traditional tarot symbolism with the Pagan and Christian symbolism that are equally significant elements of this myth.

Each card represents the Arthurian counterpart to tarot's traditional figures, such as Merlin as the Magician, Morgan le Fay as the Moon, Mordred as the King of Swords and Arthur as the Emperor. Accompanying the deck is a decorative layout sheet in the format of the Celtic Cross to inspire and guide your readings, as well as the book Keeper of Words, which lists the divinatory meanings of the cards, the cards' symbolism and the telling of the legend associated with each card.

The natural pairing of the tarot with Arthurian legend has been made before, but never with this much care, completeness and consummate artistry. This visionary tarot encompasses all the complex situations life has to offer—trials, challenges and rewards—to help you cultivate a close awareness of your past, present and future through the richness of the Arthurian legend ... a legend which continues to court the imagination and speak to the souls of people everywhere.

1–56718–267–4, Complete Kit includes: Book: 6 x 9, 272 pgs., illus., softcover, Deck: 78 full-color cards, Layout Sheet: 18" x 24", four-color $34.95

Prices subject to change without notice.

CELTIC MYTH & MAGIC
Harness the Power of the Gods & Goddesses
by Edain McCoy

Tap into the mythic power of the Celtic goddesses, gods, heroes and heroines to aid your spiritual quests and magickal goals. Celtic Myth & Magic explains how to use creative ritual and pathworking to align yourself with the energy of these archetypes, whose potent images live deep within your psyche.

Celtic Myth & Magic begins with an overview of 49 different types of Celtic Paganism followed today, then gives specific instructions for evoking and invoking the energy of the Celtic pantheon to channel it toward magickal and spiritual goals and into esbat, sabbat and life transition rituals. Three detailed pathworking texts will take you on an inner journey where you'll join forces with the archetypal images of Cuchulain, Queen Maeve and Merlin the Magician to bring their energies directly into your life. The last half of the book clearly details the energies of over 300 Celtic deities and mythic figures so you can evoke or invoke the appropriate deity to attain a specific goal.

This inspiring, well-researched book will help solitary Pagans who seek to expand the boundaries of their practice to form working partnerships with the divine.

1–56718–661–0, 7 x 10, 464 pp., softbound   **$19.95**

THE RITES OF ODIN
by Ed Fitch

The ancient Northern Europeans knew a rough magic drawn from the grandeur of vast mountains and deep forests, of rolling oceans and thundering storms. Their rites and beliefs sustained the Vikings, accompanying them to the New World and to the Steppes of Central Asia. Now, for the first time, this magic system is brought compellingly into the present by author Ed Fitch.

This is a complete source volume on Odinism. It stresses the ancient values as well as the magic and myth of this way of life. The author researched his material in Scandinavia and Germany, and drew from anthropological and historical sources in Eastern and Central Europe.

A full cycle of ritual is provided, with rites of passage, magical spells, divination techniques, and three sets of seasonal rituals: solitary, group and family. *The Rites of Odin* also contains extensive "how-to" sections on planning and conducting Odinist ceremonies, including preparation of ceremonial implements and the setting up of ritual areas. Each section is designed to stand alone for easier reading and for quick reference. A bibliography is provided for those who wish to pursue the historical and anthropological roots of Odinism further.

0–87542–224–1, 360 pgs., 6 x 9, illus., softcover   **$12.95**

Prices subject to change without notice.

LEAVES OF YGGDRASIL
Runes, Gods, Magic, Feminine Mysteries, Folklore
by Freya Aswynn

Leaves of Yggdrasil is the first book to offer an extensive presentation of Rune concepts, mythology and magical applications inspired by Dutch/Frisian traditional lore.

Author Freya Aswynn, although writing from a historical perspective, offers her own interpretations of this data based on her personal experience with the system. Freya's inborn, native gift of psychism enables her to work as a runic seer and consultant in psychological rune readings, one of which is detailed in a chapter on "Runic Divination."

Leaves of Yggdrasil emphasizes the feminine mysteries and the function of the Northern priestesses. It unveils a complete and personal system of the rune magic that will fascinate students of mythology, spirituality, psychism and Teutonic history, for this is not only a religious autobiography but also a historical account of the ancient Northern European culture.

0–87542–024–9, 288 pgs., 5¼ x 8, softcover **$12.95**

THE ONCE UNKNOWN FAMILIAR
Shamanic Paths to Unleash Your Animal Powers
by Timothy Roderick

Discover the magical animal of power residing within you! Animal "Familiars" are more than just the friendly animals kept by witches—the animal spirit is an extension of the unconscious mind, which reveals its power to those who seek its help. By using the detailed rituals, meditations, exercises and journaling space provided within this workbook, you will tap into the long-forgotten Northern European heritage of the "Familiar Self," and invoke the untamed, transformative power of these magical beasts.

This book focuses on traditional Northern European shamanic means of raising power—including drumming, dancing and construction of animal "fetiches"—and provides a grimoire of charms, incantations and spells anyone can work with a physical animal presence to enhance love, money, success, peace and more.

This is the first how-to book devoted exclusively to working with physical and spiritual Familiars as an aid to magic. Get in touch with your personal animal power, and connect with the magical forces of nature to effect positive change in your life and the lives of those around you.

0–87542–439–2, 240 pgs., 6 x 9, softcover **$10.00**

Prices subject to change without notice.

THE HANDBOOK OF CELTIC ASTROLOGY
The 13-Sign Lunar Zodiac of the Ancient Druids
by Helena Paterson

Discover your lunar self with *The Handbook of Celtic Astrology!* Solar-oriented astrology has dominated Western astrological thought for centuries, but lunar-based Celtic astrology provides the "Yin" principle that has been neglected in the West—and author Helena Paterson presents new concepts based on ancient Druidic observations, lore and traditions that will redefine Western astrology.

This reference work will take you through the Celtic lunar zodiac, where each lunar month is associated with one of the 13 trees sacred to the Druids: birch, rowan, ash, alder, willow, hawthorn, oak, holly, hazel, vine, ivy, reed and elder. Chapters on each "tree sign" provide comprehensive text on Celtic mythology and gods/desses associated with the sign's ruling tree and planet; general characteristics of natives of the sign; and interpretive notes on the locations of the planets, the Moon, the ascendant and Midheaven as they are placed in any of the three decans of each tree sign. A thorough introduction on chart construction, sign division and the importance of solstices, equinoxes, eclipses and aspects to the Moon guarantees this book will become the definitive work on Celtic astrology.

1–56718–509–6, 7 x 10, 288 pp., illus. $15.00

THE CRAFTED CUP
Ritual Mysteries of the Goddess and the Grail
by Shadwynn

The Holy Grail—fabled depository of wonder, enchantment and ultimate spiritual fulfillment—is the key by which the wellsprings of a Deeper Life can be tapped for the enhancement of our inner growth. *The Crafted Cup* is a compendium of the teachings and rituals of a distinctly Pagan religious Order—the *Ordo Arcanorum Gradalis*—which incorporates into its spiritual way of worship ritual imagery based upon the Arthurian Grail legends, a reverence towards the mythic Christ, and an appreciation of the core truths and techniques found scattered throughout the New Age movement.

The Crafted Cup is divided into two parts. The first deals specifically with the teachings and general concepts which hold a central place within the philosophy of the Ordo Arcanorum Gradalis. The second and larger of the two parts is a complete compilation of the sacramental rites and seasonal rituals which make up the liturgical calendar of the Order. It contains one of the largest collections of Pagan, Grail-oriented rituals yet published.

0–87542–739–1, 420 pgs., 7 x 10, illus., softcover $19.95

Prices subject to change without notice.

THE LLEWELLYN ANNUALS

Llewellyn's MOON SIGN BOOK: Approximately 400 pages of valuable information on gardening, fishing, weather, stock market forecasts, personal horoscopes, good planting dates, and general instructions for finding the best date to do just about anything! Articles by prominent forecasters and writers in the fields of gardening, astrology, politics, economics and cycles. This special almanac, different from any other, has been published annually since 1906. It's fun, informative and has been a great help to millions in their daily planning. New larger 5¼ x 8 format. **State year $6.95**

Llewellyn's SUN SIGN BOOK: Your personal horoscope for the entire year! All 12 signs are included in one handy book. Also included are forecasts, special feature articles, and an action guide for each sign. Monthly horoscopes are written by Gloria Star, author of *Optimum Child,* for your personal sun sign and there are articles on a variety of subjects written by well-known astrologers from around the country. Much more than just a horoscope guide! Entertaining and fun the year around. New larger 5¼ x 8 format. **State year $6.95**

Llewellyn's DAILY PLANETARY GUIDE: Includes all of the major daily aspects plus their exact times in Eastern and Pacific time zones, lunar phases, signs and voids plus their times, planetary motion, a monthly ephemeris, sunrise and sunset tables, special articles on the planets, signs, aspects, a business guide, planetary hours, rulerships, and much more. Large 5¼ x 8 format for more writing space, spiral bound to lie flat, address and phone listings, time-zone conversion chart and blank horoscope chart. **State year $7.95**

Llewellyn's ASTROLOGICAL CALENDAR: Large wall calendar of 48 pages. Beautiful full-color cover and full-color paintings inside. Includes special feature articles by famous astrologers, and complete introductory information on astrology. It also contains a lunar gardening guide, celestial phenomena, a blank horoscope chart, and monthly date pages which include aspects, Moon phases, signs and voids, planetary motion, an ephemeris, personal forecasts, lucky dates, planting and fishing dates, and more. 10 x 13 size. Set in Eastern time, with fold-down conversion table for other time zones worldwide. **State year $12.00**

Llewellyn's MAGICAL ALMANAC: This beautifully illustrated almanac explores traditional earth religions and folklore while focusing on magical myths. Each month is summarized in a two-page format with information that includes the phases of the moon, festivals and rites for the month, as well as detailed magical advice. This is an indispensable guide is for anyone who is interested in planning rituals, spells and other magical advice. It features writing by some of the most prominent authors in the field. **State year $6.95**

Prices subject to change without notice.

OMENS, OGHAMS & ORACLES
Divination in the Druidic Tradition
by Richard Webster

Although hundreds of books have been written about the Celts and the druids, no book has focused exclusively on Celtic divination—until now. *Omens, Oghams & Oracles* covers the most important and practical methods of divination in the Celtic and druidic traditions, two of which have never before been published: an original system of divining using the druidic Ogham characters, and "Arthurian divination," which employs a geomantic oracle called druid sticks.

Even if you have no knowledge or experience with any form of divination, this book will show you how to create and use the 25 Ogham *fews* and the druid sticks immediately to gain accurate and helpful insights into your life. This book covers divination through sky stones, touchstones, bodhran drums and other means, with details on how to make these objects and sample readings to supplement the text. Beautiful illustrations of cards made from the Oghams, geomantic figures and more enhance this clear and informative book, which also includes chapters on the history, lives and philosophy of the Celts and druids.

Many Celtic divinatory methods are as useful today as they were 2,000 years ago—make modern forms of these ancient oracles work for you!

1–56718–800–1, 7 x 10, 224 pp., softbound $12.95

FAERY WICCA, BOOK TWO
The Shamanic Practices of the Cunning Arts
by Kisma Stepanich

Faery Wicca, Book Two is a continued study of *Faery Wicca, Book One,* with a deepening focus on the tradition's shamanic practices, including energy work, the Body Temple, healing techniques and developing Second-Sight; meditation techniques; journeys into the Otherworld; contacting Faery Guardians, Allies, Guides and Companions; herbcraft and spellcasting; different forms of Faery divination; rites of passages; the four minor holidays; and a closing statement on the shamanic technique known as "remembering."

The Oral Faery Tradition's teachings are not about little winged creatures. They are about the primal earth and the power therein, the circles of existence, Ancient Gods, the ancestors and the continuum. *Faery Wicca, Book Two* is not a how-to book but a study that provides extensive background information and mystery teachings for both novices and adepts alike.

1–56718–695–5, 7 x 10, 320 pp., illus., softbound $17.50

BY OAK, ASH & THORN
Modern Celtic Shamanism
by D. J. Conway

Many spiritual seekers are interested in shamanism because it is a spiritual path that can be followed in conjunction with any religion or other spiritual belief without conflict. Shamanism has not only been practiced by Native American and African cultures—for centuries, it was practiced by the Europeans, including the Celts.

By Oak, Ash and Thorn presents a workable, modern form of Celtic shamanism that will help anyone raise his or her spiritual awareness. Here, in simple, practical terms, you will learn to follow specific exercises and apply techniques that will develop your spiritual awareness and ties with the natural world: shape-shifting, divination by the Celtic Ogham alphabet, Celtic shamanic tools, traveling to and using magick in the three realms of the Celtic otherworlds, empowering the self, journeying through meditation and more.

Shamanism begins as a personal revelation and inner healing, then evolves into a striving to bring balance and healing into the Earth itself. This book will ensure that Celtic shamanism will take its place among the spiritual practices that help us lead fuller lives.

1–56718–166-X, 6 x 9, est. 288 pp., illus., softcover   **$12.95**

THE SACRED MARRIAGE
Honoring the God and Goddess within Each Other
by Lira Silbury

Is your relationship with your partner everything you hoped it would be? Do you see your partner as a living manifestation of the Divine—and your sexual union as a gift to and from the Goddess and God? Or are you still trapped in old, unfulfilling relationship patterns?

The Sacred Marriage can help you transform every aspect of your relationship from the mundane to the exalted. In this book, you will learn how—within the foundation of Wicca—you can build a deeper, more meaningful relationship through sharing meditation and ritual, dreaming together, celebrating the cycles of life and practicing sacred sexuality. If you haven't yet found the right partner for such a relationship, you will discover ways to draw him or her to you through visualization, dream work and prayer. If you are already involved in a fulfilling relationship, this book will teach you more about honoring the Divine within your partnership, with over a dozen beautiful rituals written especially for couples, including the powerful "Sacred Marriage" ceremony for consecrating a long-term commitment.

1–56718–654-8, 6 x 9, 288 pp., illus., softcover   **$14.95**

Prices subject to change without notice.